THE SPIRIT OF GOD IN MISSION

A VOCATIONAL COMMENTARY ON THE BOOK OF ACTS

– SECOND EDITION –

DENZIL R. MILLER

The Spirit of God in Mission

All Scripture quotations, unless otherwise indicated, are taken from the HOLY BIBLE, NEW INTERNATIONAL VERSION. Copyright © 1973, 1978, 1984 International Bible Society. Used by permission of Zondervan Bible Publishers.

Copyright © 2013 Denzil R. Miller. All rights reserved. No part of this book may be reproduced, stored in a retrieval system, or transmitted in any form or by any means—electronic, mechanical, photocopy, recording, or otherwise—without prior written permission of the copyright owner, except brief quotations used in connection with reviews in magazines or newspapers.

ESV   Indicates scripture quotations from The Holy Bible, English Standard Version, copyright © 2001 by Crossway Bibles, a publishing ministry of Good News Publishers. Used by permission. All rights reserved.

KJV   Indicates scripture quotations from The Holy Bible, King James Version.

NASB   Indicates scripture quotations from the New American Standard Bible. Copyright © 1960, 1962, 1963, 1971, 1973, 1975, 1977, 1995 by the Lockman Foundation. Used by Permission.

NKJV   Indicates scripture quotations from The Holy Bible, New King James Version. Copyright © 1991 by Thomas Nelson, Inc.

RSV   Indicates scripture quotations from The Holy Bible, Revised Standard Version of the Bible, copyright © 1971 by the Division of Christian Education of the National Council of the Churches of Christ in the United States of America. Used by permission. All rights reserved.

Maps   reprinted with the permission of © 2005 Biblical Studies Press, http://bible.org. All rights reserved.

Library of Congress Cataloging-in-Publication Data

Miller, Denzil R., 1946–

The Spirit of God in Mission: a Vocational Commentary on the Book of Acts - Second Edition / Denzil R. Miller.

1. Biblical studies—Acts   2. Pneumatology—Lukan— Pentecostal.
3. Missions—Strategy.

ISBN 978-0-9911332-2-2

PneumaLife Publications
www.PneumaLifePublications.org
3766 N. Delaware Ave.
Springfield, Missouri, USA 65803
2013

Printed in the United States of America

– Contents –

Foreword by Loren Triplett 7

Preface 9

Table of Figures and Maps 11

Outline of Acts 13

Introduction 17

PART I: INTRODUCTORY MATTERS 21

    Chapter 1:   Interpreting Acts 23
    Chapter 2:   Getting Ready for Pentecost 35

PART II: THE JEWISH MISSION 47

    Chapter 3:   Pentecost: The First Jerusalem Outpouring 49
    Chapter 4:   Ministry in Jerusalem (Including the Second
                       Jerusalem Outpouring) 69

PART III: THE TRANSITIONAL PERIOD 87

    Chapter 5:   Persecution and Witness (Including the
                       Samaritan Outpouring) 89
    Chapter 6:   Continued Expansion (Including the
                       Damascene Outpouring) 103
    Chapter 7:   The Door is Opened for the Gentiles
                       (Including the Caesarean Outpouring) 113

PART IV: THE GENTILE MISSION 131

    Chapter 8:   Paul's First Missionary Journey
                       (Including the Antiochian Outpouring) 133
    Chapter 9:   Missionary Council in Jerusalem 153
    Chapter 10: Paul's Second Missionary Journey (Part 1) 163
    Chapter 11: Paul's Second Missionary Journey (Part 2) 177
    Chapter 12: Paul's Third Missionary Journey (Including
                       the Ephesian Outpouring) 187

PART V: JERUSALEM AND ROME 207

    Chapter 13: Jerusalem and Trials 209
    Chapter 14: To Rome 225

PART VI: APPLICATION 235

    Chapter 15: Pentecostal Baptism 237
    Chapter 16: The Message of Acts 255

Appendix 1: Episodes in Acts 261
Appendix 2: Spiritual Gifts in Acts 265
Recommended Reading 271

Other Books by the Author 275

– FOREWORD –

by Loren Triplett
Executive Director, Assemblies of God
Division of Foreign Missions
(1990-1997)

God has surely moved upon the heart of His servant, Denzil R. Miller to seek to restate the most obvious reason for the sending of His Holy Spirit to His Church. Dr. Miller has effectively revealed what I call the "lost secret of Pentecost."

Shortly before the Son of God returned to His Father in heaven, He was eating with His disciples, and He gave them this command: "Do not leave Jerusalem, but wait for the gift my Father promised, ... in a few days you will you will be baptized with the Holy Spirit. ... But you will receive power when the Holy Spirit comes on you; and you will be my witnesses in Jerusalem, and in all Judea and Samaria, and to the ends of the earth. After he said this, he was taken up ... and a cloud hid him from their sight" (Acts 1:4-5, 8).

This passage leaves no question about God's planned reason for His power to be given to those early believers. They knew they were empowered to spread the Good News everywhere, and they displayed their eagerness and success in doing God's will by employing the Holy Spirit's power to spread the Good News to near and distant regions.

History records the fact that Thomas, the disciple who at first doubted the resurrection of his Master, took the message of the resurrection to the east coast of India, where he was martyred for his faith and zeal. I once stood at the spot where it is believed that Thomas died. He gave his life for being obedient to the Master's command under the power of the Holy Spirit.

As you read the pages of this book you will rejoice with me at the clear explanation of God's intent and the eager obedience and successes of the labors of love and sacrifice by the thousands of believers at that first revival.

Again, the "lost secret of Pentecost" is the gift of power to witness. We can never fulfill Christ's Great Commission with the strategies of men. The true reason for the baptism in the Holy Spirit

Foreword

must be the clarion call for the final thrust of truth into all parts of the earth. This gospel must be preached everywhere. Our time to do it is brief. My prayer is that you will want to join the empowered army of the Great Commission in reaching our generation with the brilliant light of God's final call to the lost.

— Loren Triplett

– Preface –

This book is a revision and expansion of my book, *Acts: The Spirit of God in Mission,* published by Africa's Hope as part of their Discovery Series of textbooks. This textbook series is designed to be used in the training of African pastors and leaders in Bible and extension schools across the continent. You can find out more about the Discovery Series on the Internet at www.AfricasHope.org.

Additions to this second edition of the book, re-titled, *The Spirit of God in Mission: A Vocational Commentary on the Book of Acts,* include the "Outline of the Book of Acts" presented at the beginning of the book, the addition of Chapter 15, "Pentecostal Baptism," and the addition of "Appendix 2: Spiritual Gifts in Acts."

It is hoped that this expanded addition of the book will find a broader readership than just those receiving formal training in Bible and extension schools. It is designed to help any pastor or lay minister wanting to better understand the book of Acts. It is further hoped that the book will serve as a training manual for those wanting to be used by God in the same way as were Jesus' early disciples as recorded in the book of Acts.

Chapter 1 of this volume deals with the hermeneutical principles one should use in properly interpreting Acts. The reader wanting to know more about these hermeneutical principles and the "Seven Key Outpourings of the Holy Spirit in Acts" mentioned throughout this book should read my earlier book, *Empowered for Global Mission: A Missionary Look at the Book of Acts,* where these issues are discussed in more detail.

May the Lord richly bless you and expand your ministry as you read and apply the principles found in the book into your own life and ministry.

— Denzil R. Miller, D.Min.

– Table of Figures and Maps –

Figure 1.1	Luke's Empowerment Witness Motif	29
Figure 2.1	The Seven Key Outpourings as They Relate to the Jewish and Gentile Missions	40
Figure 8.1	Map: Paul's First Missionary Journey	134
Figure 8.2	"Pneuma Events" and Paul's Missionary Journeys	135
Figure 10.1	Map: Paul's Second Missionary Journey	164
Figure 12.1	Map: Paul's Third Missionary Journey	188
Figure 12.2	The New Testament "Strategy of the Spirit"	195
Figure 14.1	Map: Paul's Journey to Rome	226

– OUTLINE OF ACTS –
(As Presented in this Study)

INTRODUCTORY (1:1-11)

1. GETTING READY FOR PENTECOST (1:1-26)
   a. The Spirit is Promised (1:4-8)
   b. Jesus Taken Up into Heaven (1:9-11)

THE JEWISH MISSION (1:12–8:1a)

2. PENTECOST—THE FIRST JERUSALEM OUTPOURING (2:1– 4:22)
   a. In the Upper Room (1:12-26)
   b. The Spirit Is Poured Out (2:1-13)
   c. Peter's Spirit-inspired Witness (2:14-36)
      1) Prophecy Fulfilled (vv. 14-21)
      2) The Gospel Proclaimed (2:22-36)
      3) The Promise of the Spirit (2:37-41)
   d. A New Prophetic Community (2:42-47)
      1) Spirit-empowered Witness in Jerusalem (3:1-26)
      2) A Miracle at the Beautiful Gate (3:1-10)
      3) Peter's Second Spirit-inspired Message (3:11-26)
   e. Spirit-inspired Witness Before the Sanhedrin (4:1-22)

3. MINISTRY IN JERUSALEM—INCLUDING THE SECOND JERUSALEM OUTPOURING (4:23–8:1a)
   a. A Powerful Missionary Prayer (4:23-30)
   b. A Second Outpouring in Jerusalem (4:31-37)
   c. Revelation and Witness (5:1-16)
      1) A Conspiracy Is Unmasked (5:3-11)
      2) Ongoing Witness in Jerusalem (5:12-16)
   d. Imprisonment, Release and Witness (5:17-42)
   e. A Spirit-guided Decision (6:1-7)
   f. Stephen's Spirit-empowered Witness (6:8-15)
   g. Stephen's Speech and Martyrdom (7:1–8:1a)

THE TRANSITIONAL PERIOD (8:1b–12:25)

4. PERSECUTION AND WITNESS—INCLUDING THE SAMARITAN OUTPOURING (8:1b–40)
   a. The Witness of the Scattered Believers (8:1b-4)
   b. Philip's Spirit-empowered Witness in Samaria (8:5-8)
   c. The Samaritan Outpouring (8:9-25)
      1) A Missing Ingredient (8:14-16)
      2) Simon the Sorcerer (8:9-11, 13; 18-24)
   d. Philip's Spirit-directed Ministry in Gaza (8:26-40)

5. CONTINUED EXPANSION—INCLUDING THE DAMASCENE OUTPOURING (9:1–43)
   a. Saul's Conversion (9:1-7)
   b. Saul's Healing, Commissioning, and Empowering (9:8-19)
   c. Saul's Witness in Damascus and Jerusalem (9:20-30)
   d. The Church Is Strengthened and Grows (9:31)
   e. Peter's Spirit-empowered Ministry in Judea (9:32–43)

6. THE DOOR IS OPENED FOR THE GENTILES— INCLUDING THE CAESAREAN OUTPOURING (10:1–12:25)
   a. A Divine Appointment (10:1-26)
   b. Peter Goes into the Gentiles (10:27-33)
   c. Peter's Spirit-inspired Message (10:34-43)
   d. The Holy Spirit Is Poured out on Gentiles (10:44-48)
   e. The Door Is Opened (11:1-18)
   f. The Church Strengthens and Expands (11:19–12:25)
   g. Missionary Witness in Antioch (11:19-30)
   h. Persecution, Prayer, Deliverance, and Witness (12:1-25)

THE GENTILE MISSION (13:1–20:38)

7. PAUL'S FIRST MISSIONARY JOURNEY—INCLUDING THE ANTIOCHIAN "OUTPOURING" (13:1–14:28)
   a. The Antiochian "Outpouring" (13:1-3)
   b. Cyprus: Spirit-empowered Ministry (13:4-12)
   c. Antioch: The Gospel Is Proclaimed (13:13-52
   d. Iconium: Signs and Wonders (14:1-7)
   e. Lystra: Gifts in Operation (14:8-20a)
   f. Derbe: Soul Harvest (14:20b-23)
   g. Antioch: The First Missions Convention (14:24-28)

8. MISSIONARY COUNCIL IN JERUSALEM (15:1-21)
   a. Dissension in Antioch (15:1-5)
   b. Peter, Barnabas, and Paul Testify (15:6-12)
   c. A Word from the Lord (15:13-21)
   d. An Encouraging Letter (15:22-35)

9. PAUL'S SECOND MISSIONARY JOURNEY—PART 1 (15:36–16:40)
   a. Paul's Second Journey Begins (15:36-39a)
   b. Galatia: Pastoral Visits (15:39b–16:5)
   c. The Spirit Guides the Missionaries (16:6-10)
   d. Philippi: the Gospel Goes to Europe (16:11-15)
   e. A Slave Girl Is Delivered (16:16-18)
   f. Opposition and Deliverance (16:19-28)
   g. The Jailer's Household Is Saved (16:29-34)
   h. Apologies and Departure (16:35-40)

10. PAUL'S SECOND MISSIONARY JOURNEY— PART 2 (17:1–18:22)
    a. Thessalonica: Success and Turmoil (17:1-9)
    b. Berea: the Message Is Received (17:10-15)
    c. Athens: A Few Believe (17:16-34)
    d. Corinth: An Extended Stay (18:1-17)
    e. Ephesus: A Brief Stopover (18:18-21)

11. PAUL'S THIRD MISSIONARY JOURNEY—INCLUDING THE EPHESIAN OUTPOURING (18:23–20:6)
    a. Pastoral Visits to Galatia and Phrygia (18:23)
    b. Apollos, Priscilla, and Aquila (18:24-28)
    c. The Ephesian Outpouring (19:1-7)
    d. The Ephesian Campaign (19:8-10)
    e. Further Ministry in Ephesus (19:11-41)
       1) Spirit-empowered Ministry (vv. 11-20)
       2) Riot and Vindication (vv. 12-41)
    f. Final Ministry in Europe and Asia (20:1-38)
       1) International Missionary Team (vv. 1-6)
       2) Eutychus Raised from the Dead (vv. 7-12)
       3) Farewell to the Ephesian Elders (20:13-38)

JERUSALEM AND ROME (21:1–28:31)

12. JERUSALEM AND TRIALS (21:1–25:32)
    a. To Jerusalem: Journey Arrival and Arrest (21:1-36)
        1) Journey to Jerusalem (21:1-16)
        2) Arrival (21:17-26)
        3) Arrest (21:27-36)
    b. Paul's Speeches in Jerusalem (21:37-23:11)
        1) Paul Addresses the Crowd (21:37–22:21)
        2) Paul the Roman Citizen (22:22-29)
        3) Before the Sanhedrin (22:30-23:11)
    c. Plot and Escape (23:12-35)
        1) The Plot to Kill Paul (23:12-22)
        2) Paul Transferred to Caesarea (23:23-35)
    d. Paul's Trial Before Felix (24:1-27)
    e. Paul's Trial Before Festus (25:1-12)
    f. Paul's Trial Before Agrippa (25:13–26:32)
        1) Festus Consults King Agrippa (25:13-22)
        2) Paul Before Agrippa (25:23–26:32)

13. TO ROME (27:1–28:31)
    a. The Journey to Rome (27:1– 44)
        1) A Warning from the Spirit (27:1-12)
        2) Hurricane (27:13-26)
        3) Shipwreck (27:27-44)
    b. Ministry in Malta (28:1-10)
        1) Divine Protection (28:1-6)
        2) The Sick Are Cured (28:7-10)
    c. Open Doors in Rome (28:11-31)
        1) Arrival at Rome (28:11-16)
        2) Preaching the Kingdom in Rome (28:17-31)

– INTRODUCTION –

The year was 1909. The place was Valparaiso, a city high in the Chilean Andes. The members of the First Methodist Church had gathered for their weekly Sunday school class. Their pastor, Dr. Willis Hoover, was teaching them from the book of Acts. One of the members asked him, "What prevents our being a church like the early church?" "Nothing," Dr. Hoover answered, "except something within ourselves." Thus challenged, the congregation set itself to praying for an outpouring of the Spirit upon their church and upon their country. Soon a Pentecostal revival broke out, with hundreds of church members being baptized in the Holy Spirit. The revival continues until today.

Today the Pentecostal Methodist Church, which sprang from that revival, is the largest Protestant denomination in Chile, with more than 1.5 million members more than 3,250 congregations. One local church, the Jotabeche Pentecostal Methodist Church, has more than 350,000 members. Roughly two-thirds of all Protestants in Chile are either Pentecostal or charismatic, and approximately one quarter of all Catholics are charismatic. There are almost two million denominational Pentecostals in Chile, amounting to 12 percent of the total population.

The Chilean revival is a clear example of what can happen when a people take seriously the book of Acts. *That's what we intend to do in this book.*

Acts is one of the most exciting books in the Bible. It tells the story of the beginning of the church. In Acts we learn that the church did not begin timidly, nor apologetically, but with a mighty explosion of God's power and grace. The book is filled with thrilling stories of true commitment and courage. As we move through this study, we will be looking at those stories.

It has often been said that the title, "The Acts of the Apostles," which appears in many of our Bibles, is not the best name for the book. I agree. As others have suggested, a better name would be "The Acts of the Holy Spirit," since He is the central character and champion of the book. As the story of Acts progresses, the human protagonists change (i.e., Peter, Stephen, Philip, Paul, etc.), but the divine Protagonist, the Holy Spirit, remains constant. Throughout Acts He takes center stage, filling, empowering, enabling, and

Introduction

directing the work.

In Acts the Holy Spirit is revealed as the Spirit of Missions. Missions is, in fact, a central theme of both Luke's gospel and the book of Acts, sometimes called Luke-Acts. We have, therefore, chosen to entitle this book *The Spirit of God in Mission: A Vocational Commentary on the Book of Acts.*

An explanation or two will be helpful here. Throughout this book we
will use the words *mission* and *missions.* When we speak of *mission* we are speaking of God's mission—sometimes called the *missio Dei*. God's mission is to bless all the peoples of the earth through the seed of Abraham, that is, through Jesus Christ (Gen. 12:3; 22:18; cf. Gal. 3:16). Stated another way, God's mission is to redeem and call unto Himself a people out of "every tribe and language and people and nation" on the earth (Rev. 5:9; 7:9). Jesus gave the Great Commission to direct the church in fulfilling that mission (Matt. 28:18-20; Mark 16:15-16; Luke 24:47-48; John 20:22; Acts 1:8). When we speak of *missions,* we are talking about all the church does to fulfill the mission of God. This would include such things as giving, going, and praying for missions.

Some read Acts only as history. They say, "Wasn't it wonderful how the Spirit worked in New Testament times?" They believe, however, that we should not expect Him to work in the same manner today. Others, however, ask, "Why not today? Why can't the twenty-first century church receive the same Spirit in the same way and thus experience the same power, glory, and guidance as did the early church?" I believe that it can, and should.

This study of Acts will have a distinct orientation, as stated above. It is a *vocational* commentary, meaning it is purposely oriented toward those actively involved in ministry. As we examine the ministries of the apostles and other believers in Acts, we will again and again be asking the question, "How should their ministries impact and influence our ministries today?" In doing this, we hope to learn many valuable lessons about our own ministries and how we should conduct them. The goal of our study will be more than to simply gain knowledge about the early church. It will be to have the same spiritual experiences as did those first believers, and to put into practice in our own lives and ministries the same practices they implemented into theirs.

This book divided into six parts. Parts I-V reflect the natural divisions of the book of Acts. They trace the progress of the church from its Jewish roots in Jerusalem, through its Gentile formation, to

Introduction

its eventual arrival in Rome, the capital city of the Roman Empire. There is also included in Part I an introductory chapter, which will familiarize the reader to the unique hermeneutical issues surrounding the interpretation of Acts. Part IV contains a chapter that interprets and applies some of the concepts learned in the study of Acts.

It is strongly recommended that, at this point in your study, you take time to read through the entire book of Acts in one setting. This should take about three to four hours. This exercise will give you a broad overview of the book. You will begin to get a feeling of the character of the book and the flow of the narrative. As you read, note recurring themes that appear in the book, such as the work of the Holy Spirit in empowering and directing believers, the proclamation of the gospel, the triumph over persecution, and the kingdom of God. You may want to indicate these themes in your Bible margin or in a notebook.

You will notice that each chapter is divided into subdivisions, as follows:

Pre-Lesson Reading Assignment. Here you will be given a reading assignment from the book of Acts. It is the portion of Acts that will be covered in that particular chapter. It is essential that, at this point, you lay aside this book, pick up your Bible, and carefully read this portion of Scripture. There are parts of the chapter that cannot be fully understood without a clear and current recollection of the biblical text. This is especially true of the "Commentary" subdivisions in each chapter. It is also advisable that you keep your Bible open to the place in Acts being covered in the lesson under study.

Reading Assignment. In the "Reading Assignment" you will be asked to read again the portion of Acts that will be immediately addressed. If you have followed the plan laid out in this study, this will be the third time you will have read this portion of Scripture. Having done this, you will be ready to begin a thoughtful study of these verses.

The Story. In the "Story" subsections of each chapter you will find, in narrative form, a summary of the portion of the book of Acts indicated in the "Reading Assignment" immediately preceding. A thoughtful reading of these subsections will help you to engage directly with the Acts narrative.

Commentary. In these subsections we will make pertinent comments on selected portions of the text under discussion. Our goal, as previously mentioned, will be to give insight into the ministries of the apostles and other Christian workers in Acts, and to apply these

Introduction

insights to our ministries today. All Scripture quotations cited in bold italics are taken from the New International Version of the Bible.

It is my hope that, as you read this book, your life and ministry will be transformed by the lives and ministries of those first-century missionaries. I further hope that you will be filled with the Spirit as they were, and that you too will become a Spirit-empowered witness of Christ and His gospel.

QUESTIONS FOR REFLECTION AND REVIEW

1. Why would the "Acts of the Holy Spirit" be a more appropriate title for the book of Acts than the "Acts of the Apostles"?
2. Distinguish between the two concepts of *mission* and *missions.*
3. Why does the author call this textbook a "vocational" commentary?

QUESTIONS FOR CLASSROOM DISCUSSION

1. Why is it important how one approaches a study of the book of Acts? What difference does it make whether he or she sees it as a book simply describing the history of the early church or a book of present-day missionary strategy?
2. How can one's personal experience with God affect the way he or she interprets the book of Acts? Should it? Give reasons for your answer.

– Part I –
Introductory Matters

– CHAPTER 1 –

INTERPRETING ACTS

Before plunging into the text of Acts, it is important that we take time to ask and answer a few important questions concerning the book, such as, "Who wrote Acts and when? To whom was it written and why?" Another important question is "What is the unique hermeneutical principle that we should employ in interpreting Acts?" In this chapter we will address these and other interpretative issues. We will begin by asking, "Why study Acts?"

WHY STUDY ACTS?

We study Acts for several reasons: First, a proper understanding of the book will greatly enhance our understanding of the rest of the New Testament. Acts serves as an essential bridge between the Gospels and the New Testament epistles. Just think, if there were no book of Acts, we would be left wondering who Paul was, and where the churches to whom he wrote came from. There would be many gaps in our knowledge of the church, and our understanding of the rest of the New Testament books would be greatly diminished.

Second, we study Acts because it helps us to see what the early church looked like, and it gives us a model of what the church should look like today. It answers many questions, such as,

- What were the core values and priorities of the first believers?
- How did they minister?

- What moved them to do as they did?
- What were the secrets of their great evangelistic and missionary successes?
- What were the essential experiences and common practices of the first church?
- What challenges did they face, and how did they meet those challenges?

The answer to each of these questions has profound implications for us today as we answer our own questions about ministry, such as,

- What should be our core values and central priorities?
- How are we to conduct our ministries?
- How can we ensure success in our own evangelistic and missionary efforts?
- What essential spiritual experiences must we have, and what practices should we implement?
- What challenges do we face today, and how can we successfully address those challenges?

These and many more questions can be answered in a study of the book of Acts. How foolish any church or Christian would be to dismiss or neglect this essential resource.

A final reason we study is Acts is because it gives us a divinely-inspired strategy for missionary outreach. It is, in fact, a training manual for twenty-first century Christians! Luke intended for the book of Acts to be a lasting model of how the kingdom of God will advance until Jesus comes again. It the gospels we read about what Jesus did; in the Acts we read about what Jesus expects us to do until He returns. The book of Acts not only tells of how the early church preached the gospel and evangelized the then-know world, it gives us an enduring strategy of how we can effectively do missions today.

BACKGROUND

Authorship

Most New Testament scholars identify Luke as the author of Acts. This is the same Luke who wrote the Gospel bearing his name. Although Luke never names himself as the author (as Paul often does in his epistles, Rom. 1:1; 1 Cor. 1:1; Gal. 1:1), both external and internal evidence bear witness to his authorship. External evidence includes the testimony of early church writings such as the

Chapter 1: Interpreting Acts

Muratorian Canon (A.D. 170) and the writings of Irenaeus (A.D. 180).

Internal evidence—i.e., evidence from within the New Testament text itself—also supports Luke's authorship. For instance, both the Gospel of Luke and Acts are addressed to the same person, Theophilus (Luke 1:3; Acts 1:1), indicating that Luke is the author of both volumes. In addition, the famous "we passages" in Acts suggest that Luke was a fellow traveler and missionary associate of the apostle Paul. These passages almost certainly refer to Luke, since he was with Paul at Rome (Col. 4:14; 2 Tim. 4:11).

From these "we passages" we learn that Luke traveled and ministered with Paul during Paul's Second Missionary Journey (16:10-18) and on his journey from Philippi to Jerusalem (20:5-15). We further learn that Luke likely stayed with Paul during the apostle's imprisonment in Caesarea (21:27-26:32) and was with him on his perilous sea journey to Rome (27:1-28:16). From one of Paul's letters we discover that Luke remained with him during his imprisonment in Rome (2 Tim. 4:10-11). It is no wonder that Paul called Luke his "dear friend" (Col. 4:14). In the same passage Paul identifies Luke as a medical doctor, calling him "the beloved physician" (KJV). Paul mentions Luke one other time, where he calls him one of his "fellow laborers" (Phm. 24). Luke is the only Gentile writer in the New Testament, and, for that matter, the entire Bible.

Date and Purpose in Writing

Acts was written around A.D. 65, about 37 years after the Spirit was first poured out on the Day of Pentecost. Luke was, therefore, writing to a second generation of Christians. These believers were not present at Pentecost and probably had little accurate knowledge about the beginnings of the church or its dynamic spread during its early years.

Luke possibly wrote from Rome, since it was there where the book of Acts ends, and since Luke spent considerable time with Paul while Paul was in prison there. The believers to whom he wrote were probably Gentiles and Hellenized Jews who lived remotely from Jerusalem, far from where the early events of Acts occurred. Further, from the internal evidence, it seems evident that the believers to whom Luke wrote were undergoing persecution, and possibly, as a result, had lost their missionary vision and zeal. There also seems to have been among them a waning emphasis on the empowering work of the Spirit. Luke wrote these late-first-century Christians to address these unacceptable conditions.

Although Acts is addressed to one, Theophilus, it is clear that Luke's message was not just for that one person, but for a much wider readership. It was common during the first century for writers to address their works to one person. Theophilus was possibly Luke's patron and helped to finance the writing and distribution of the book.

Certainly, Luke wrote to teach history. He wanted these early believers to know about the beginnings of the church and its eventual spread from Jerusalem to Rome. His primary intent, however, was not simply to teach history. Luke wrote to call the church back to its Pentecostal and missionary roots. By telling these believers how the church began, and how, even in the midst of severe persecution, it triumphed in the power of the Spirit, he hoped to encourage them to do the same. Luke wanted them to know that this could happen if they, like those first disciples, would understand the purpose of the church and the necessity of being empowered by the Holy Spirit. Luke's primary purpose in writing Acts is encapsulated in Acts 1:8, as we will discuss in more detail later in this chapter. Luke further wrote to teach his readers that the empowering presence of the Spirit comes from a powerful spiritual experience he calls the baptism in the Holy Spirit (Luke 3:16; Acts 1:5; 11:16).[1] In Acts Luke presents this experience as separate from salvation and accompanied by speaking in tongues. Its purpose is to empower believers for effective witness.

HERMENEUTICAL ISSUES

Interpreting Historical Narrative

To properly interpret Acts one must understand that it belongs to the literary genre of historical narrative. As a historical narrative, Acts must be approached somewhat differently than other types of literature in the New Testament, such as, gospels (Matthew–John), epistles (Romans– Jude), and apocalyptic writing (Revelation). Each of the four New Testament genres requires its own interpretative approach. As historical narrative, Acts tells the true Spirit-inspired story of the beginning of the church. There are three important insights, and two important hermeneutical tools, that can help us in interpreting historical narrative:

---

[1] Luke also refers to this experience as "the gift of the Holy Spirit," "receiving the Spirit," being "filled with the Holy Spirit," and the Holy Spirit "coming upon" or "falling on" a person or group.

Three Important Insights

When interpreting Acts one should keep in mind three important insights. When these insights are ignored, one's interpretation can go astray. These three insights are (1) the literary unity of Luke-Acts, (2) the theological character of Acts, and (3) the theological independence of Luke.[2] Let's look briefly at each of these important concepts:

The literary unity of Luke-Acts. To properly interpret Acts one must recognize that it is the second part of a two-part work, often called Luke-Acts, the first part being the Gospel of Luke. The unity of Luke-Acts is indicated in Acts 1:1, where Luke calls his Gospel "my former book." This insight is important because we discover much about Luke's understanding of the role of the Holy Spirit in missions by comparing the Gospel of Luke with the book of Acts. This understanding helps us to properly interpret the purpose and meaning of the baptism in the Holy Spirit.

The theological character of Acts. Second, one must understand the theological character of Acts. Some have taught that, since Acts is historical narrative, it cannot be used as a source for normative doctrine.[3] They say that we can only get history from Acts and nothing more. To get normative doctrine, they say, we must go to the New Testament epistles, which were written for that purpose. Therefore, according to this teaching, the Pentecostal doctrines of subsequence[4] and initial evidence[5] cannot be supported, since these doctrines come primarily from a study of Acts. Today, however, most evangelical biblical scholars reject this theory. They teach that Luke not only wrote as a historian but as a Spirit-inspired theologian. Therefore, Acts, if properly interpreted, is a legitimate source for normative doctrine.

The theological independence of Luke. Finally, Luke must be

---

[2] You can read more about these concepts in *The Charismatic Theology of St. Luke* by Roger Stronstad, pp. 1-12.

[3] Normative doctrine is teaching that applies equally to all people of all times.

[4] The doctrine of subsequence is the teaching that the baptism in the Holy Spirit is an experience separate from and following the new birth.

[5] The doctrine of initial evidence is the teaching that those who are baptized in the Holy Spirit will speak in tongues as the Spirit gives utterance.

given theological independence from Paul. This means that we must not take what Paul teaches about the work of the Holy Spirit in his epistles and impose his teaching on Luke without first letting Luke speak for himself. After we hear from Luke, and thoroughly understand what he is teaching, we can then harmonize his teaching with Paul's. By doing this we can get the New Testament's full teaching on the Holy Spirit.

Two Important Tools

Further, two important hermeneutical approaches, or tools, must be employed to properly interpret Acts. One is the use of biblical theology; the other is the use of narrative theology.

Biblical theology. Biblical theology is a different approach to interpreting Scripture than systematic theology, which is the traditional way of interpreting the Bible. In doing systematic theology, a theologian first chooses a topic. Next, he gathers texts relating to the topic from throughout the Bible. He then lays out the texts side by side for investigation. In doing this, the systematic theologian often does not consider the historical background or literary context from which the text is taken. Having done this, he then seeks to interpret and synthesize what these texts teach on the subject.

Biblical theology is done differently. The biblical theologian approaches Scripture diachronically, that is, across time. He seeks to discover how God has progressively revealed Himself and His plan throughout sacred history. He does not seek to harmonize Scripture, as in systematic theology, but rather seeks to allow each biblical author to speak for himself. The writer is allowed to speak out of his own theological agenda and out of his own historical and cultural background. Using this method in interpreting Acts allows Luke to speak for himself without unduly imposing upon him the theological agenda of either Paul or John.

Narrative theology. A second tool that we must employ in interpreting Acts is narrative theology. Narrative theology is an orderly approach to interpreting the historical portions of Scripture. It uses an understanding of the literary principles and rules an author employs in composing historical narratives. Narrative theology interprets the narrative by understanding such narrative devices as narrative rhetoric, inclusion-exclusion, redaction, didactic segments, and parenthetical commentary. *Narrative rhetoric* is the storyteller's intentional attempt to influence the beliefs and attitudes of his readers. He does this through the way he tells his story. *Inclusion-exclusion* refers to the author's conscious choice to include or exclude certain facts and events from his story. He includes those facts and events that help him to achieve his purpose in writing, and excludes the ones that do not help him to achieve his purpose. *Redaction* is a tool used by biblical authors whereby they, under the inspiration of the Holy Spirit, edit or interpret certain passages of Scripture they cite. They sometimes do this to emphasize their purpose in writing. *Didactic segments* are those portions of a story where the narrative writer seeks to deliberately teach certain truths. He often does this by using the words of the characters of the story. *Parenthetical commentary* uses comments added to the story by the author to help the reader to understand the meaning of what is taking place. Luke uses all these devices in Acts. Identifying and understanding them helps us to understand why Luke wrote the book.[6]

The Interpretative Key

Many Bible commentators have cited Acts 1:8 as the key verse of the book. As such, it serves as the key to understanding Acts. We thus call it the *interpretative key* to Acts. By this we mean that this verse helps to "unlock" our understanding of the entire book. It does this by introducing two key concepts, as follows:

1. Empowerment-witness motif. The first and most important concept is found in the first half of the verse, which reads, "But you will receive power when the Holy Spirit comes on you; and you will be my witnesses ..." We call this Luke's *empowerment-witness motif.* A motif is a pattern of words, concepts, or events repeated throughout a work. As we progress through Acts, we will observe this pattern being repeated again and again. The pattern can be charted as follows:

Luke's Empowerment-Witness Motif

The Empowering of the Holy Spirit → results in → Missional Witness

---

Figure 1.1

This pattern reveals Luke's primary intent in writing the book. He wrote to call the church of his day, and ultimately the church of

---

[6] For a fuller discussion of these and other narrative concepts see the author's book, *Empowered for Global Mission,* pp. 25-53.

every day, back to its Pentecostal and missionary roots.

2. Table of contents. The second part of Acts 1:8 serves as an outline—or a sort of table of contents—for the book. Jesus said that His followers would be His witnesses "... in Jerusalem, and in all Judea and Samaria, and to the ends of the earth." Using this statement we can outline the book of Acts as follows:

- Acts 1:1–11   Introduction
- Acts 1:12–8:1a   The church's witness in Jerusalem (The Jewish Mission)
- Acts 8:1b–12:25   The church's witness in Judea and Samaria (The Transitional Period)
- Acts 13:1– 28:31   The church's witness to the ends of the earth (The Gentile Mission)

Note that we call the church's witness in Jerusalem, the Jewish Mission; the church's witness in Judea and Samaria, the Transitional Period; and the church's witness to the ends of the earth, the Gentile Mission. The second part of Acts 1:8 also reveals the book's missionary orientation. It is about the missionary advance of the church to the ends of the earth. (These concepts will be discussed more in Chapter 2.)

Guidelines for Interpreting Acts

As we move through the book of Acts, eight important hermeneutical principles will guide our study. They are as follows:

1. All Scripture (including the historical portions) is inspired by God and is useful for doctrine (2 Tim. 3:16).
2. Luke's writings belong to the literary *genre* of historical-narrative.
3. Luke wrote as a Spirit-inspired historian, a Spirit-inspired theologian, and a Spirit-inspired missiologist.
4. The disciplines of biblical theology and narrative theology must be employed in interpreting Acts.
5. Luke had his own Spirit-inspired agenda and purposes in writing Luke-Acts.
6. Luke, like any biblical writer, must first be understood on his own terms, and only then should his teachings be related to those of other biblical writers.

7. In writing his histories, Luke, under the guidance of the Holy Spirit, was selective and subjective in his choice of material.
8. Luke's primary intent for writing Acts is revealed in Acts 1:8.[7]

THE MISSIOLOGICAL CHARACTER OF ACTS

Luke wrote Acts, not only as a Spirit-inspired historian and theologian, but also as a Spirit-inspired missiologist. Missionary themes dominate the book. In it Luke has much to say about the Gentile nations (the *ethne*) and the church's responsibility to reach them (Acts 1:8; 13:46; 26:20; 28:28).[8] He further talks about missionary strategy. He structures the entire book of Acts around Jesus' strategic missionary pronouncement in Acts 1:8. Also, in chapter 19 he summarizes Paul's missionary strategy, a strategy the apostle used throughout the Roman empire. Understanding the missiological character of Acts is essential in understanding the message of Acts.

CONCLUSION

Acts can, therefore, be properly viewed as a missions manual. In it we can find methods and strategies that can guide us in fulfilling the Great Commission of Christ. It is more than the simple story of the missionary advance of the first-century church; it is a divinely-inspired guidebook of how that advance was accomplished in the first century, and should be accomplished today. As we proceed through this study, we will be looking at the experiences, attitudes, strategies, and methods that caused the first church to quickly become a force in the earth. We will learn many things that will help us in fulfilling the ministries to which God has called us.

---

[7] For a fuller explanation of these principles, see Anthony Palma, *The Holy Spirit: A Pentecostal Perspective* (Springfield, MO: Gospel Publishing House, 2001), 91-96.

[8] The *ethne* are mentioned 44 times in Acts, including 2:5; 4:25, 27; 7:7, 45; 8:9; 9:15; 10:22, 35, 45; 11:1, 18; 13:19, 42, 46, 47, 48; 14:2, 5, 16, 27; 15:3, 7, 12, 14, 17, 19, 23; 17:26; 18:6; 21:11, 19, 21, 25; 22:21; 24:2, 10, 17; 26:4, 17, 20, 23; 28:19, 28.

Chapter 1: Interpreting Acts

QUESTIONS FOR REFLECTION AND REVIEW

1. Give three reasons why it is important to study the book of Acts.
2. How does Acts serve as a bridge between the gospels and the epistles?
3. How can the book of Acts serve as a book of missionary strategy for the church today?
4. Who is the author of Acts? Give internal and external evidence to support your answer.
5. When was Acts written? To whom was it written? From where was it written?
6. What were the circumstances of the people to whom Luke wrote? How did these circumstances influence Luke's intent in writing to them?
7. According to the author, what was Luke's primary intent in writing Acts?
8. In what verse does Luke indicate his intent in writing Acts?
9. What powerful spiritual experience does Luke emphasize as being necessary for one to be empowered to participate fully in God's mission?
10. To what genre of literature does the book of Acts belong?
11. List and explain three important insights necessary for one to properly interpret Acts.
12. What is meant by the literary unity of Luke-Acts.
13. Did Luke write only as a historian, or did he also write as a Spirit-inspired theologian? Explain your answer.
14. Why is it important that Luke be given theological independence from Paul?
15. State two important hermeneutical tools that can be helpful in interpreting Acts.
16. How does biblical theology differ from systematic theology?
17. Define the following hermeneutical concepts used in interpreting historical narratives:
    - Narrative theology
    - Narrative rhetoric
    - Inclusion-exclusion
    - Redaction
    - Didactic segments
    - Parenthetical commentary.
18. How does Acts 1:8 serve as the interpretative key to the book of Acts?
19. Describe the *empowerment–witness motif* first introduced in the first half of Acts 1:8 and further developed throughout the book of Acts.
20. Explain how the second half of Acts 1:8 serves as a table of contents for the book.
21. What three "missions" are introduced in 1:8?
22. Cite eight important guidelines that should be followed in order to properly interpret Acts.

23. What do we mean when we say that Luke wrote as a Spirit-inspired missiologist?

QUESTIONS FOR CLASSROOM DISCUSSION

1. Other than to simply gain historical knowledge of the church's beginnings, why is it important for ministers of the gospel to carefully study the book of Acts?
2. Do you agree or disagree with C. Peter Wagner's statement that Acts is "God's training manual for modern Christians"? Why or why not?
3. How does one's understanding of the audience to whom Luke wrote Acts help him or her to properly interpret the message of the book?
4. Why is a proper understanding of Acts 1:8 essential to a correct interpretation of Acts?

Chapter 1: Interpreting Acts

– Chapter 2 –

Getting Ready for Pentecost

PRE-LESSON READING ASSIGNMENT

Acts 1:1-26

INTRODUCTION

The first eleven verses of Acts serve as a programmatic introduction to the entire work. As such, they set the tone and "write the program" for all that will follow. They perform at least five important functions in Luke's narrative:

- They summarize and finalize the work of Jesus as presented in the Gospel of Luke (vv. 1-2).
- They serve as a narrative bridge between Luke's two volumes (cf. Luke 24:44-53).
- They reveal Luke's authorial intent and introduce the key theme of the work (1:8a).
- They provide a "table of contents" for the book (1:8b).
- They introduce five overarching themes that will reappear throughout the book (vv. 1-11).

This chapter will look at how these verses fulfill these functions.

FIRST WORDS

Reading Assignment: Acts 1:1-3

The Story
Luke begins his book by reminding his readers of his former work, that is, the gospel of Luke. He summarizes Jesus' ministry as a ministry of "doing" and "teaching." After His resurrection, Jesus remained with His disciples for forty days, teaching them about the kingdom of God. Then, as His concluding act of ministry, Jesus, through the Holy Spirit, gave final instructions to His apostles.

Commentary
1:1 Theophilus. Luke addresses his book to Theophilus. This is the same man to whom he addressed his gospel, where he calls him "most excellent Theophilus" (Luke 1:3). In Acts the title "most excellent" is used of nobility and political leaders (Acts 24:3; 26:25). Theophilus, which means "lover of God," was probably a Greek believer, a man of considerable wealth and influence, and Luke's literary patron. Although Luke and Acts are addressed to a single person, they were obviously written to a larger audience. Luke had a specific community of believers in mind when he wrote, as was discussed in Chapter 1. Even more broadly, Acts has a message for all "lovers of God."

In my former book ... I wrote about all that Jesus began to do and to teach. Luke's "former book" is his gospel. According to Luke, that book described what Jesus *began* to do and teach before His ascension. The implication is that this second volume would be about what Jesus *continued* to do and teach after His ascension. In Luke, Jesus carried out His ministry through the direction and power of the Holy Spirit (Luke 4:18-19; cf. Acts 10:38). In Acts He will continue His ministry through His church, which will also be directed and empowered by the Spirit. The words "do and teach" summarize and characterize Jesus' entire ministry. It was a ministry of powerful words and mighty works.

1:2 instructions through the Holy Spirit. Even after His death and resurrection Jesus still carried out His ministry under the impulse of the Spirit. He gives instructions ("commandments," KJV) "through the Holy Spirit." The Holy Spirit's active role in empowering and inspiring ministry is a key theme of both the Gospel of Luke and Acts. As the Superintendent of the Harvest, the Holy Spirit, who anointed and guided Jesus' ministry, will now anoint and guide the global mission of the church.

1:3 After his suffering, he showed himself ... that he was alive. Here, at the very beginning of Acts, Luke refers to the death and resurrection of Jesus. These two pivotal events represent the core of the gospel (1 Cor. 15:1-6) and the paramount message of the church, as Luke will portray throughout Acts (1:22; 2:23-24, 31-32; 3:15, 26; 4:2, 33; 5:30; 10:39-40; 13:29-30, 34; 17:18, 31-32; 23:6; 24:15-21). Luke immediately informs his readers that the church's witness is to the gospel, and, that the marrow of the gospel is the death and resurrection of Christ. This is the message we must forcefully and faithfully proclaim to the nations.

spoke about the kingdom of God. The kingdom of God is the overarching context for the book of Acts.[9] One way Luke demonstrates this fact is by employing a common narrative strategy known as *inclusio*. In using this strategy a narrator will frame his story (or part of that story) inside key parallel statements. These statements will reveal a concept or idea which is to be superimposed onto all that occurs between them. In Acts Luke frames his entire book between key statements concerning the kingdom of God (1:3; 28:23, 31).[10] Once he does this, it is no longer necessary for him to mention the kingdom each time it applies. It is assumed that the kingdom of God is the context of everything within the frame. For Luke, to proclaim the kingdom is equivalent to preaching the gospel (Acts 8:12; 28:23, 31).

THE SPIRIT IS PROMISED

Reading Assignment: Acts 1:4-8

The Story

During His last meeting with His disciples, Jesus gave them final instructions. They were to wait in Jerusalem for the promised outpouring of the Spirit. In a few days they would be baptized in the Holy Spirit. As a result, they would receive supernatural power, enabling them to take the gospel to Jerusalem, all Judea and Samaria, and to the ends of the earth. When the disciples asked Jesus about Israel's future participation in the kingdom of God, He put them off and pointed them to the task at hand—Spirit-empowered witness to the nations.

---

[9] For a full treatment of the kingdom of God, see the author's book, *The Kingdom of God: A Pentecostal Interpretation.*

[10] Luke uses the phrase "kingdom of God" 32 times in his gospel (4:43; 6:20; 7:28; 8:1, 10; 9:2, 11, 9:27, 60, 62; 10:9, 11; 11:20; 13:18, 20, 28-29; 14:15; 16:16; 17:20-21; 18:16-17. 24-25, 29; 19:11; 21:31; 22:16, 18; 23:51) and six times in Acts (1:3; 8:12: 14:22; 19:8; 28:23, 31).

Commentary

1:4 On one occasion. This phrase reminds us of the episodic[11] nature of biblical history. Luke, like all biblical historians, is very selective in what he chooses to include in (or exclude from) his narrative. He carefully chooses only those incidents that will aid him in conveying the special message he wants to convey. Out of the many times Jesus met with His disciples during the forty days between His resurrection and His ascension, Luke chooses to begin his narrative with this specific incident. Luke's selectivity can be seen by that fact that he tells his story of the beginning of the church in only seventy episodes (and 14 episodic series).[12]

He gave them this command. Jesus issues a final command before returning to the Father: "Do not leave Jerusalem, but wait for the gift my Father promised." This command parallels Jesus statement in Luke 24:49: "Stay in the city until you have been clothed with power from on high." Jesus had, during the past forty days, repeatedly told His disciples to "Go!"[13] But now, in His final word to His disciples, He commands them to "Stay!" In other words, they must "go into all the worlds and preach the good news to all creation" (Mark 16:15), but first they must "stay" in Jerusalem and "wait for the gift [His] Father promised" (v. 4). The lesson is this: before they could effectively obey the first command, they would have to explicitly obey the second. Jesus left His church with a humanly impossible task, the evangelization of all nations before He comes again. It was a job beyond their (and our) capability. They would, therefore, need supernatural help. They were thus to "stay in the city until [they had] been clothed with power from on high" (Luke 24:49). We too, if we are to effectively reach the lost with the gospel, must carefully obey both commands.

the gift my Father promised. The phrase here translated "the gift my Father promised" (Gk. *tēn epangelian tou patros*) is literally "the promise of the Father" (ESV, NKJV, RSV). To what specific promise of the Father is Jesus referring? He is likely referring to the promise of the outpouring of the Spirit in Joel 2:28-29, since that

---

[11] An episode is a specific event or story that occurs as part of a larger series of events or stories.

[12] See Appendix 1.

[13] With each restatement of the Great Commission is an explicit or implicit command to go (Matt. 28:18-20, cf. 24:14; Mark 16:15-18; Luke 24:46-49; John 20:21-22; Acts 1:8).

was the passage Peter quoted to explain the outpouring of the Spirit at Pentecost (Acts 2:17-18). Jesus could have also been referring to His earlier promise that the "Father in heaven [will] give the Holy Spirit to those who ask him" (Luke 11:13). Joel generalized the promise: it is for "all people." Jesus specified: although the promise is potentially for all people, it is specifically for those children of the Father who earnestly ask for it (Luke 11:9-13).

1:5 baptized with the Holy Spirit. This phrase could be better translated "baptized *in* (Gk. *en*) the Holy Spirit." Just as John baptized *in* water, Jesus would baptize *in* the Holy Spirit. This statement of Jesus is referencing the statement of John the Baptist in Luke 3:16. In this metaphor Jesus is the baptizer and the Holy Spirit is the element into which one is baptized. Paul uses the same metaphor to describe another baptism, baptism into the body of Christ (1 Cor. 12:13). In Paul's metaphor the Spirit is the baptizer and the body of Christ is the element.

1:6 restore the kingdom to Israel. The disciples were correct in connecting Jesus' teaching concerning the Holy Spirit with the kingdom of God; however, their timing and focus were amiss. Jesus' immediate concern was that they would be baptized in the Holy Spirit so they might receive power to participate in advancing God's kingdom in the earth.

1:8 you will receive power ... you will be my witnesses. Acts 1:8 serves as the hermeneutical key to the book of Acts. As discussed in the last chapter, this verse can be divided into two parts, roughly corresponding to the first and second halves of the verse. The first half reveals Luke's *empowerment–witness motif* (i.e., "you will receive power" and as a result "you will be my witnesses"). This motif is the key to understanding Luke's primary intent in writing Acts. It is repeated many times in Acts. The pattern is most dramatically demonstrated in seven key outpourings in Acts:

1. Pentecost, the First Jerusalem Outpouring (2:1-4)
2. The Second Jerusalem Outpouring (4:31)
3. The Samaritan Outpouring (8:14-17)
4. The Damascene Outpouring (9:15-18)
5. The Caesarean Outpouring (10:44-48)
6. The Antiochian Outpouring (13:1-3)
7. The Ephesian Outpouring (19:1-7).

Each of these outpourings resulted in powerful missional witness. As we move through this study, we will observe how, in accordance with 1:8, every evangelistic and missionary advance of the church is preceded by one or more empowerings with the Holy Spirit. Through these outpourings the church is again and again empowered and equipped for its missional task. This is to be the church's pattern for witness during the entire Age of the Spirit, until Jesus comes again.

The second half of Acts 1:8 ("... in Jerusalem, and in all Judea and Samaria, and to the ends of the earth") functions as a programmatic outline for Acts. In other words, it writes a program or "table of contents" for the entire book. The following chart helps us to understand how Acts 1:8 interprets and structures the entire book of Acts:

The Seven Key Outpourings as They Relate to the Jewish and Gentile Missions

Introductory 1:1-11	The Jewish Mission *Jerusalem*	Transitional Period *Judea and Samaria* (Extending to Galilee, Cyprus, Cyrene, and Antioch)	The Gentile Mission *The Remotest Part of the Earth*
	1:12–8:1a Fulfilling the Jewish Mission	8:1b–12:25 Preparation for the Gentile Mission	13:1-28:31 Carrying out the Gentile Mission
Acts 1:8 "You will receive power... you will be my witnesses..."	❶ Pentecost ❷ The Second Jerusalem Outpouring	❸ The Samaritan Outpouring ❹ The Damascene Outpouring ❺ The Caesarean Outpouring	❻ The Antiochian "Outpouring" ❼ The Ephesian Outpouring

Figure 2.1[14]

Acts 1:8 thus discloses Luke's primary intent in writing Acts. Luke wrote to call the church back to its Pentecostal and missionary roots, and to demonstrate the absolute necessity of the Spirit's empowering if one is to effectively participate in the mission of God. He further wrote to teach that this empowering comes as the result of

---

[14] Figure 2.1 is taken from the author's book *Empowered for Global Mission: A Missionary Look at the Book of Acts,* p. 164.

a powerful life-altering experience, the baptism in the Holy Spirit.

The second part of the verse reveals Luke's secondary purpose: to trace the church's geographical progress from Jerusalem to Rome. It was also to show how the church moved from being a localized Jewish sect into a universal body of believers, encompassing both Jews and Gentiles.

to the ends of the earth. The ultimate scope of God's mission is "the ends of the earth" (Gk. *eschátou teés geés*). Every person, of every age, and of every language and nation is the object of His loving concern and grace. Every person must therefore hear the good news of Christ. It is for this great purpose that the Spirit empowers Christ's disciples.

Life Application

The command of Jesus to wait for the promise of the Father was not only for those first disciples in Jerusalem; it is for all believers of every age until Jesus comes again (cf. Luke 11:9-13). We, like those early believers, must seek the face of God until the Holy Spirit comes upon us as He did upon them. Only then will we be adequately equipped to be His witnesses at home and "to the ends of the earth."

JESUS TAKEN UP INTO HEAVEN

Reading Assignment: Acts 1:9-11

The Story

Having promised His disciples power, Jesus ascended into heaven. As He disappeared from their sight, two men (angels) appeared before them. The angels challenged them, "Why are you standing here staring into the sky? This same Jesus will come again in the same way you have seen him go into heaven."

Commentary

1:9 He was taken up. Jesus' ascension receives only brief mention in the gospels (Mark 16:19; Luke 24:51). Here, however, Luke adds more detail concerning the event. Jesus was taken up "before their very eyes," that is, He ascended visibly and bodily into heaven. In Acts this story sets the stage for the outpouring of the Spirit at Pentecost (2:33). It is an important aspect of Luke's theology and one of the "many convincing proofs" that Jesus was alive (cf. 1:3).

1:10 Why do you stand looking? These words of the angels seem to come as a challenge to the gawking disciples. While there is an appropriate time to stand and gaze on the Lord's glory (2 Cor. 3:18), such activity, however, can never serve as a substitute for obedience to His clear commands. The disciples had been commanded to return to Jerusalem and wait to receive power from on high (Luke 24:49; Acts 1:4-5), and they were required to quickly obey. Throughout Acts angels are seen intervening into the mission of God. They often urge the disciples on to "go" and bear witness to Christ (5:19-20; 8:26).

1:11 This same Jesus ... will come back. This statement of the angels introduces the eschatological context of the book of Acts. Since this same Jesus will come back, there is an urgency about the disciples' mission. The entire book of Acts (as well as the entire New Testament) has an eschatological, or last-days, context: "He must remain in heaven until the time comes for God to restore everything..." (Acts 3:21). Luke spoke often on eschatology and the second coming of Christ (Luke 12:35-40; 13:34-35; 21:25-36; 22:16; Acts 1:10-11; 2:17; 3:19-21).

Further Insight
The first eleven verses function in Acts much as does a legal or academic abstract. They outline the major elements of what is to follow in the rest of the book. Five key themes are introduced that repeatedly recur throughout Acts. In this study we will often cite these themes as they appear in the text. However, now, to prepare the reader for what is to come, we will briefly state them:

1. The kingdom of God. Luke mentions the kingdom of God twice in these verses: In verse 3 Jesus "spoke about the kingdom of God." In verse 6, His disciples inquired about the restoration of "the kingdom to Israel." As mentioned, the kingdom of God is a key theme in Acts.

2. The global mission of the church. Jesus told His disciples that "you will be my witnesses in Jerusalem, and in all Judea and Samaria, and to the ends of the earth" (v. 8). Acts is principally the story of the church fulfilling its God-ordained mission to take the gospel to the nations.

3. The necessity of Spirit empowering. In verses 4-5 Jesus commanded His disciples, "Do not leave Jerusalem, but wait for the gift my Father promised, which you have heard me speak about. For John baptized with water, but in a few days you will be baptized with the Holy Spirit." In verse 8, He promised them, "You will receive power when the Holy Spirit comes on you." The mission of God can only be successfully accomplished in the power of the Spirit. This theme is repeated often in Acts.

4. The Holy Spirit guiding the work of missions. Verse 2 says that Jesus gave orders to the disciples "by the Holy Spirit." He continued to minister in the Spirit's power, even after His resurrection. Throughout Acts one reads of the Spirit inspiring, guiding, and directing the work of missions. Luke presents Him as the Superintendent of the Harvest.

5. The urgency of the missionary task. In verse 11 the angels chided the disciples: "Men of Galilee,... why do you stand here looking into the sky? This same Jesus ... will come back." In Acts the work of missions is carried out in anticipation of Christ's soon return.

IN THE UPPER ROOM

Reading Assignment: Acts 1:12-26

The Story

In obedience to Jesus' command, the disciples returned to Jerusalem. There they entered an upper room where they resided, prayed, and conducted business. The group included the eleven apostles: Peter, John, James, Andrew, Philip, Thomas, Bartholomew, Matthew, James the son of Alphaeus, Simon the Zealot, and Judas son of James. Also with them were Mary, the mother of Jesus, Jesus' brothers, and a group of women. The believers numbered about 120. These all continued together in prayer.

One day Peter stood and proposed to the group that Judas Iscariot, who had betrayed Jesus and then committed suicide, be replaced. His replacement would have to be a man who had been with the disciples during Jesus' entire ministry. The group then nominated two men, Joseph called Barsabbas and Matthias. After prayer, they cast lots, and the lot fell to Matthias, who was added to the eleven apostles.

Commentary

1:13 upstairs to the room where they were staying. There were about 120 disciples who gathered with the apostles in the upper room (v. 15). Their time was divided between this venue and the temple courts. In the upper room they gathered for prayer and business. They also "stayed continually at the temple, praising God" (Luke 24:53).

1:14 constantly in prayer. Luke consistently associates the reception of the Holy Spirit with earnest prayer. The Holy Spirit descended upon Jesus "as He was praying" (Luke 3:21). Before the day of Pentecost the disciples were "continually ... in praise" (Luke 24:53) and "constantly in prayer" (Acts 1:14). Saul spent three days in prayer before Ananias laid hands on him to receive the Spirit (9:9, 11). Cornelius "prayed to God regularly" (10:2), and Peter also prayed in preparation for the outpouring of the Spirit at Caesarea (v. 9). At Antioch the Spirit moved as the church worshiped, prayed, and fasted (13:1-2). The Holy Spirit came upon the Samaritans, Saul, and Ephesian disciples when they were being prayed for (8:17; 9:17-18; 19:6). Further, it was in the context of teaching about prayer that Jesus instructed His disciples to pray to their heavenly Father and ask Him for the Holy Spirit (Luke 11:1-2, 9-13). Anyone who desires to be filled with the Holy Spirit should, thus, commit himself or herself to earnest and expectant prayer to God. Further, prayer should mark the lifestyle of all Spirit-filled Christians (Luke 18:1; Acts 3:1; Rom. 1:10-11; 8:26-27; Eph. 1:16; 1 Thess. 5:17). The prayer of faith is a powerful spiritual weapon available to all believers (Mark 11:24; James 5:15).

along with the women. Women were among those who were filled with the Spirit at Pentecost. Throughout his two-volume work Luke often focuses on the significance of women in fulfilling the mission of God (Luke 8:1-3; 23:49, 55; 24:1-12, 22; Acts 5:14; 8:12; 16:13-15; 17:4). He makes it clear that women can be filled with the Spirit and effectively used by God in ministry (Acts 1:14; 2:17-18; 18:18-19, 26; 21:9).

1:22 one of these must become a witness with us of his resurrection. In the upper room Peter makes it clear that "it is necessary" to choose a replacement for Judas. While one reason for this necessity was to return the number of disciples to the original twelve, the key reason for the choice seems to be witness to the gospel, for Peter said that the one chosen "must become a witness ... of his resurrection."

CONCLUSION

In the first chapter of Acts Luke linked his second volume to his first. He also revealed his purpose in writing the book and introduced some key themes of his work. Luke thus set the stage for the outpouring of the Spirit that would take place on the Day of Pentecost. In the next chapter we will examine that epochal event and its meaning for us today.

QUESTIONS FOR REFLECTION AND REVIEW

1. In what ways do the first eleven verses of Acts serve as a programmatic introduction to the rest of the book?
2. To whom is the book of Acts addressed? Was it meant only for him?
3. What is the "former book" that Luke mentions in 1:1?
4. How is the Spirit of God introduced as the "Superintendent of the Harvest" in verse 2?
5. How important is the message of Jesus' death and resurrection to Luke?
6. How does the literary device of *inclusio* help us to understand that the kingdom of God is the overarching theme of Acts?
7. What was Jesus' final command to His church before returning to heaven? How can this command be reconciled with His repeated command to "go"?
8. To what promises was Jesus referring in 1:5 when. He spoke of "the gift my Father promised"?
9. Describe the metaphor "baptized in the Holy Spirit."
10. According to 1:8, what would be the result of the Holy Spirit coming upon the disciples?
11. List seven key outpourings of the Holy Spirit in Acts, each of which demonstrates Luke's empowerment–witness motif introduced in 1:8.
12. Study Figure 2:1 and answer the following questions:
    - Which verses in Acts are introductory?
    - Which chapters cover the Jewish Mission? The Transitional Period?
      the Gentile Mission?
    - Which outpourings of the Spirit occurred during the Jewish Mission? the Transitional Period? the Gentile Mission?
13. According to 1:8, what is the ultimate scope of God's mission?
14. What question did the angels ask the disciples at Jesus' ascension? What promise did they make? Why did they ask the question?
15. List five key missiological themes introduced in Acts 1:1-11.
16. Prior to Pentecost, what were the disciples doing in the upper room? What were they doing in the temple courts? (cf. Luke 24:53).
17. Cite several texts in Luke-Acts that associate prayer with receiving the Holy Spirit.
18. Why does Luke point out that women were also present before the Day of Pentecost?

Chapter 2: Getting Ready for Pentecost

QUESTIONS FOR CLASSROOM DISCUSSION

1. How is it significant that Jesus' final instruction to His disciples was to wait in Jerusalem until they had been empowered by the Holy Spirit? What present-day applications can be made?
2. Is it important whether one calls the Pentecostal experience the baptism *of* the Holy Spirit, the baptism *with* the Holy Spirit, or the baptism *in* the Holy Spirit? Which is the best designation? Why? What are the implications?
3. In this chapter the author states that, in accordance with 1:8, each of seven key outpourings of the Spirit in Acts resulted in powerful missional witness. He further states that "every evangelistic and missionary advance of the church is preceded by one or more empowerings with the Holy Spirit." What are the implications of these truths?
4. What are the missional implications of the angels' question to the disciples, "Men of Galilee, why do you stand here looking into the sky?"
5. In the upper room the disciples were constantly in prayer. How important is prayer to one's living the Spirit-empowered life? How important is prayer in fulfilling the *missio Dei?*

– Part II –
The Jewish Mission

– CHAPTER 3 –

PENTECOST
THE FIRST JERUSALEM OUTPOURING

PRE-LESSON READING ASSIGNMENT

Acts 2:1–4:22

INTRODUCTION

In the last chapter we observed the church getting ready for Pentecost. Jesus commanded His disciples to remain in Jerusalem until they had been baptized in the Holy Spirit. This baptism would result in their being empowered for witness, both locally and globally. In this chapter we will examine the outpouring of the Spirit on the Day of Pentecost and observe how it resulted in immediate, powerful prophetic witness in the city. We will also look at the nature of that witness, which included Spirit-inspired proclamation and Spirit-empowered demonstration.

THE SPIRIT IS POURED OUT

Reading Assignment: Acts 2:1-13

The Story

On the Jewish feast of Pentecost God poured out His Spirit on the gathered disciples. The Spirit's coming was accompanied by two remarkable phenomena: a sound from heaven like the blowing of a mighty wind, followed by the appearance of a mass of flames that came to rest above the group. The mass then divided itself into individual tongues of fire, with one tongue lighting over the head of each disciple. They were all filled with the Holy Spirit and began to proclaim the wonders of God in various Gentile languages. These languages were recognized by Jewish pilgrims who had gathered for Pentecost from throughout the then-known world. The crowd's reaction to the disciples' speaking in tongues was mixed: some were amazed, asking, "What does this mean?" Others mocked.

Commentary

The outpouring of the Spirit at Pentecost is the defining event in the book of Acts. It sets the stage and gives meaning and definition to everything that follows. A clear understanding of the meaning of Pentecost is essential for an accurate interpretation of Acts.

2:1 When the day of Pentecost came. Pentecost was one of three annual pilgrim feasts of the Jews in which every Jewish male in the area was required to attend.[15] The word "Pentecost" (Gk. *pentecostos*) means fiftieth. Pentecost took place fifty days after Passover. It was also called the Feast of Weeks (Exod. 34:22), the Feast of Harvest (Exod. 23:16), and the Feast of Firstfruits (v. 19). Tens of thousands of Jewish pilgrims gathered from all over the Roman empire to attend this important feast.

they were all together in one place. The place where the disciples gathered is traditionally believed to be the upper room mentioned in 1:13. However, more recent scholarship has generally located the place of the Spirit's outpouring as the temple mount, probably in the Court of the Gentiles, since this was the only venue in Jerusalem large enough to contain the crowd of possibly thirty to forty thousand people who gathered to hear Peter's sermon.[16] Luke also says that the disciples spent considerable time in the temple before Pentecost (Luke 24:53). Wherever the disciples gathered, they were there in obedience to the command of Jesus to wait in Jerusalem to be "clothed with power from on high" (Luke 24:49; cf. Acts 1:4-8).

2:2-3 a violent wind ... tongues of fire. The outpouring of the Spirit was accompanied by two supernatural wonders, one "in the heaven above," the other "on the earth below" (2:19). These wonders

---

[15] The other two pilgrim feasts were Passover and Tabernacles.

[16] About three thousand were saved at the conclusion of Peter's sermon (2:42). If that number represented ten percent of the crowd, then the size of the crowd must have been at least thirty thousand.

indicate that a theophany (a visual manifestation of the presence of God) was occurring. The first wonder was a sudden sound from heaven "like the blowing of a violent wind." This deafening blast was likely heard throughout Jerusalem—especially on the temple mount, where it occurred (v. 6). The origin of the sound being "from heaven" indicates that God had come powerfully on the scene. It reminds us of the words of Jesus: "The wind blows where it wishes, and you hear the sound of it" (John 3:8, NKJV). As Jesus had earlier breathed on the eleven disciples, God was now breathing on the 120 (cf. John 20:20-22; also Job 4:9, 33:4), and His breath sounded like a violent wind from heaven!

The "sound like the blowing of a mighty wind" also speaks to the missional purpose of the Spirit's outpouring, as first revealed in 1:8. Wind is one of the most powerful elements in all of nature, as recent hurricanes have underlined. Jesus said that the global missionary work of the church is to be carried out in the power of the Spirit. He also described the Spirit's redemptive works as like the wind, sovereign in its movement and ceaseless in its activity (cf. John 3:8). The Spirit works tirelessly throughout the world inspiring and empowering the church, revealing Christ to the lost, and drawing people unto Him.

A second wonder occurred at Pentecost: the appearance of "what seemed to be tongues of fire that separated and came to rest on each of them." Judging from the wording of the text, it seems that the appearance of fire first came to rest over the disciples' heads as one great fiery mass. It then divided itself, and an individual tongue of fire came to rest on each of the waiting disciples. What did it mean? In the Old Testament fire is sometimes used as a symbol of God's presence (Exod. 3:2; 19:18). According to Stanley Horton, "The fire here signified God's acceptance of the Church Body as the temple of the Holy Spirit (Eph. 2:21, 22; 1 Cor. 3:16), and then, the acceptance of the individual believers as also being temples of the Spirit (1 Cor. 6:19)."[17] No longer would people be required to come to the temple in Jerusalem to meet the living God, but now "living temples" of God would take the gospel to all nations in the power of the Spirit (Acts 1:8).

2:4 All of them were filled with the Holy Spirit. The Holy Spirit who had come upon the disciples now entered into them and filled them with His power and presence. The disciples' being "filled

---

[17] Stanley M. Horton, *The Book of Acts: The Wind of the Spirit* (Springfield: MO: Gospel Publishing House), 1996, p. 31.

Chapter 3: Pentecost: The First Jerusalem Outpouring

with the Spirit" is a direct fulfillment of Jesus command and prophecy in Acts 1:4-8. In these verses, He described their coming experience with the Spirit as receiving "the gift my Father promised" (v. 4), being "baptized with [in] the Holy Spirit" (v. 5), and as the moment "when the Holy Spirit comes upon [them]" (v. 8). In Acts Luke often uses these and other select terms interchangeably in describing the experience of Spirit baptism.

The purpose of their being filled with the Spirit is not for conversion but empowerment for missional witness, as Jesus predicted in 1:8: "But you will receive power when the Holy Spirit comes upon you; and you will be my witnesses…" The metaphor of being "filled with the Spirit" suggests the pervasiveness of the experience. When one is baptized in the Spirit, the Spirit fills and pervades every area of his or her being.

Further, it is significant that each time in Acts that the Spirit of God is poured out on a group of people, they are *all* filled (2:4; 4:31; 8:17, 10:44; 19:6, implied), thus indicating that the experience is for all believers. Every believer must be filled with the Spirit because every believer is called to be a witness for Christ (Acts 1:8).

began to speak in other tongues. The 120 disciples' speaking in tongues at Pentecost was the immediate and direct effect of their being filled with/baptized in the Holy Spirit. This is the first of three explicit mentions of people being filled with the Spirit and speaking in tongues in Acts (cf. 10:46; 19:6). On two other occasions in Acts where people are initially filled with the Spirit, speaking in tongues is a logical implication (8:17-19; 9:17-18 with 1 Cor. 14:18). Luke presents speaking in tongues as the universal sign of one's being baptized in the Holy Spirit.

The disciples' speaking in the tongues of the surrounding Gentile nations (fifteen are mentioned) testifies to the purpose of the gift. It reminds us of Jesus' ultimate focus in Luke 24:47 and Acts 1:8 on "all nations" and "the ends of the earth." The purpose of Spirit baptism, as presented by Luke both in his gospel and in Acts, is empowerment for missional witness.

2:5 *from every nation under heaven.* Luke informs his readers that people "from every nation under heaven" were gathered on the Day of Pentecost. Luke uses hyperbole to make a point. According to John R. W. Stott, "Although all the nations of the world were not present *literally,* they were *representatively.*"[18] The list of nations in

---

[18] John R. W. Stott, *The Message of Acts: The Spirit, the Church and the World* (Downers Grove, IL: Inter-Varsity Press, 1990), 68.

verses 9-11 harks back to the Table of the Nations in Genesis 10, and includes descendants of all three of Noah's sons: Shem, Ham, and Japheth. We are reminded of Jesus' words that "repentance and forgiveness of sins will be preached in his name to all nations, beginning at Jerusalem" (Luke 24:47).

2:6 each … in his own native language. The missional purpose of Spirit baptism is again emphasized in this verse. We are subtly reminded that those who spoke in these fifteen languages—as well as those who speak in the thousands of other languages throughout the world—are all objects of God's loving concern. They must all, therefore, remain the focus of the church's mission (Matt. 24:14; Rev. 5:9; 7:9).

2:11 declaring the wonders of God. Having been filled with the Spirit, the 120 begin to declare the wonders of God to the gathering crowd in their own native tongues. While many have interpreted the disciples' speaking in tongues as Spirit-inspired praise, the text clearly indicates Spirit-empowered proclamation. Whether worship or proclamation, the purpose is witness, for why else would the Spirit have caused them to speak in the languages of those gathered for the Feast of Pentecost?

Life Application

Jesus commanded His disciples to go into all the world and preach the gospel. And yet, He was insistent that they not begin the task until they had first been "clothed with power from on high" (Luke 24:49). We, like those first-century disciples, have also been commanded to take the gospel to all nations. And we, as they, must obey the command of Jesus to wait for the Spirit's empowering. This empowering comes as a result of one's being baptized in the Holy Spirit. This powerful experience is as essential a requirement for ministry today as it was for the disciples then.

FURTHER INSIGHT: THE SIGNIFICANCE OF PENTECOST

Is Pentecost the "birthday of the church?" This is a widely accepted opinion concerning the Day of Pentecost. Many biblical scholars, however, reject this view, pointing out that there is no scriptural text stating that this is the case. The church, rather than being born at Pentecost, emerged when Jesus first began to call His disciples to follow Him (cf. Matt. 4:18-22; 9:9; 18:17).

Pentecost, rather than being the birthday of the church, is the moment in time when the already existent church was first empowered by the Spirit to carry out its God-given mandate to take the gospel to all nations (Luke 24:46-49; Acts 1:8). Pentecost should thus serve as a lasting model for the church of every age until Jesus comes again (Acts 1:11). Believers today should ask for, and expect to receive, the same empowering experience as those first-century believers at Pentecost. And they should expect it for the same purpose, empowerment for mission.

Further, Pentecost is an early indication in Acts that Spirit baptism is an experience distinct from conversion. The disciples were already converted before Pentecost. They had been cleansed (John 15:3), called (Matt. 4:19; Luke 5:27-28; John 10:27-28), and commissioned (Matt. 28:18-20; Mark 16:15-16) by Jesus to take the gospel to the nations. Their command from Jesus was not to wait for the new birth, but to wait until they were empowered by the Spirit (Luke 24:49; Acts 1:4-8). The experience, in Luke's view, is not for sinners, but for God's children (Luke 11:9-13; cf. John 14:7).

PETER'S SPIRIT-INSPIRED WITNESS

Reading Assignment: Acts 2:14-36

The Story

Responding to the cry of the gathered crowd ("What does this mean?") Peter, full of the Holy Spirit, stood and addressed them. He informed them that the disciples were not drunk, as some had charged, but full of the Spirit, as prophesied by the Hebrew prophet Joel. According to Peter, these disciples' filling with the Spirit, evidenced by speaking in tongues, was a fulfillment of Joel's prophecy. It was also an indication that the last days had surely arrived. Quoting the ancient prophet, Peter proclaimed that the experience was not only for these disciples, but for all people: men and women, old and young, rich and poor, until Jesus comes again. As a result of this outpouring, the door is opened for all people to call on the name of the Lord and be saved.

Having explained the meaning of the events of Pentecost, Peter boldly proclaimed the gospel. He began by recounting the ministry of Jesus, noting that it was accredited by miracles, wonders, and signs. His crucifixion, though carried out by wicked men, was part of God's plan. And His resurrection was inevitable, since it was "impossible for death to keep its hold on him." Peter cites two Davidic Psalms (16:8-11; 110:1), claiming that these prophecies could only have been speaking of Christ, who alone was resurrected

Chapter 3: Pentecost: The First Jerusalem Outpouring

and exalted to the right hand of God. There He received from the Father the promise of the Holy Spirit, which He had now poured out on these disciples. Peter concluded his message: "Therefore let all Israel be assured of this: God has made this Jesus, whom you crucified, both Lord and Christ."

COMMENTARY

Prophecy Fulfilled (vv. 14-21)

Just as Jesus' Nazareth Proclamation (Luke 4:18-19) interpreted and explained the meaning of His anointing with the Holy Spirit at the Jordan River (3:21-22), Peter's Pentecost Proclamation interpreted and explained the meaning of the Spirit's outpouring at Pentecost. Just as Jesus' anointing was for missional witness ("The Spirit of the Lord is on me, because he has anointed me to preach good news to the poor..."), the disciples' empowering at Pentecost was also for missional witness (Acts 1:8).

2:14 Peter ... raised his voice and addressed the crowd. As Jesus had promised, the outpouring of the Spirit resulted in powerful Spirit-anointed witness. Peter, raising his voice to be heard above the gathering throng, addressed the crowd. The Greek word from which "addressed" is translated (*apophtheggomai*) is the same word translated "enabled" in 2:4. Peter was not merely preaching a sermon, at least not in the traditional sense. He was uttering forth (literal meaning) a Spirit-inspired prophetic message. This is thus a Lukan example of the gift of prophecy in action. Luke here depicts prophecy as Spirit-empowered proclamation of the gospel. The primary purpose of Spirit baptism is kerygmatic,[19] that is, it brings inspiration and empowerment to bear effective witness to the gospel.

2:16 this is what was spoken by the prophet Joel. In explaining the meaning of the disciples reception of the Spirit, Peter quoted from Joel 2:28-29. The disciples' speaking in tongues and resulting Spirit-inspired proclamation evidenced the fulfillment of Joel's prophecy that God would "pour out [His] Spirit on all people" (Acts 2:17-18).

2:17 the last days. The context of Acts is eschatological[20]—just as is the context of the entire New Testament. The events of Pentecost demonstrate conclusively that the last days had indeed

---

[19] Kerygma is the Greek word meaning proclamation.

[20] Eschatology is the biblical study of the last days.

dawned. They began with the first coming of Christ, the anointed One, and will continue until He comes again. The last days are thus defined as the Age of the Spirit. The missionary ministry of the church in Acts is carried out in anticipation of Christ's soon coming (cf. 1:11).

I will pour out my Spirit on all people. Under the Old Covenant the Spirit was given to select individuals, at select times, for select purposes. Now the Spirit is poured out generously on all humankind. The gift of the Spirit is thus universally available to all who will sincerely ask for it (Luke 11:9-13).

Your sons and daughters will prophesy. The gift of the Spirit, and its empowering result, is equally available to women as well as men. Luke sees women as co-participants in the church's prophetic mission of taking the gospel to all nations (cf. Luke 1:41-42; 2:36; Acts 18:26; 21:9).

2:18 and they will prophesy. These words are not found in Joel's prophecy, but were added by Peter (and recorded by Luke) as he spoke under the Spirit's inspiration. The apostle seems to be making the point that the disciples' speaking in tongues was part and parcel of the fulfillment of Joel's prophecy. Speaking in tongues is thus identified as prophetic, or Spirit-inspired, speech. Pentecost is, therefore, the initial fulfillment of Moses' wish that "all the LORD's people were prophets and that the Lord would put his Spirit on them" (Num. 11:29). The age of the prophethood of all believers had dawned.[21] The unique sign of this new community of prophets is speaking in tongues, and, by implication, its primary vocation is Spirit-inspired proclamation of the gospel to all nations.

2:20 the coming of the great and glorious day of the Lord. Luke again emphasizes the eschatological context of the book of Acts. Spirit-empowered witness to the nations must continue until Christ returns.

2:21 everyone who calls on the name of the Lord will be saved. The ultimate purpose of the Spirit's outpouring is to bring people to faith in Christ. The Spirit-empowered witness of the church will result in people calling on the name of the Lord and being saved.

The Gospel Proclaimed (2:22-36)

Peter's Spirit-anointed message at Pentecost, along with his message in 3:11-26, establishes a pattern for preaching the gospel in

---

[21] Roger Stronstad, *The Prophethood of All Believers* (Sheffield, ENG: Sheffield Academic Press, 2003).

Acts. This pattern is often called the "apostolic kerygma." It includes such elements as (1) the proclamation that Jesus is Lord and Christ, who was crucified, raised from the dead, and exalted to the right hand of the Father (2:22-36; 3:13-15); (2) an announcement that the Spirit has been poured out on all believers (2:16-18, 32-33; 3:19); (3) an encourage-ment to expect the promised gift of the Holy Spirit (2:38-39); (4) a declaration that Jesus will return (3:20-21); and (5) a call to faith and repentance (2:36-38; 3:19).[22] All these elements should be found in our gospel proclamation today.

2:22 Jesus ... *a man accredited by God to you by miracles, wonders, and signs.* Jesus was the central message of all apostolic preaching. Here, Peter is saying that God placed His stamp of approval on Jesus' life, ministry, and message by working through Him in miracles, wonders, and signs. These miraculous works, according to Luke, were done through the power of the Spirit (Acts 10:38). The Spirit who had worked through Jesus was now working through His Spirit-empowered servants. The Spirit would accredit their message in the same way He had accredited Jesus'. A "miracle" (Gk. *dunamis*) is a demonstration of God power. A "wonder" (Gk. *teras*) is the effect of the miracle on the hearts and minds of the observers. A "sign" (Gk. *semeion*) is a miracle that attests to or confirms the message of the gospel and demonstrates the power of the kingdom of God.

2:24 *nailing him to the cross ... God raised him from the dead.* The death and resurrection of Christ are two essential elements of all gospel preaching (cf. 1 Cor. 15:1-4). (See comments on 1:3.)

2:32 *we are all witnesses.* Witness is a central theme in Acts. The theme was first introduced in 1:8. In Acts, Jesus' disciples are called witnesses at least thirteen times (1:8, 22; 2:32; 3:15; 5:32; 10:39, 41, 43; 13:31; 14:17; 22:15; 23:11; 26:16).

2:33 *the promised Holy Spirit.* This phrase references Jesus' command in 1:4 to wait for the "promise of the Father" (1:4: NKJV; cf. Luke 11:13; 24:49, Acts 2:33, 39). The promise of the Father is the promise that God's people will be baptized in and empowered by the Holy Spirit (Acts 1:4-8; cf. Luke 3:15-16; 24:49).

he has ... poured out what you now see and hear. The outpouring of the Holy Spirit on the Day of Pentecost was Jesus' final redemptive act, which included His death, resurrection,

---

[22] See the note on "[Acts] 2:14–40 PETER'S PENTECOST SERMON," in the *Life in the Spirit Study Bible* (Grand Rapids, MI: Zondervan, 2003), 1665-1666.

ascension, and the pouring out of His Spirit. This outpouring fulfilled His promises made in John 14:16 and Acts 1:4-5.

2:36 both Lord and Christ. The conclusion of the matter is that Jesus is both Lord (Gk. *Krion*) and Christ (Gk. *Christon*), or Messiah.

Life Application

God's will for His church is that it be a Spirit-empowered community of last-days prophets dedicated to carrying the message of Christ to the ends of the earth before He comes again. If that is the case, then we must each dedicate ourselves to that all-important task.

The gospel, which is the message of Jesus, must remain the central message of the church today. At the heart of the message is Christ's death, burial, and resurrection (cf. 1 Cor. 15:1-7). We must never forget that it is this message, preached in the power of the Spirit, that will open the door for people to be saved. We must never neglect this message. We must never be so foolish and shortsighted as to replace it with other less important messages, no matter how appealing they may seem at the time.

THE PROMISE OF THE SPIRIT

Reading Assignment: Acts 2:37-41

The Story

Hearing Peter's Spirit-inspired explanation of the events of Pentecost and his proclamation of the gospel, many in the crowd were deeply moved and began to cry out to the apostles, "Brothers, what shall we do?" Peter replied that they must repent of their sins and follow Christ in water baptism. Then they, too, could receive the gift of the Holy Spirit. Not only could they receive, but everyone from every place and age, who will meet these conditions can receive the same gift. Because of the powerful demonstrations at Pentecost, and Peter's powerful proclamation of the gospel, about three thousand people believed on Christ, repented of their sins, were baptized in water, and added to the church.

Commentary

Pentecost is the first example in Acts of Luke's *empowerment–witness motif* introduced in Acts 1:8. The disciples' being filled with the Holy Spirit resulted in powerful prophetic proclamation of the gospel (2:14-41), which then resulted in an immediate and ongoing harvest of souls (vv. 41, 47).

2:37 Brothers, what shall we do? Those who listened to Peter's Spirit-anointed message were "cut to the heart," that is, they were brought under strong conviction by the Holy Spirit (cf. John 16:8-11). As a result, they cried out, "What shall we do," that is, "What can we do to receive the Messiah and to experience what we have seen?"

2:38 Repent and be baptized. The imperative "repent" (Gk. *metanoeésate*) occurs five times in preaching in Acts (2:38; 3:19; 8:22; 17:30; 26:20). Repentance and faith are the essential requirements for salvation (Acts 20:21; cf. Matt. 21:32; Mark 1:15), and water baptism is the first step of obedience. It is "the pledge of a good conscience toward God" (1 Pet. 3:21) and an outward symbol of the inner work of conversion.

the gift of the Holy Spirit. Those who had been born again could now receive the gift of the Holy Spirit. The gift (singular) of the Holy Spirit is not to be confused with the gifts (plural) of the Spirit. This is the gift of the Spirit Himself. In Luke's usage, the gift of the Spirit is an empowering experience separate from conversion whose purpose is empowerment for witness. In Acts 1:4-5 Jesus equates it with the promise of the Father and the baptism in the Holy Spirit, which the disciples would receive at Pentecost. He said that the reception of this gift would result in power to witness (v. 8). It is the same gift that the new believers will receive in Samaria (8:20) and the Gentiles will receive in Caesarea (10:45; 11:17).

2:39 for you and your children and for all who are far off. The gift of the Spirit is for all people of every generation until Jesus comes again. The phrase, "all who are far off," is a reference to the Gentiles (cf. 22:21).

2:41 three thousand were added. As a result of the outpouring of the Spirit at Pentecost, and the powerful Spirit-empowered witness that followed, three thousand people followed Peter's instructions and were added to the church. It is also likely that these same three thousand people were baptized in the Holy Spirit on the same day, since they followed the instructions of Peter in verse 38 (cf. v. 41).

Life Application

As preachers of the gospel, we have two great responsibilities: the first is to clearly proclaim the gospel of Christ and point people to salvation. The second is to immediately lead these same people into the baptism in the Holy Spirit. Being born of the Spirit will prepare them for heaven. Being filled with the Spirit will prepare them for Christian service.

A NEW PROPHETIC COMMUNITY

Reading Assignment: Acts 2:42-47

The Story

The outpouring of the Spirit at Pentecost resulted in the creation of a new prophetic community. This community of Spirit-baptized prophets was characterized by devotion to God, to the truth, and to one another. It was also characterized by the divine presence, evidenced by signs and wonders. Their powerful inner and outer witness produced continual growth as "the Lord added to their number daily those who were being saved."

Commentary

2:42 They devoted themselves. The inner life of the new prophetic community was one of devotion. This devotion was fourfold: to the apostles' teaching, to fellowship, to the breaking of bread, and to prayer. This dynamic community life was the result of the Spirit's working in them individually and in their relationships with one another. Their devotion was sustained through ongoing prayer and commitment to the mission of God.

2:43 many wonders and miraculous signs. Just as Jesus' ministry was attested to by miraculous signs, so were the ministries of His followers. According to Luke, both were the result of their being filled with, and empowered by, the Spirit.

2:44 every day they continued to meet together. The inner life of the new prophetic community was also marked by a strong bond of unity and togetherness. This togetherness included daily gatherings in homes and in the temple courts. In their home cells they ate and shared communion together. In their public meetings they gave kerygmatic witness to Christ. Always, their gatherings were filled with praise and joy.

2:47 enjoying the favor of the people. In accordance with Luke's missionary and pneumatic theme in Acts, the believers' Spirit-generated community life served as a powerful witness to those outside the community of faith. That is, people were attracted to the church and "the Lord added to their number daily those who were being saved."

Chapter 3: Pentecost: The First Jerusalem Outpouring

Life Application

Our witness to the world involves more than proclamation; it also involves being the community of Christ. As God's Spirit-filled prophetic community, our association with one another and the world must be characterized by devotion to Christ, to one another, and to the word of God. Our gatherings should be filled with the presence of God and the joy of the Lord. Christ must be at the center of all we do. His life and presence should be demonstrated by wonders and miraculous signs. Such a church will be a powerful witness to those outside and will draw people into itself.

SPIRIT-EMPOWERED WITNESS IN JERUSALEM

Reading Assignment: Acts 3:1-26

The Story

At the hour of prayer Peter and John met a beggar at the Beautiful Gate (the entrance to the Court of the Women) in the temple at Jerusalem. The beggar asked them for money. Peter, however, gave him something better. He took the beggar by the hand and in the name of Jesus Christ of Nazareth lifted him up. The man's feet and ankles were immediately healed. In excitement he began running through the temple courts praising God.

Because of the excitement caused by the beggar's healing, the people gathered around him, Peter, and John. Just as he had done on the Day of Pentecost, Peter seized the opportunity to preach the gospel. He told the people that it was not his nor John's own power or holiness that had made the man walk. It was the power of the name of the resurrected Jesus! He then declared the gospel to them, saying that Jesus' death and resurrection were foretold by all the prophets, and calling on them to repent of their sins. If they would do this, their sins would be blotted out and God would send "times of refreshing" upon them. They should also look for Jesus to come again from heaven. All of this, said Peter, had been foretold by Moses, Samuel, and the other holy prophets. God had even promised Abraham that through his offspring (that is, Jesus) all the peoples of the earth would be blessed. They must now repent. If, however, they did not turn from their wicked ways, they would be cut off.

COMMENTARY

Luke concluded his account of the outpouring at Pentecost with a summary statement: "Everyone was filled with awe, and many wonders and miraculous signs were done by the apostles" (v. 43). Now, he gives a more detailed account of one of those miraculous signs, the healing of a crippled beggar. It follows from the natural flow of the narrative that this healing occurred as a direct result of the disciples being filled with the Spirit at Pentecost. And, as on the Day of Pentecost, it resulted in powerful witness to Christ.

A Miracle at the Beautiful Gate (3:1-10)

3:6 what I have I give you. This phrase spoken by Peter is a reference to the power of the Holy Spirit that he and the other disciples had received on the Day of Pentecost. It is only because they had been baptized in the Holy Spirit that they could say with confidence, "Look at us!" (v. 4). What they had received, however, was not for their own personal blessing. It was power to give away—to bless others. It was primarily to bear witness to Jesus.

In the name of Jesus Christ of Nazareth. All the ministry of the early church was done in the name of Jesus (Acts 2:38; 3:16; 4:10, 18, 30; 5:40; 8:12, 16; 9:27; 10:48; 15:26; 16:18; 19:5, 13, 17; 21:13; 26:9). This means that the disciples operated under His authority and followed His directions. As they submitted themselves to Jesus and His mission, they received authority from Him to act in His name.

3:10 filled with wonder and amazement. Seeing the lame beggar leaping and praising God in the temple courts, the people were filled with wonder and came running together to find out what had happened. At that moment a "faith shift" took place in their hearts. These people who had previously been hostile to, or disinterested in, the message of Christ suddenly became vitally interested. This illustrates the value of miraculous signs and wonders in the evangelistic and missionary work of the church.

Peter's Second Spirit-Inspired Message (3:11-26)

Luke presents a second example of prophetic (Spirit-inspired) preaching in the New Testament. As at Pentecost, Jesus is the central theme of the message. Also, as in Peter's Pentecost message, there is a promise of the Spirit for those who will repent and follow Christ.

3:15 You killed the author of life, but God raised him from the dead. Again Peter's message centers on the death and resurrection of Jesus. To neglect this essential theme is to miss the very heart of the gospel. (See comments on 1:3.)

We are witnesses of this. Spirit-empowered witness is a central theme of Acts (see comments on 2:32). We know that Peter's witness in this instance is Spirit-empowered because it was predicated by the miracle of healing the crippled beggar (3:1-6).

3:19 Repent, then, and turn to God. As in all apostolic proclamation, Peter calls his hearers to repentance. The call to repentance and faith is an essential component of all true preaching. The call is to "repentance toward God and faith toward our Lord Jesus Christ" (Acts 20:21, NKJV; cf. Matt. 21:32; Mark 1:15; Acts 19:4; Heb. 6:1).

times of refreshing may come from the Lord. This metaphor refers to the outpouring of the Holy Spirit. We can expect God to continue to send times of refreshing (outpourings of the Spirit) on the church until "he may send the Christ," that is, until Jesus comes again. This verse echoes Acts 2:38 in that it calls on people to first be saved ("repent ... and turn to God, so that your sins may be blotted out") and then to receive the Holy Spirit. This turning to God, and the resultant outpouring of the Spirit, can be both individual and corporate.

3:20 *that he may send the Christ.* This phrase reminds us of the eschatological (last days) context of the book of Acts. Because Jesus is coming again, the church must go quickly to fulfill the mission of Christ (cf. 1:11).

3:25 *Through your offspring all peoples on earth will be blessed.* The global mission of Christ, as expressed in 1:8, was not a new development in God's redemptive plan. It was rather a restatement of God's eternal mission from the beginning. Here, Peter is referring to God's promise to Abraham that through his "offspring" (Christ) "all peoples on the earth will be blessed" (cf. Gen. 12:6; 18:18; 22:18; 26:4; Gal. 3:8, 16). From the beginning, God's concern has always been for all the nations of the earth. The book of Acts is the story of how the early church went about fulfilling that mission. It is a model of how the church should go about fulfilling the mission of God until Jesus comes again.

Life Application

Believers today, like Peter, should be able to say to nonbelievers in need, "What I have I give you." Like Peter, we must remain full of the Holy Spirit so that, when the need presents itself, we will be ready to minister in His power. We can do this only as we act in the name of Jesus, that is, under His authority and in obedience to His commands. If we will do this, we, too, can expect the Lord to do signs and wonders in confirmation of His word.

As we go about preaching the gospel, we should think very carefully about the content of our message. It is not enough that we simply "preach the Bible." Certainly, we must preach the "whole counsel of God" (Acts 20:27, NKJV); however, we must center our message on Christ. We must clearly explain the meaning of His death and resurrection. The apostolic kerygma, as found in Acts, must serve as a model for our evangelistic and missionary teaching and preaching today.

SPIRIT-INSPIRED WITNESS BEFORE THE SANHEDRIN

Reading Assignment: Acts 4:1-22

The Story

Peter and John were arrested for preaching Christ in the temple courts and placed in jail for the night. The next morning they were asked to explain their actions. Peter, again filled with the Holy Spirit, answered that it was "by the name of Jesus of Nazareth" that the crippled beggar had been healed, and it is by that same name that they were preaching to the people. He boldly declared, "Salvation is found in no one else, for there is no other name under heaven given to men by which we must be saved." The Jewish leaders again commanded the two apostles to stop preaching and teaching in the name of Jesus. Peter and John, however, replied that they could not help speaking about what they had seen and heard. After being threatened again, they were released.

Commentary

The jailing and threatening of Peter and John in these verses is the first incident in Acts of overt persecution against the church. The church's ability to resist and triumph over persecution is a dominant theme of the book. Luke's message seems to be this: As the church moves in the power of the Spirit, and remains focused on the mission of God, it can triumph and progress, even in the face of persecution.

4:2 teaching the people and proclaiming in Jesus the resurrection of the dead. Note that the apostles' focus remained on the teaching and proclamation of the gospel.

4:4 the number of men grew to about five thousand. The growth of the church is an important concern of Luke in Acts. In a short time it has grown from the original 120 (1:15), to 3,120 (2:41), and now to 5,000, excluding women and children. As the church moved in the power and guidance of the Holy Spirit, it continued to grow and prosper (2:47; 5:14; 6:1-7; 8:6-8; 9:35-42; 11:21-26; 12:24; 13:49; 14:1, 21; 16:5; 17:4; 19:18-26). It had now grown to the point that it became a threat to the religious establishment in Jerusalem.

4:8 *Peter, filled with the Holy Spirit.* Luke again emphasizes the fact that the ministry of the early church was energized and empowered by the Spirit. This, of course, was not the first time Peter had been filled with the Spirit, since he had already been filled at Pentecost. He is now *re*-filled, or anointed, by the Spirit for ministry. Peter's being filled with the Spirit, as at Pentecost, results in bold proclamation of the gospel.

4:10 *It is by the name of Jesus Christ of Nazareth.* When asked by what power or what name they had healed the lame man, Peter focused the people's attention on the real star of the show, that is, on Jesus Christ of Nazareth. It was through His power and His holiness that the man was healed. The people were not to look to Peter or to the other apostles, but only to Jesus, who was the real power and authority behind their ministry.

4:12 *no other name ... by which we must be saved.* Jesus is humankind's only means of salvation. He is the Savior of the world (John 4:42; 1 Tim. 4:10; 1 John 4:14) and the one Mediator between God and man (1 Tim. 2:5). There is no salvation apart from Him (John 14:6).

4:20 *we cannot help speaking.* The disciples could not restrain themselves. They were driven by an inner compulsion to testify concerning Jesus. This inner compulsion came from knowing who He was and what He had commissioned them to do, and from being filled with the Holy Spirit.

Life Application

Sometimes persecution comes, often as a direct result of our missionary and evangelistic successes. If we are to remain faithful to the proclamation of the gospel, we, like Peter and John, must learn to walk and minister in the power of Spirit. We must also remain open to fresh refillings of the Spirit. All along, we must not veer from our commitment to clearly and boldly proclaim the gospel of Christ, for the message of Jesus is the only message that will lead people to heaven.

CONCLUSION

Pentecost is the exciting story of how the first disciples were empowered by the Holy Spirit to fulfill Christ's mandate to bear witnesses to Christ in the city of Jerusalem. It thus began the fulfillment of Christ's promise in Acts 1:8: "But you will receive power when the Holy Spirit comes on you; and you will be my witnesses *in Jerusalem...*" Once empowered by the Spirit, these believers gave powerful witness to the gospel through bold, Spirit-anointed proclamation and through mighty demonstrations of God's power. In the next chapter, we will observe how that witness continued to spread throughout Jerusalem and the surrounding areas. We will also see how the church in Jerusalem was again empowered by a second outpouring of the Spirit in Jerusalem.

QUESTIONS FOR REFLECTION AND REVIEW

1. Give the historical background to the Day of Pentecost.
2. Where is it traditionally believed that the disciples were gathered when the Spirit was poured out at Pentecost? Where does the author believe they were more probably gathered?
3. How do the sound of the violent wind and the tongues of fire point to the missional purpose of the Spirit's outpouring at Pentecost?
4. When did these two phenomena occur, before or after the 120 were filled with the Spirit?
5. When did the 120 speak in tongues, before or after they were filled with the Spirit? What is the significance of these facts?
6. For what purpose was the Spirit given at Pentecost? (cf. 1:8)
7. Of the 120 present at Pentecost, how many were filled with the Spirit? How many spoke in tongues? What is the significance of these facts?
8. In what kind of tongues did the 120 speak at Pentecost? Why is this significant?
9. According to 2:5, where did the pilgrims at Pentecost come from? Why is Luke's terminology significant?
10. According to the author was the speaking in tongues at Pentecost praise or proclamation?
11. Should Pentecost be considered the birthday of the church? Give reasons for your answer.
12. Why do we say that Peter's Pentecost "sermon" was really a prophetic utterance?
13. Which prophet did Peter quote at Pentecost? According to this prophecy, what would be the result of the Spirit being poured out on people?
14. According to 2:21, what is the ultimate purpose of Pentecost?

Chapter 3: Pentecost: The First Jerusalem Outpouring

15. Who is the central message of Peter's preaching at Pentecost—as well as the central theme of all apostolic preaching?
16. According to 2:37, what was the crowd's response to Peter's prophetic address? What were Peter's instructions to them?
17. How does the context of Acts 2 indicate that Peter in vv. 38-39 is taking about empowerment rather than conversion?
18. What was the result of the outpouring of the Spirit followed by Peter's Spirit-anointed message at Pentecost?
19. Describe the new prophetic community created by the outpouring of the Spirit at Pentecost (2:42-47).
20 Give two examples of Spirit-empowered ministry in Jerusalem that resulted from the outpouring of the Spirit at Pentecost.
21. What does Peter's refilling with the Spirit in 4:4 indicate about the Spirit-filled walk?

QUESTIONS FOR CLASSROOM DISCUSSION

1. At Pentecost the sound from heaven and the tongues of fire occurred before the disciples were filled with the Spirit. Speaking in tongues occurred afterward. What is the significance of this sequence of events?
2. Why is it important how one interprets Spirit baptism—as conversion-initiation or as empowerment for witness? How will one's interpretation of the experience affect the way he or she carries out the Great Commission of Christ?
3. Is there any significance to the fact that in Acts each time that the Spirit of God is poured out on a group of people they are *all* filled (2:4; 4:31; 8:17; 10:44; 19:6, implied)? Explain your answer.
4. When Peter told the lame man at the Beautiful Gate, "What I have I give you," to what was he referring? How can we ensure that we too have something to give to others as we minister?
5. In 4:8 Peter, who was first filled with the Spirit at Pentecost, is again filled with the Spirit. What present-day implications flow from this fact?

Chapter 3: Pentecost: The First Jerusalem Outpouring

– CHAPTER 4 –

MINISTRY IN JERUSALEM

(INCLUDING THE SECOND JERUSALEM OUTPOURING)

PRE-LESSON READING ASSIGNMENT

Acts 4:23–8:1a

INTRODUCTION

After the outpouring of the Holy Spirit on the Day of Pentecost, the church became a powerful evangelistic force in Jerusalem. On the very first day, three thousand people were saved and baptized in water (and probably baptized in the Holy Spirit). A powerful Spirit-anointed witnessing community was created, with new believers being added to the church daily. The disciples' witness was characterized by powerful preaching and miraculous signs and wonders. One such miracle took place at the Beautiful Gate of the temple. A forty-year-old man who had been crippled from birth was miraculously healed through the ministry Peter and John. In the excitement of the moment, a huge crowd gathered to see what had happened. Peter used the opportunity to proclaim the gospel, and the church grew to five thousand men, besides women and children.

Such success brought persecution from the Jewish religious leaders. The apostles were captured, threatened, and released. As the days went by, the persecution mounted. The disciples, however, were not alone; the Holy Spirit was with them. Jesus had promised them power, and they had received that power when they were baptized in the Holy Spirit on the Day of Pentecost.

Being filled with the Spirit, however, is not a one-time-only experience; it is a repeatable and ongoing experience. God was about to again pour out His Spirit mightily in Jerusalem. This second outpouring, which we are calling the "Second Jerusalem Outpouring," would result in ongoing Spirit-empowered witness in the city.

A POWERFUL MISSIONARY PRAYER

Reading Assignment: Acts 4:23-30

The Story

After being threatened and released by the Jewish religious authorities, Peter and John returned to the company of believers and reported what the chief priests and elders had done to them. They then prayed a powerful God-centered missionary prayer, expressing their confidence in God and His providential dealings with man. They concluded their prayer with two requests: that God would give them boldness to preach the word, and that He would perform miraculous signs and wonders through the name of Jesus.

Commentary

4:24 they raised their voices together in prayer to God. Throughout Acts there is a strong emphasis on prayer. It is mentioned thirty-three times. Here, the disciples were in prayer when the Spirit was poured out. Note how the disciples' prayer in this instance was a God-centered, rather than a problem-centered prayer. They focused their attention, not on their own problems, but on the greatness and sovereignty of God.

4:25 You spoke by the Holy Spirit. This phrase is an affirmation that Old Testament Scriptures were inspired by the Holy Spirit. That same Spirit was now inspiring and empowering the apostles and other disciples to fulfill God's mission.

4:28 They did what your power and will had decided beforehand should happen. What had happened to Christ, and by implication, what was happening to the disciples at this moment, was not happenstance. It was rather part of God's providential dealings with humankind, and with them. As we seek to fulfill Christ's mandate to take the gospel to all nations, we can be assured that we are in God's hands and that He will direct our paths, both by His

Spirit and by His providence.

4:29 enable your servants to speak your word with great boldness. The disciples did not ask for deliverance, or even protection from harm. They rather asked for boldness to speak the gospel in the face of danger and threats. God answered their prayer by filling them with the Holy Spirit. Boldness is one manifestation of the power to witness promised in 1:8.

4:30 Stretch out your hand. To ask God to stretch out His hand is to ask Him to manifest His presence through the power of the Holy Spirit, for when the disciples asked God to stretch out His hand, He answered by sending His Spirit (v. 31). In Scripture the hand (or arm, or finger) of the Lord is a metaphor often used for the power of the Holy Spirit (Josh. 4:24; 2 Kings 3:15; Isa. 59:1; Ezek. 3:14; 37:1; Luke 11:20; Acts 11:21; 13:11).

Life Application

As we go into the world to preach the gospel, we can anticipate resistance. Sometimes we will even experience threats and persecution. When this happens, we should remain focused on the task that God has given to us. We should go to God and seek Him for a fresh infilling of the Holy Spirit. Our prayer should not focus on our problems, but rather on God and His ability to take care of us and meet our every need.

A SECOND OUTPOURING IN JERUSALEM

Reading Assignment: Acts 4:31-37

The Story

The Lord answered the church's prayer in a dramatic way. He manifested His presence among them by shaking the place where they had gathered. God then filled everyone present with the Holy Spirit and, as on the Day of Pentecost, they began to boldly proclaim the message of Christ.

Because of this and other outpourings of the Holy Spirit in Jerusalem, great grace rested on the apostles, and they continued to preach the resurrected Christ. This fresh bestowal of the Holy Spirit, as on the Day of Pentecost, drew the church together in unity and loving concern for one another. Some even sold their houses and lands and gave the proceeds to the apostles to distribute to the needy among them. One man by the name of Joseph (or Barnabas) sold a field and gave the proceeds to the apostles.

Commentary

The disciples' prayer was answered with a second powerful outpouring of the Spirit in Jerusalem. As with the first outpouring at Pentecost, this outpouring resulted in powerful Spirit-anointed witness. This is the second of seven key outpourings of the Spirit in Acts (cf. p. 16). Like the other six, it graphically illustrates Luke's *empowerment– witness motif,* first presented in 1:8.

4:31 After they prayed. The Holy Spirit came in response to the disciples' heartfelt prayer. Jesus had previously taught them to ask for the Holy Spirit: "So I say to you: Ask and it will be given to you; seek and you will find; knock and the door will be opened to you" (Luke 11:9; cf. v. 13).

the place where they were meeting was shaken. Just as He had done on the Day of Pentecost, the Holy Spirit manifested His coming with a powerful demonstration of His power and presence. This is a second theophany in Acts, the first being at Pentecost. Some have identified the "place" (Gk. *topos*) as the temple mount (cf. Acts 2:46; 3:1; 4:1; 5:21, 25, 42). If this is the case, the shaking of the great stone walls and pillars of the temple must have been an awesome sight.

they were all filled with the Holy Spirit. The immediate consequence of the Spirit's coming, as it was on the Day of Pentecost, was that the disciples were "filled with the Holy Spirit." Luke uses the term ten times in Luke-Acts (Luke 1:15, 41, 67; Acts 2:4; 4:8, 31; 9:17; 13:9, 52). Each time he uses the term, he uses it to describe an experience separate from conversion whose purpose is empowerment for prophetic vocational witness. Paul, on the other hand, uses the term only once in the context of Spirit-filled worship (Eph. 5:18-20).

spoke the word of God boldly. The result of the believers being filled with the Spirit was bold powerful Spirit-anointed witness (v. 33). The subject of their witness was the resurrection of the Lord Jesus (i.e., the gospel). This is the same result as at Pentecost: they were first filled with the Spirit and they spoke in tongues "declaring the wonders of God" (2:11). Peter then preached a Spirit-inspired message resulting in three thousand people coming to Christ (vv. 14-41). Finally, a powerful witnessing community was formed, and many signs and wonders were done by the apostles (vv. 42-47). This pattern is repeated throughout Acts: every time there is an outpouring of the Spirit, the result is Spirit-anointed missional witness.

4:32 *one in heart and mind.* Unity was both a requisite and a result of their being filled with the Spirit. Before Pentecost "they were all with one accord in one place" (Acts 2:1, NKJV). After Pentecost they were "one in heart and mind." Their unity was around the mission of Christ. Such unity is essential to reaching the nations with the gospel.

4:33 *much grace was upon them all.* This phrase is a reference to their being filled with the Spirit (Luke 2:40; Acts 6:8). The preposition "upon" reminds us of Jesus' promise in 1:8 that the Holy Spirit would come "upon" them and give them power to witness (cf. Luke 24:49).

Life Application

The apostles were first filled with the Spirit on the Day of Pentecost (2:4). Peter was again filled with the Spirit in 4:8. Now, they are once again filled with the Spirit. It is essential that Christian workers realize that they must experience frequent infillings with the Holy Spirit. They must not make the mistake of thinking that once they have been baptized in the Spirit, they have somehow "arrived." Rather, the Spirit-empowered life must be maintained. While Spirit baptism does, indeed, bring a Christian into a new relationship with God, that relationship must be continually renewed. No matter how powerful one's initial infilling may be, if the experience does not find further expression in a life of sincere devotion, disciplined prayer, and committed witness, the power of the experience will soon fade. The Christian worker will lose the spiritual power he or she received.

REVELATION AND WITNESS

Reading Assignment: Acts 5:1-16

The Story

The church's expanding witness was now threatened by wrongdoing from within. A man by the name of Ananias, along with his wife, Sapphira, were moved by Satan and conspired to deceive the congregation. They pretended to give the entire proceeds from the sale of a piece of property to the church; however, they held back part of the sale price for themselves. The Holy Spirit revealed their conspiracy to Peter, who challenged their deception, saying that they were lying, not only to men, but to the Holy Spirit as well. God then struck them dead. As a result, great fear came upon the church and

Chapter 4: Ministry in Jerusalem

all who heard the story.

In spite of such wrongdoing from within, and continued opposition from without, the church continued to prosper and grow. The apostles, still anointed by the Spirit, did many miraculous signs and wonders among the people, and the believers continued to meet together in the temple under Solomon's Colonnade in the Court of the Gentiles. Because of the Spirit's mighty presence upon them, they were feared by some, yet held in high regard by all. Their numbers continued to swell as new believers, both men and women, joined their ranks. God worked extraordinary miracles through them. The sick were laid in the streets so that Peter's shadow might pass over them. Multitudes began to gather from the surrounding towns, and many brought their friends and loved ones to be healed and set free from demons. As had often happened in the ministry of Jesus, all were healed.

COMMENTARY

A Conspiracy Is Unmasked (5:3-11)

Not only did the Holy Spirit empower believers to effectively proclaim the gospel to the lost, He also enabled them to challenge threats to the spread of the gospel from within their own ranks. The story of Ananias and Sapphira is one such example.

5:3 Satan has so filled your heart. Just as one can be filled with the Spirit, there exists the possibility that Satan (or his demonic agents) can also fill or influence one's heart (cf. Luke 22:3; 31). The Holy Spirit revealed to Peter the conspiracy of Ananias and Sapphira, for how else could he have known what was in their hearts? This incident is a Lukan example of the operation of the gift of distinguishing between spirits (1 Cor. 12:10).

5:3, 9 you have lied to the Holy Spirit ... you agree to test the Spirit of the Lord. To sin against the work and mission of God is to sin against and test the Holy Spirit.

5:11 Great fear seized ... all who heard about these events. As with previous Spirit-directed acts, this one resulted in witness. This time fear seized the people who heard. Such fear can be the beginning of the knowledge of the Lord (Pr. 1:7; 9:10) In Acts the manifestation of God's power results in various reactions, including utter amazement (2:7; 3:10), being filled with awe (2:43), perplexity (2:12), hearts filled with praise to God (4:21), great fear (5:5, 11), great joy (8:8), astonishment (8:13), and saving faith (9:42, cf., 1 Cor. 2:4-5). We, like the first-century believers, should pray that

God will "stretch out [His] hand to heal and perform miraculous signs and wonders through the name of [His] holy servant Jesus" (Acts 4:30).

Ongoing Witness in Jerusalem (5:12-16)
Acts 5:12-16 is one of fifteen summary passages that Luke inserts into the story of Acts.[23]

5:12 many miraculous signs and wonders among the people. Signs and wonders are an essential part of true proclamation. According to Paul, the gospel has not been fully proclaimed until it has been clearly presented and powerfully demonstrated (cf. Rom. 15:18-19). Proclamation and demonstration are two sides of the same gospel coin. In evangelistic ministry signs and wonders help to open the hearts of people to the message of the gospel. For an explanation of "miracles, wonders, and signs," see comments on 2:22.

5:14 more and more men and women believed in the Lord. Again, the result of Spirit-induced signs and wonders was witness, resulting in saving faith.

5:15 Peter's shadow. Though the text does not explicitly state that anyone was actually healed by Peter's shadow, we can reasonably assume that some were. This manifestation of God's power fits into the category of "extraordinary miracles," such as the curing of illnesses and exorcism of evil Spirit by cloths that touched Paul's body (Acts 19:11-12). If God grants such miracles, we rejoice; however, they are not to be viewed as normative practice in the church.

5:16 from the towns around Jerusalem. Witness in Jerusalem had now extended into the towns round about Jerusalem, that is, into Judea. The fulfillment of Jesus' prophecy in 1:8 continues.

Life Application
We are called to be "competent as ministers ... of the Spirit" (2 Cor. 3:6). God wants to demonstrate his grace and power through us in the manifestation of spiritual gifts and fruit. Such manifestations should occur both in the church (as with Ananias and Sapphira) and in the marketplace (as when the apostles performed many signs among the people). For this to happen, we must remain full of the Spirit and open to His voice. Such a release of spiritual gifts can

---

[23] Other summary passages are 2:43-47; 4:4, 32-35; 5:42; 6:7; 8:4; 9:31; 12:24; 13:52; 14:6-7; 14:28; 15:35; 16:4-5; 19:20.

bring great blessing to the church and result in a dramatic advance of the gospel.

IMPRISONMENT, RELEASE AND WITNESS

Reading Assignment: Acts 5:17-42

The Story
Filled with jealousy, the Jewish religious leaders arrested the apostles and put them into jail. That same night an angel of the Lord freed them, commanding them, "Go, stand in the temple courts,... and tell the people the full message of this new life." The next morning, the apostles obeyed the angel's command and went into the temple courts. There they began teaching the people. When the Jewish leaders heard that the apostles were again in the temple teaching the people, they had them seized and brought before the council, where they ordered them to stop preaching in the name of Jesus. However, Peter and the apostles answered, "We must obey God rather than men," and began witnessing to the council concerning the death, resurrection, and exaltation of Christ. They then told the Jewish leaders to repent, declaring, "We are witnesses of these things, and so is the Holy Spirit, whom God has given to those who obey him."

Some in the council wanted to have them executed. Calming them down, Gamaliel reasoned with them, saying, "If this movement is from God, we cannot stop it; we will find ourselves fighting against God." The council then had the apostles flogged, ordered them to stop speaking in the name of Jesus, and let them go. The apostles, however, rejoiced that they had been counted worthy to suffer for "the Name." Day after day the continued proclaiming Christ in the temple courts and from house to house.

Commentary
The apostles were again hauled before the Jewish authorities and commanded not to preach the gospel. And again they refused, saying that they were subjects of a higher authority—God. In both instances, Luke attributes their boldness to the Holy Spirit (4:8, cf. v. 31; 5:32).

5:17 filled with jealousy. As the church's numbers continued to increase in Jerusalem, so did the jealousy and resentment of the local religious authorities. Persecution continued to mount against the church. Throughout Acts, the gospel advanced in the midst of persecution.

5:19 angel of the Lord. The ministry of angels is mentioned at least eighteen times in Acts. The writer of Hebrews describes them as "ministering spirits sent to serve those who will inherit salvation" (Heb. 1:14). Angels have not been commissioned to preach the gospel. That is the job of the redeemed. However, in Luke-Acts angels do participate in advancing the kingdom of God by observing (Luke 15:10), informing (Luke 1:11-19; 26-38; 2:8-14; 24:4-8; Acts 7:38, 53, 27:23-24), directing (Acts 1:10-11; 8:26; 10:3-6, 22: 11:13), comforting (Luke 1:26; 2:10; Acts 27:23), strengthening (Luke 22:43), and delivering (Acts 5:19; 12:7) the children of God.

5:20 Go, stand ... and tell. The command of the angel to "Go" reminds us of Jesus' Great Commission where He instructs His disciples to go to all nations and preach the gospel (cf. Matt. 28:18-20; Mark 16:15-18; Luke 24:46-48; John 20:21-22; Acts 1:8). As we *go,* we are to take our *stand* for Christ and *tell* His message to all who will listen.

5:32 We are witnesses of these things, and so is the Holy Spirit. It is the Spirit who empowers us to witness for Christ (1:8). The Spirit Himself also bears witnesses to Christ. He convicts the lost of their sins (Gen. 6:3; John 16:8), reveals Christ to them (John 16:15), and then regenerates those who repent and believe the gospel (John 3:6; Tit. 3:5). The "things" to which we are called to witness are the message of Jesus' crucifixion, resurrection, and exaltation to the right hand of God. In doing this we must urge the people to repent and receive forgiveness for their sins (vv. 30-31).

the Holy Spirit ... whom God has given to those who obey him. In context, the obedience spoken of here is not a general obedience to the commands of God (though that application may be made), but specific obedience to the command to be Christ's witnesses (cf. vv. 28-29). The implication is that God will fill with the Spirit and empower those who are prepared to obey His command to preach the gospel to the lost (1:8).

5:40 They ... had them flogged ... and ordered them not to speak in the name of Jesus. The persecution is escalating. The disciples received yet another ultimatum to stop preaching Christ. This time, however, the authorities had them flogged to emphasize their seriousness.

5:42 they never stopped teaching and proclaiming the good news. Before, Peter was afraid to witness for Christ (Luke 22:54-62); now he preaches boldly, even in the face of persecution and death.

What made the difference? He had been empowered by the Holy Spirit (2:4), and he continued to walk in the Spirit. With this empowering came great zeal and boldness to preach the gospel (Acts 4:20; 30-31).

Life Application

When the apostles were threatened and commanded to stop preaching the gospel, they did not stop. This was because they were full of the Holy Spirit and focused on the mandate of Jesus that they should be His witnesses. We too must remain full of the Spirit and focused on the mandate of Christ. If we will, we will courageously preach the gospel in the face of adversity.

A SPIRIT-GUIDED DECISION

Reading Assignment: Acts 6:1-7

The Story

As the church in Jerusalem continued to grow, another dispute arose in their midst. Some of the Grecian Jews complained that their widows were being neglected in the daily distribution of food. Directed by the Holy Spirit, the apostles developed a plan to address the issue. They said to the people, "It's not right for us to neglect the preaching and teaching of the word or prayer." They then instructed the church to choose seven men "full of the Spirit and wisdom" whom they would put in charge of the matter. The proposal pleased the church, and seven Spirit-filled men were chosen and appointed to the task. Because of this Spirit-guided action, the word of God spread, and the number of disciples in Jerusalem increased rapidly. Even a large number of priests became obedient to the faith.

Commentary

6:1 the number of disciples was increasing. In spite of the hostility the church was facing, it continued to increase in numbers. The church's growth, however, brought new challenges. The many needs of the people began to distract the apostles from the ministry to which Jesus has called them—the proclamation of the gospel.

6:2 not be right for us to neglect the ministry of the word of God. Like the apostles, our primary calling as ministers of the gospel is to proclaim the word of God. No matter what other responsibilities he or she may be given, it is never right for a minister or missionary to neglect the ministry of the word. When this happens, the preacher of the gospel must take immediate steps to delegate the work to others so that he can remain focused on preaching and teaching the word of God and prayer.

6:3 seven men ... full of the Spirit and wisdom. Those chosen for leadership in the church should be full of the Holy Spirit and wisdom.

6:6 laid their hands on them. In Acts, the laying on of hands often indicates that someone is being commissioned to service, as in this instance. Other such instances could include Ananias' laying hands on Paul (Acts 9:15-18; cf. 26:15-18), and Paul's laying hands on the Ephesian disciples (19:6, cf. 10). (See note on 8:17.)

6:7 the word of God spread. As a result of the apostles' Spirit-directed decision to appoint seven "deacons" to help them in the work, the word of the Lord continued to spread in Jerusalem. "The number of disciples ... increased rapidly" in Jerusalem and a "large number of priests became obedient to the faith." Two of these deacons (Stephen and Philip) will emerge as powerful evangelists and prophetic witnesses to the gospel of Christ.

Life Application

The Spirit of the Lord not only empowers us to preach the gospel to the lost, He also directs us in administrating the work of the church. If the leaders of the church will be filled with the Spirit and follow the leadership of the Spirit, this will result in the church becoming more effective in its primary mission of taking the gospel to the lost and planting other Spirit-empowered missional churches. Pastors should not try to hold their lay people back from ministry. They should rather ensure that they are filled with the Spirit, and then release them to be used by God in whatever way He may choose.

STEPHEN'S SPIRIT-EMPOWERED WITNESS

Reading Assignment: Acts 6:8-15

The Story

Stephen was one of the seven chosen to take care of the Grecian widows. He was "a man full of God's grace and power," and through him the Spirit did great signs and wonders among the people. Stephen's witness was opposed by a radical sect of Jews known as the Synagogue of the Freedmen. They were unable, however, to stand up against the Spirit or the wisdom by which Stephen spoke. As a result, they began to stir up the Jewish elders and teachers, accusing him of blasphemy. Soon after this, they seized him and brought him before the Sanhedrin, where false witnesses testified against him. As Stephen testified, his accusers saw the Spirit come upon him so that his face appeared "like the face of an angel."

Commentary

Having introduced his readers to the seven Spirit-filled "deacons," Luke now turns his attention to the Spirit-empowered ministry of two of them. The first is Stephen.

6:8 Stephen, a man full of God's grace and power. Being full of God's grace and power are the result of one's being filled with the Spirit (cf. 4:31-33). Before Luke describes Stephen's ministry, he wants his readers to know that Stephen was full of the Holy Spirit (see also v. 3). This is a consistent pattern in Acts. Luke always prefaces the description of one's ministry by showing that he was first filled with the Spirit. This includes Peter (2:4; 4:8), Stephen (6:3, 5), Philip (6:3), Paul (9:17-18), Barnabas (11:22-24), and Silas (15:32, implied).

6:10 his wisdom or the Spirit by whom he spoke. Stephen's ministry was characterized by Spirit-inspired preaching. The Spirit gave to him supernatural wisdom to confound his detractors. This could be a manifestation of the spiritual gift of the word of wisdom spoken of by Paul (1 Cor. 12:8).

Life Application

Spirit-empowered ministry is not for apostles only; it is for all of God's people. Stephen was not an apostle, but God used him mightily. We have all been called to be His witnesses, and we have all been promised His power (1:8; 2:4, 38). God can use anyone who will open his or her life to Him, be filled with the Spirit, and obey His command to share the gospel with others.

STEPHEN'S SPEECH AND MARTYRDOM

Reading Assignment: Acts 7:1–8:1a

The Story

When Stephen was given the opportunity to speak, he launched into a discourse detailing the history of the Jewish people. He told the Jews that, although God continually reached out to them and sent them leaders and prophets, they continually rejected His messengers. God called Abraham and made a covenant with him to bless his

Chapter 4: Ministry in Jerusalem

decedents. He blessed Isaac and Jacob, and used Joseph to save their nation. God also called Moses to deliver them from Egyptian bondage. Yet some Israelites still rejected Moses, saying to him, "Who made you ruler and judge over us?" Moses, however, continued to lead them, and was used by God to do wonders and miraculous signs in Egypt, at the Red Sea, and in the wilderness. Moses prophesied, "God will send you a prophet like me from your own people."

Stephen then told them of their fathers' rebellion against Moses and God: "They rejected him and in their hearts turned back to Egypt." Neither did their fathers appreciate God's many other kind acts toward them, such as the tabernacle in the wilderness or the temple, which He led Solomon to build. Even so, they should know "that the Most High does not live in houses made by men."

At this point Stephen began to drive his message home. He called his accusers "stiff-necked people, with uncircumcised hearts and ears." He told them that they were just like their fathers who always resisted the Holy Spirit. Their fathers even persecuted the prophets who predicted the coming of the Righteous One. And now they had committed the ultimate wrong; they had betrayed and murdered their promised Messiah!

Stephen's bold accusation infuriated his accusers. They became so enraged that they began to grind their teeth at him. Stephen, however, was full of the Spirit. He looked up to heaven and saw God's glory, and Jesus standing at the right hand of the Father. He cried out, "Look, I see heaven open and the Son of Man standing at the right hand of God!"

This incensed his opponents all the more. They covered their ears and began to shout at the top of their voices. They then dragged him out of the city and began to stone him. As the stones fell upon Stephen, he prayed, "Lord, do not hold this sin against them." Then he uttered a final prayer, "Lord Jesus, receive my spirit," and died.

Those who took part in the murder of Stephen laid their coats at the feet of a young Jewish Pharisee, named Saul of Tarsus, who was consenting to Stephen's death.

COMMENTARY

Stephen's Speech

Stephen's speech is not so much a sermon as the inspired words of a prophet. Stephen did not try to plead his own cause, or to mitigate his impending punishment. Rather, he spoke by the Spirit, boldly declaring God's message for the day. His message had strong missionary overtones. Stephen reminded the Jews of how God had often spoken to the fathers outside Jerusalem. Quoting from Isaiah, he insisted that the temple is not the way to God, for God is far too vast to be housed in any man-made building.

The violent response Stephen received from the crowd was not unanticipated. After all, these were the same people who had condemned Christ to death. In fact, they leveled the same accusation against Stephen as they had against Jesus—blaspheming the temple. Stephen, however, felt that it was more important to declare the true message of God than to preserve his own life. By killing him, they did to him what they had always done to God's prophets.

7:37 God will send you a prophet like me. This is a reference to Moses' prophecy in Deuteronomy 18:15. Peter identified the "prophet like Moses" as Jesus, the Messiah (Acts 3:19-22). Both Jesus and Moses were Spirit-anointed charismatic prophets, for the Spirit of God rested upon both of them (Num. 11:16-29; Luke 4:18-19), and by the Spirit both performed miraculous signs and wonders (Acts 7:36; 10:38). Unlike Moses, however, the Spirit rested upon Jesus' ministry in full measure (Luke 4:18-19; John 1:32; 3:34, KJV). There are other similarities between Jesus and Moses. For instance, just as God took the Spirit who rested on Moses and placed Him on the seventy elders in the wilderness, at Pentecost—and since Pentecost—God has taken the Spirit who rested on Jesus and put Him on Jesus' disciples. Moses' longing expressed in Numbers 11:29 ("I wish that all the Lord's people were prophets and that the Lord would put his Spirit on them!") was first fulfilled at Pentecost (Acts 2:17-18). The purpose of this transfer of the Spirit is the same for us and Jesus' disciples as it was for Moses' seventy elders—empowerment for service.

7:51 You always resist the Holy Spirit! Stephen, full of the Spirit, was very bold. He reminded the Jews how their fathers refused to obey the words of Moses who "was sent to be their ruler and deliverer by God Himself" (v. 35). Now they were rejecting the Greater than Moses, and in doing this, they were resisting the Holy Spirit just as their fathers had.

7:52 the Righteous One ... you have betrayed and murdered him. They had committed the ultimate transgression: they had betrayed and murdered the Righteous One, their promised Messiah.

Stephen's Martyrdom

7:55 Stephen, full of the Holy Spirit. Stephen is described as being "filled with" or "full of" the Spirit on this and two other occasions in Acts (6:3, 5). "Filled" indicates the process, "full," the resulting state. Stephen was full of the Spirit when he preached to the Jews. Now, as they begin to stone him, he remains full of the Spirit. The Spirit not only empowered Stephen's teaching and preaching, He also enabled him to stay true to God and the mission God had given him, even in the time of great trial.

Jesus standing at the right hand of God. As he was dying, Stephen had a vision of the ascended Christ. When Jesus ascended, He sat down at the right hand of the Father (Luke 22:69; Eph. 1:20; Col. 3:1; Rev. 3:21). It is from this exalted position that He received from the Father the promised Holy Spirit, whom He poured out at Pentecost (Acts 2:33). What can account for Jesus, in this instance, standing at the right hand of God? It can only be that He is standing in honor of His faithful servant Stephen, the church's first martyr.

7:59-60 Lord Jesus, receive my spirit ... Lord, do not hold this sin against them. Stephen died as Jesus died: both were full of the Spirit (cf. Heb. 9:14), both prayed for their executors (cf. Luke 23:34), and both offered up their spirits to God (cf. Luke 23:46). Stephen not only bore witness to Christ in his life and in his preaching, he also bore faithful witness to Christ in his death.

8:1 Saul was there, giving approval to his death. In 7:58 Luke said that "the witnesses laid their clothes at the feet of a young man named Saul." This young man would later, after he encountered the resurrected Christ on the road to Damascus, become Paul, the apostle to the Gentiles. However, on this occasion, Saul was present "giving approval to [Stephen's] death." The courage and grace that Stephen displayed at this time must have profoundly affected Saul, and was likely a key element in His eventual surrender to Christ.

Life Application

There are times when God calls upon us to preach the word, even in uncomfortable and dangerous situations. At such times we must never compromise the gospel message. We must be bold and always "speak the truth in love" (Eph. 4:15). Such boldness in the face of danger comes when we are totally committed to the mission of God and, like Stephen, "full of God's grace and power" (Acts 6:8).

We learn another lesson from these verses: we should guard ourselves against becoming like the Jews who "always resisted the Holy Spirit." It is possible that we, too, can resist the Holy Spirit. Just as the Pharisees rejected the Spirit-anointed ministry of Jesus, church leaders today can be tempted to reject the demonstration of the Spirit's power and the manifestation of spiritual gifts in the name of "sound doctrine" or social respectability.

Another lesson: we should realize that the Holy Spirit will never abandon us in our times of great trial. And neither will Jesus! Just as He honored Stephen in his death, He will honor us—if we will remain faithful unto Him. Jesus promised, "Be faithful until death, and I will give you the crown of life" (Rev. 2:10, NKJV). Sometimes a Christian's death or martyrdom has an even greater impact for Christ than his life. Truly, *the blood of the martyrs is the seed of the church!*

CONCLUSION

In this unit we have looked at two powerful outpourings of the Holy Spirit that took place in Jerusalem: Pentecost (i.e., the First Jerusalem Outpouring, 2:1-4) and the Second Jerusalem Outpouring (4:31). Both outpourings resulted in immediate Spirit-empowered witness in the city, and both demonstrate Luke's *empowerment-witness motif* introduced in 1:8: "You will receive power ... and you will be my witnesses." The powerful witness resulting from these two outpourings also began the fulfillment of the second part of Jesus' evangelistic agenda revealed in the second part of the verse: "You will be my witnesses in Jerusalem, and in all Judea..."

The outpourings of the Spirit in Jerusalem served a second purpose. They prepared the church for the great persecution that was to come. Unknown to the believers in Jerusalem, a frenzy of violent persecution would soon break out against them. We will discuss that persecution and the church's response in the next chapter.

QUESTIONS FOR REFLECTION AND REVIEW

1. Describe the disciples' prayer in Acts 2:24-30.
2. How is the Second Jerusalem Outpouring similar to the first outpouring at Pentecost?
3. What was the result of the Second Jerusalem Outpouring in Jerusalem?
4. Why did Luke include a second outpouring of the Spirit in Jerusalem in his narrative?
5. What personal and ministry lessons can we learn from this outpouring?
6. How is the story of Ananias and Sapphira connected with the two outpourings of the Spirit in Jerusalem?
7. How are signs and wonders related to the Holy Spirit? How are they related to the evangelistic success of the church?

8. Describe the angel's instructions to the apostles in 5:20. What role do angels have in the missionary advance of the church?
9. To whom does God give the Holy Spirit according to 5:32? Obedience to do what?
10. Why was it important that seven men be chosen to take care of the feeding of the widows in Acts 6? What kind of men were chosen? What was the result of this Spirit-guided action?
11. What was the source of Stephen's grace and power for ministry?
12. Who was there to observe Stephen's martyrdom? How did Stephen's dying impact his life?

QUESTIONS FOR CLASSROOM DISCUSSION

1. How does the disciples' God-centered, faith-filled prayer during their time of persecution compare with many prayers we hear today? How could we learn to pray more effectively during times of trial and persecution?
2. What is the significance of Luke's including the account of a second powerful outpouring of the Spirit on the church in Jerusalem? What are the implications for our churches today?
3. Why is obedience to Christ's command for us to be His witnesses essential to our remaining full of the Holy Spirit?
4. What does Luke show to be the source of Stephen's great boldness, wisdom, and grace? Can we attain that same boldness, wisdom, and grace today? How?

Chapter 4: Ministry in Jerusalem

Part III
Transitional Period

– CHAPTER 5 –

PERSECUTION AND WITNESS

(INCLUDING THE SAMARITAN OUTPOURING)

PRE-LESSON READING ASSIGNMENT

Acts 8:1b-40

INTRODUCTION

In the last two chapters we investigated how, as a result of two (and probably many more) mighty outpourings of the Holy Spirit on the church in Jerusalem, it became a mighty evangelistic force in the city. Not only was the church equipped to fulfill its mission of reaching the people of Jerusalem (1:8), it was also prepared for what lay ahead. The Jerusalem Christians were soon to experience a savage outbreak of persecution that would cause them to flee for their very lives. The believers were unaware of what was to come, but God knew. And He was preparing them by filling them again and again with His Holy Spirit. In this chapter we will look at how the church responded to that persecution.

The time had come for the church to move to the next item on Jesus' "Acts 1:8 Agenda," the evangelization of Judea and Samaria. As previously stated, we are calling this the Transitional Period of the book of Acts (see Figure 2.1, page 30). It is the time period when the church "transitioned" from being a purely Jewish sect to an international missionary force. During this period three powerful outpourings of the Holy Spirit occurred. Each served to prepare the church for its upcoming Gentile Mission, which will be discussed in Part IV.

THE WITNESS OF THE SCATTERED BELIEVERS

Reading Assignment: Acts 8:1b-4

The Story

On the same day Stephen was stoned, a great persecution, led by Saul of Tarsus, broke out against the church in Jerusalem. Saul began moving from house to house, assaulting and arresting Christian men and women, putting them into prison. Many believers fled for their lives from Jerusalem, scattering throughout the regions of Judea and Samaria. Amazingly, they preached the gospel everywhere they went! The apostles, however, remained in Jerusalem, enduring the full brunt of the persecution.

Commentary

The Jews' pent-up anger and resentment against the church suddenly erupted into a frenzy of violent persecution. Until now, the church had reached out to Jews only. Later, in 13:1-4, the church will launch its Gentile Mission. However, before that can happen, it must go through a period of transition.

8:1 persecution broke out against the church. The persecution was fierce and violent. Its source was the Jewish religious elite. The church's response to persecution is a major theme in Acts. Luke records how persecution came repeatedly against believers (cf. 4:1-22; 5:17-40; 6:12-15, 7:54-60; 8:1-3; 9:23-30; 11:19;12:1-19;13:49-50; 14:5-7; 16:16-24; 17:5-9, 13-15; 18:12-13; 19:23-41; 21:27ff; 23:12-22). This realization helps us to understand Luke's intent in writing Acts. His original audience was likely enduring persecution, and as a result, it had significantly curtailed its evangelist and missionary work. Luke wrote to address this unacceptable situation. He wrote to show how the church could triumph over persecution. It could do this by being filled with the Spirit and by remaining committed to Christ's mission to witness to all peoples before He comes again.

8:3 scattered throughout Judea and Samaria. Because of the persecution, the church was scattered throughout Judea and Samaria. This scattering represents a major step forward in the church's developing from a regional Jewish sect to a universal body of believers. It is the next step in the fulfillment of Jesus' agenda as stated in Acts 1:8 ("you will be my witnesses in ... Judea and Samaria"). It is also the church's first venture into non-purely-Jewish missions. It thus challenged the long-held prejudices that Jewish Christians had brought into the church from their religious and cultural past.

8:4 [They] preached the word wherever they went. The persecution of the church did not have the result hoped for by the Jewish authorities. Instead of stamping out the movement, it only scattered the embers of evangelism. Those who were scattered faithfully preached the gospel wherever they went. Some have said that the persecution was an act of God designed to force the church to do what it was otherwise unwilling to do, that is, preach the gospel outside Jerusalem. The true message of this story, however, is that any church, if it will be filled with the Spirit and remain true to Christ's commission, can triumph over adversity and remain an effective witnesses for Christ. What caused these persecuted believers to keep preaching, even during a time of great persecution and trauma? It is because they had been empowered by the Holy Spirit! (cf. 2:4; 4:31).

Life Application

Although we do not welcome persecution, sometimes it will come, especially if we are faithful to boldly proclaim the message of Christ. When persecution does come, we must be ready. We can do this, if we, like those first Christians in Jerusalem, will stay focused on Christ's mission and remain full of the Holy Spirit.

PHILIP'S SPIRIT-EMPOWERED WITNESS IN SAMARIA

Reading Assignment: Acts 8:5-8

The Story

Philip, one of the scattered believers, went to a city in Samaria and began preaching Christ. His Spirit-empowered preaching was accompanied by miraculous signs, including the healing of paralytics and cripples, and the deliverance of people from demonic possession. Because of this, great crowds of people gathered and listened intently to his message. A great soul harvest resulted as people believed Philip's message about the good news of the kingdom of God and the name of Jesus Christ. Philip baptized those men and women who received Christ as Savior.

Commentary

8:5 Philip went down to a city in Samaria and proclaimed the Christ there. The proclamation of Christ (i.e., the gospel) is again emphasized. Jesus said that His disciples would be *His* witnesses (1:8). Two implications flow from this truth: (1) They would be witnesses for Him, that is, they would be His representatives, and (2) He would be the subject of their witness. Philip represents both concepts.

8:6 crowds heard Philip and saw the miraculous signs he did. Philip's witness, like that of Jesus, was not in word only, but also in works (cf. Acts 1:1). His Spirit-inspired proclamation was accompanied by powerful Spirit-generated miraculous signs. The value of signs and wonders in evangelism is illustrated in this story. Because the crowds saw the miraculous signs of Philip, they gave heed to what he said. True gospel preaching always involves both powerful proclamation of the gospel—truth encounter—and mighty demonstrations of kingdom power—power encounter (cf. Rom. 15:18-19).

8:8 great joy. The Samaritans' great joy is the result of their experience of salvation and the knowledge of sins forgiven. Joy is also a sign of the Spirit of God working in one's life (Luke 10:21; Acts 8:39; 13:52; Rom. 14:17; 15:13; Gal. 5:22; 1 Thess. 1:6).

8:12 they believed Philip as he preached the good news of the kingdom of God and the name of Jesus Christ. We have here a description of true saving faith: the Samaritans put their faith in Jesus Christ for salvation (cf. 16:31). The preaching of the good news of the kingdom of God is synonymous with preaching Christ (28:23, 31).

baptized, both men and women. Philip, a man "full of the Spirit and wisdom" (Acts 6:3), would have never baptized these new believers in water had they not been truly converted. Luke again specifically mentions women. Since they were baptized in water, it must also be true that they, along with the men, were converted and later received the Holy Spirit when Peter and John prayed for them (v. 17; cf. 2:38). It further follows that the women received the Spirit for the same purpose as the men, power to proclaim Christ (1:8).

Life Application

We must never forget that our primary message is the gospel, the message of Christ, and we must always strive to preach that message in the power of the Holy Spirit. If we will faithfully do this, we can expect God to confirm His word through signs and wonders. Further, we should anticipate that women as well as men will be saved, baptized in water, and filled with the Holy Spirit, and as a result they too will become full participants in the ministry of the Spirit (cf. 2:17-18; 21:9; 1 Cor. 11:13; 14:31).

THE SAMARITAN OUTPOURING

Reading Assignment: Acts 8:9-25

The Story

News soon arrived in Jerusalem that Samaria had accepted the word of God. None of the Samaritans, however, had received the Holy Spirit (that is, in the Lukan sense of empowering for witness). This circumstance so concerned the apostles that they then sent Peter and John to pray with them to receive the Holy Spirit.

Upon arriving in Samaria, Peter and John began laying their hands on the new Samaritan Christians. One after another they received the Holy Spirit. Then, after praying with them, the apostles joined the Samaritans in proclaiming the gospel to the residents of the city. On their way back to Jerusalem, Peter and John preached the gospel in many Samaritan villages.

Among those who responded to Philip's preaching in Samaria was a sorcerer by the name of Simon. Because of his occultic displays of power, Simon was revered by many. He was known as the "Great Power of God." Simon, nevertheless, believed Philip as he preached, and was baptized. He followed Philip everywhere, amazed by the miracles God was working through him. Later, when Peter and John arrived in Samaria and prayed with the Samaritans to receive the Spirit by laying their hands on them, Simon was especially impressed. He offered to buy this ability from the apostles. But Peter rebuked him, saying, "May your money perish with you, because you thought you could buy the gift of God with money!" Peter told Simon that he could have no part in such a ministry because his heart was not right with God, being full of bitterness and captive to sin. He should, therefore, repent of his wickedness. Simon was filled with fear and asked Peter to pray for him.

COMMENTARY

A Missing Ingredient (8:14-16)

How the apostles must have rejoiced when they received the news of the great soul harvest in Samaria. The gospel had been clearly and powerfully proclaimed, and people had been miraculously healed and delivered. Many had been baptized in water. Upon closer examination, however, the apostles in Jerusalem realized that a vital ingredient was missing from the Samaritan revival—no one was being filled with the Holy Spirit. In the apostles' minds this was a serious issue, for everyone who receives the gospel must also become a proclaimer of the gospel. The same applies to communities of believers. Wherever the gospel goes *to,* it must go *from.* For this to happen, those who receive the gospel must also be empowered by the Spirit, as was promised by Jesus in Acts 1:8. According to the plan of Jesus, the church's witness was to begin in Jerusalem and then proceed into Judea and Samaria. It was not, however, to stop there. It was to spread from there until it reached the "ends of the earth." The issue was so serious that the apostles sent their two most prominent members, Peter and John, to Samaria to pray with the Samaritans to receive the Holy Spirit.

8:14 Samaria ... accepted the word of God. There is no indication in the text that the Samaritans' conversion was defective in any way, as some have claimed. They had truly believed in Christ and acted on the demands of the gospel.

8:15 they prayed for them that they might receive the Holy Spirit. As will later be the case with Paul in Ephesus, the apostles' first order of business upon arriving in Samaria was to see that those who had received Christ were immediately baptized in the Holy Spirit, as were the believers on the Day of Pentecost. The reason for this insistence was not to complete the Samaritans' salvation, but rather to ensure that they had been empowered by the Spirit to carry the gospel to others.

8:16 the Holy Spirit had not yet come upon any of them. Though these Samaritans had been truly converted, they had not been baptized in the Holy Spirit as prescribed by Jesus in Acts 1:8. Note that Luke uses the same terminology here ("come upon") as Jesus used in 1:8, where He said, "But you will receive power when the Holy Spirit comes on you," indicating that their experience with the Spirit was the same, and for the same purpose, as the believers at Pentecost.

they had simply been baptized into the name of the Lord Jesus.

The Samaritans' baptism in water is a clear indicator that they had been truly converted before the arrival of Peter and John. Philip, a man "full of the Spirit and wisdom" (Acts 6:3), would have never baptized them in water had they not been truly converted.

Samaritans Receive the Spirit (8:17, 25)

The Samaritan Outpouring is the third key outpouring of the Spirit in Acts. It is the first outpouring during the Transitional Period (see Figure 2.1, page 30).

8:17 placed their hands on them. The apostles laid hands on the Samaritans for them to receive the Holy Spirit. Some have said that people can only receive the Spirit if the apostles (or their representatives) lay hands on them. Is this true? No, since in Acts some were filled with the Spirit without the laying on of hands (2:4; 10:44), and one was filled when someone other than an apostle laid hands on him (9:17-18). What then is the meaning and purpose of laying on hands to receive the Spirit as revealed in Acts? We lay hands on people to encourage them to be filled and, to a certain degree, to impart the Spirit to them. Another important reason we lay hands on people to receive the Spirit is to commission them into service, as was the case with the seven deacons (6:6), Saul (9:15-17), and the Ephesian believers (19:6). This was probably the case here also. Peter and John were not only praying for the Samaritans to receive the Spirit, they were also commissioning them to missional witness (cf. 1:8). Everyone who receives the Spirit is thus commissioned as Christ's witness.

they received the Holy Spirit. This is not the moment of the Samaritans' conversion. That had already occurred when they believed and received the message of Christ preached by Philip. This is rather the moment when they were empowered by the Spirit for witness.

8:25 testified and proclaimed the word of the Lord. The Samaritan Outpouring is another important example of Luke's *empowerment– witness motif* as stated by Jesus in Acts 1:8: "You will receive power ... you will be my witnesses." The apostles' testimony and proclamation in this case seems to be directed, not at the Samaritan Christians (they had likely taught them on other occasions), but toward the non-Christian residents of Samaria. Proclamation in Acts is always directed at those who are lost (4:2; 5:42; 8:5, 25; 13:5, 38; 17:3, 23; 20:27; 26:23). This verse contains the first mention of the phrase *word of the Lord* in Acts. In Acts the phrase is synonymous with the gospel (cf. Acts 13:44, 48-49; 15:35-

36; 16:32; 19:10, 20). It is used interchangeably with the phrase *word of God* (Acts 4:31; 6:2, 7; 8:14; 11:1; 12:24: 13:5, 7, 46; 17:13; 18:11). The "Lord" in the phrase "word of the Lord" is to be understood as the Lord Jesus Christ.

preaching the gospel in many Samaritan villages. Not only did the apostles join with the Samaritans in preaching the gospel in Samaria, but also on their return trip to Jerusalem they began preaching the gospel in many Samaritan villages. This is the first time the apostles preached to anyone other than pure-blooded Jews. It seems that they received a "reciprocal blessing" when they prayed with the Samaritans to receive the Spirit. They, too, were re-empowered and inspired to preach the gospel to the lost. Those who pray with others to receive the Spirit are themselves blessed.

Simon the Sorcerer (8:9-11, 13; 18-24)

Why did Luke include the story of Simon the Sorcerer in the book of Acts? It seems that he included this narrative as a warning to those who would be tempted to seek God's power for personal gain. The practice of Simon is contrasted with the ministries of Philip, Peter, and John, who were used by the Spirit to bring life and blessing to others. Simon, on the other hand, sought the power of God for personal gain.

8:13 Simon himself believed ... And he followed Philip. It is difficult to determine whether Simon was truly converted. If he was, his commitment to Christ was very shallow. It seems that he was more interested in following Philip and observing his miracles than he was in following Christ.

8:18 Simon saw that the Spirit was given. The Samaritans' experience of receiving the Spirit must have been dramatic and observable, for when Simon saw what had happened, he wanted to buy the power from the apostles (v. 18). It is likely that Simon saw the Samaritans speaking in tongues as did the 120 on the Day of Pentecost (2:4), the Gentiles at Caesarea (10:46), and the twelve Ephesian believers (19:6).

8:20 the gift of God. The "gift of God" mentioned here is the baptism in the Holy Spirit promised by Jesus in 1:4-8. Since it is a gift, the experience, like the experience of salvation, is not earned or merited. It is freely given by the Heavenly Father to any child of God who will humbly and sincerely ask for it (Luke 11:9-13). (See note on 2:38.)

FURTHER INSIGHT: SAMARIA: A NEW CENTER OF MISSIONS

A few paragraphs after the Samaritan episode Luke states that "the church throughout Judea, Galilee and Samaria enjoyed a time of peace. It was strengthened; and encouraged by the Holy Spirit, it grew in numbers, living in the fear of the Lord" (9:31). This verse is a summary statement concerning the progress of the church from the persecution and disbursement of the Jerusalem Christians in 8:1 through the conversion and early ministry of Saul (Paul). It gives us insight into the missional result of the outpouring of the Holy Spirit in Samaria. In 9:31 Luke notes how, along with the churches in Judea and Galilee, the church in Samaria enjoyed a time of peace and growth as it was strengthened and encouraged by the work of the Holy Spirit. It further demonstrates that a Spirit-empowered missional church was planted in Samaria as a result of the ministry of Philip and the apostles.

Life Application

In our evangelism and church planting efforts it is important that we address the issue of Spirit baptism. It is essential that those involved in gospel work—whether it be pastoral, evangelistic, or missionary— understand the importance of immediately leading those who have been born again into the experience of Spirit baptism. This work must not be delayed for at least two reasons: The first is personal: The new convert will need the power of the Spirit to resist the temptations and attacks he or she will encounter from the world, the flesh, and the devil. The second reason is missional: Every believer must be empowered by the Spirit because every believer must be Christ's witness to the lost (1:8).

The gospel worker must further understand that everywhere the gospel goes *to,* it must proceed *from.* This can only happen if believers in that new church are empowered by the Holy Spirit and taught about their responsibility to win others to Christ. We must, therefore, ensure that the churches we plant are Spirit-empowered missional churches, that is, churches willing and capable of planting other Spirit-empowered missional churches. Only then will the gospel spread spontaneously throughout a community or region.

PHILIP'S SPIRIT-DIRECTED MINISTRY IN GAZA

Reading Assignment: Acts 8:26-40

Chapter 5: Persecution and Witness

The Story

In the midst of the great revival in Samaria an angel of the Lord appeared to Philip and directed him to go south to a certain road in Gaza in southwestern Judea. There he encountered an Ethiopian eunuch riding in a chariot. The man was a high governmental official in the court of Candace, queen of Ethiopia. He was returning home after a pilgrimage to worship at the temple in Jerusalem.

As he rode along, the man was reading from the book of Isaiah. The Spirit of God then directed Philip to draw near to the chariot. As he did, he heard the man reading aloud from Isaiah 53:7-8. Philip asked him if he understood what he was reading. The Ethiopian replied, "How can I unless someone explains it to me." Philip then joined him in his chariot and explained to him how this passage was talking about Jesus. Soon they passed a body of water where Philip baptized the Ethiopian.

Immediately the Spirit of the Lord whisked Philip away, and the eunuch continued on his journey rejoicing. Philip was next seen in Azotus, about twenty miles (thirty-two kilometers) to the north. He continued his journey northward along the coastline. He preached the gospel in all the towns until he arrived in Caesarea.

Commentary

The story of Philip and the Ethiopian eunuch is a good example of what has been called a "divine appointment," when God providentially arranges the circumstances and divinely leads His servants into situations where the gospel can be presented with maximum effect.

8:26 an angel of the Lord said to Philip, Go. This is the fifth appearance of an angel of the Lord in Luke-Act (cf. Luke 1:11, 28; 2:9; Acts 5:19), and the second appearance in Acts. Three more appearances will follow (10:4; 12:7-11, 23). Luke presents angels as active participants in the advancement of God's kingdom. They are, however, never seen preaching the gospel. This task is left solely to Spirit-filled believers. Here, as elsewhere, the angel is the Lord's agent urging a believer to "go" and bear witness to Christ (cf. 5:19-20).

8:27 an Ethiopian. This man is the first pure Gentile to receive the gospel in Acts. As the Holy Spirit did with the Samaritans, He again uses Philip to open a new door for the gospel. A black African man becomes the first representative in Acts of those at "the ends of the earth" (1:8), as well as those "who are far off" (2:39), who were to receive the gospel and the gift of the Holy Spirit.

8:29 The Spirit told Philip, Go. As before, the Holy Spirit is acting as the Superintendent of the Harvest. As such, He inspires and directs the work of missions. He will soon act again in this story, where He will suddenly take Philip away (v. 39). Six times in Acts the Lord, through the Spirit, directs the disciples to "go" (9:11, 15; 10:20; 22:10, 21; 28:26).

8:32 The eunuch was reading. For Luke, Scripture plays an essential role in the advancement of God's kingdom. The Spirit does not work independently of what is written; rather, He works in the fulfillment of Scripture (cf. 1:20; 7:42; 13:29, 33; 15:15; 23:5; 24:14).

8:35 Philip ... told him the good news about Jesus. As a Spirit-anointed evangelist, Philip remained true to his calling of preaching Christ (8:40; 21:8).

8:39 the eunuch ... went on his way rejoicing. The eunuch's rejoicing is an indication that he not only received Christ as Savior, but also that he was possibly filled with the Spirit in conjunction with his water baptism. Luke often connects joy with being filled with the Spirit (Luke 1:44, 47; 10:21; Acts 8:8; 13:52), as does Paul (Rom. 14:17; Gal. 5:22; 1 Thess. 1:6).

Life Application

From Philip's ministry to the Ethiopian eunuch we learn some important ministry lessons: We must follow the leading of the Holy Spirit in performing our work as ministers of the gospel. Had Philip not been full of the Spirit and open to the Spirit's voice, this opportunity would have been missed. Further, had he not understood the great importance of presenting Christ, the opportunity would have been wasted. We can also take great encouragement from this story, knowing that, when the Lord leads us into a ministry opportunity, He has also been at work providentially arranging circumstances and preparing the recipients to receive the gospel.

CONCLUSION

Two powerful outpourings of the Spirit in Jerusalem prepared the church for its Spirit-empowered ministry in Jerusalem (2:4, 4:31). These same outpourings helped to prepare the church for the coming persecution (8:1). So, when the time of trial did come, and the church was scattered, it was ready. It was not diverted from its primary calling, but continued to preach the gospel in the power of the Spirit. Philip went down to Samaria and preached Christ (v. 4). In Samaria many were saved, healed, and delivered. Then, when the apostles arrived in Samaria, they prayed with the new believers to be empowered by the Spirit, just as the church in Jerusalem had been empowered.

With the evangelization and empowering of the Samaritans, the church took its first step in moving from its Jewish to its Gentile mission (see Figure 2.1, page 30). In the next chapter we will look at the church's second step. As the church continued to expand throughout Judea, Galilee, and Samaria, another outpouring of the Spirit occurred. This outpouring, which we call the Damascene Outpouring, further helped prepare the church for its coming Gentile mission. The next chapter explores the outpouring of the Spirit that took place in Damascus and the church's continued expansion that resulted.

QUESTIONS FOR REFLECTION AND REVIEW

1. Why would Luke include the story of the persecution and scattering of the Jerusalem church in his narrative?
2. How does the church's scattering into Judea and Samaria relate to Jesus' statement in Acts 1:8?
3. What gave the Christian refugees the zeal and moral courage they needed to preach the word, even under the most trying circumstances?
4. What was the central theme of Philip's preaching in Samaria? What should our central theme of preaching be today?
5. How did miraculous signs contribute to Philip's evangelistic success? What was his source of spiritual power?
6. What indications are there in the text that the Samaritans were truly saved as a result of Philip's ministry?
7. Why did the apostles in Jerusalem send Peter and John to Samaria?
8. What reasons could the apostles have had for laying hands on the Samaritans?
9. Did the Samaritans receive the Holy Spirit at the time of, or after, their conversion?
10. Describe some missional results of the Samaritan Outpouring.
11. How does Acts 9:31 indicate that a new center of missions was formed in Samaria as a result of the Samaritan Outpouring?
12. What two means of divine direction did Philip receive in ministering to the Ethiopian eunuch? (vv. 26-29).
13. How is the story of Philip and the Ethiopian eunuch an example of a "divine appointment"?

QUESTIONS FOR CLASSROOM DISCUSSION

1. Because the scattered Jerusalem believers had been filled with the Spirit, they faithfully preached Christ, even in the midst of severe trial. What important lessons can we learn from this story?
2. Philip was full of the Spirit and he faithfully preached Christ. How did each of these factors contribute to his evangelistic success in Samaria? What other factors could have contributed?
3. What important lessons can we learn from the apostles' insistence that the newly-saved Samaritan believers be immediately baptized in the Holy Spirit? How does our practice today square with that of the apostles? What are the results of our present-day practices? What steps could we take to address the situation?
4. The Samaritans' being filled with the Spirit shows that God wants to include every people group as full participants in His mission—even those who may be considered "unworthy" by others. Is there any ethnic or social group you may be tempted to exclude from God's mission? How has your attitude been affected by this story?
5. After a person is saved, how long should we wait before we lead him or her into the baptism in the Holy Spirit? Give reasons for your answer.

Chapter 5:Persecution and Witness

– Chapter 6 –

Continued Expansion

(Including the Damascene Outpouring)

PRE-LESSON READING ASSIGNMENT

Acts 9:1-43

INTRODUCTION

The church's expansion from Jerusalem into Judea and Samaria was a significant step in the development of its mission. Indeed, Philip's evangelistic ministry in Samaria was the first time since Pentecost the gospel was preached to non-purely-Jewish people. Peter and John's ministry to the newborn church in Samaria demonstrated that, not only could non-Jews be saved and fully included in the family of God, but, by being filled with the Spirit, they could become full participants in the mission of God. In Samaria the church began its transition from a localized Jewish sect into the worldwide omni-cultural missionary institution Jesus intended it to be.

In this chapter the church will take yet another giant step forward in fulfilling its missionary mandate to take the gospel to "the ends of the earth." The conversion and empowering of Saul of Tarsus will prepare the way for him to become God's instrument in opening wide the door to Gentile inclusion into the family and mission of God.

Chapter 6: Continued Expansion

Since Saul's infilling with the Spirit occurred in the city of Damascus, we call it the Damascene Outpouring. It is the fourth of seven key outpourings of the Holy Spirit in Acts. It is also the second of three outpourings occurring during the Transitional Period (see Figure 2.1, page 30). Like the Samaritan Outpouring, the Damascene Outpouring helped to prepare the church for its upcoming Gentile Mission. Each of these outpourings also contributed to the fulfilling of Luke's primary intent in writing Acts, that is, to call the church back to its Pentecostal and missionary roots. To emphasize this concept Luke repeatedly shows how, when people are filled with the Spirit, they become powerful witnesses for Christ.

SAUL'S CONVERSION

Reading Assignment: Acts 9:1-7

The Story
Saul of Tarsus continued to persecute the church in Jerusalem. Then, upon hearing of a group of Christians in the Syrian city of Damascus, he obtained official permission from the high priest to go there to arrest them and bring them back to Jerusalem as prisoners. As he and his party neared the city of Damascus, Jesus appeared to them in brilliant light, blinding Saul and causing him to fall to the ground. The Lord called out to him, "Saul, Saul, why are you persecuting me?" "Who are you, Lord?" Saul replied. The voice responded, "I am Jesus, whom you are persecuting. Now get up and go into the city, and you will be told what you must do." The men with Saul heard the sound, although they did not understand what was happening. They led him by the hand into the city, where he remained blind for three days. During that time he neither ate nor drank.

Commentary
Luke again focuses the reader's attention on Saul of Tarsus. Previously, in Acts chapter 7, Saul was seen giving his assent to the murder of Stephen, and in chapter 8, he began to violently persecute and destroy the church. Now, on the Damascus Road, the direction of Saul's life was dramatically altered. There, he had a powerful life-changing encounter with the resurrected Christ. The arch-persecutor of the church was to become its ardent proclaimer.

9:1 Saul was still breathing out murderous threats. In

Jerusalem Saul had been systematically moving from house to house, capturing believers and putting them into prison (8:3). He later described his work in this way: "I persecuted the followers of this Way to their death, arresting both men and women and throwing them into prison" (22:4). On another occasion he said, "I put many of the saints in prison, and when they were put to death, I cast my vote against them. Many a time I went from one synagogue to another to have them punished, and I tried to force them to blaspheme. In my obsession against them, I even went to foreign cities to persecute them" (26:10-11).

9:3 *suddenly a light from heaven.* This phrase echos the phrase in 2:2: "Suddenly a sound ... from heaven." The phrase "from heaven" indicates the light's divine or supernatural origin (cf. Luke 20:4-5; Acts 11:9). The light emanated from the resurrected Jesus, the One who had been exalted to the right hand of God, and who, from there, had poured out the Holy Spirit (2:33). He now appears to Saul in person. This appearance is yet another theophany in Acts (cf. 2:1-3; 4:31).

9:4 *Saul, Saul, why do you persecute me?* By persecuting the church, Saul was persecuting Christ. This fact demonstrates Jesus' close identification with His church. Paul said that Jesus loved the church so much that He died for it (Eph. 5:25). He often referred to the church as the "body of Christ" (1 Cor. 12:12, 27; Eph. 4:12; 5:23).

9:5 *Who are you, Lord?* In response to this question from Saul, Jesus answered, "I am Jesus who you are persecuting." Years later, in Paul's testimony before King Agrippa, he revealed that he actually called Jesus "Lord" twice (22:8-10). In the second instance Paul used the title after Jesus had clearly identified Himself. Then, Saul asked, "What shall I do, Lord?" (v. 10). Saul's double use of the title "Lord" indicates that he was truly converted at this moment on the Damascus Road. He later wrote that "no one can say, 'Jesus is Lord,' except by the Holy Spirit" (1 Cor. 12:3).

Life Application

Saul was saved when he met the resurrected Christ. It is the same today. To be saved one must also have a personal encounter with the living Christ. Not everyone's experience will be as dramatic as Saul's; nevertheless, it is essential that each person meets Christ personally. As ministers of the gospel, our primary job is to call people to faith in Him. They can meet Christ personally by repenting of their sins and putting their trust in Him alone for salvation.

Chapter 6: Continued Expansion

SAUL'S HEALING, COMMISSIONING AND EMPOWERING

Reading Assignment: Acts 9:8-19

The Story

The Lord appeared in a vision to a disciple named Ananias. He told Ananias to go to the house of Judas, who lived on Straight Street. There he should inquire for Saul, whom he would find in prayer. The Lord also informed Ananias that Saul had seen a vision. In the vision he had seen a man named Ananias coming to him and healing him of his blindness. At first Ananias objected, since he had heard stories of how Saul had been persecuting the saints in Jerusalem, and how Saul had come to Damascus to arrest Christians there. The Lord, however, assured him by telling him that Saul was His chosen instrument to proclaim His name among the Gentiles and their kings and before the people of Israel.

Obeying the Lord, Ananias went to the house of Justus. There, he laid his hands on Saul, calling him "Brother." He told Saul how Jesus had sent him to pray with him that he might be healed and be filled with the Spirit. Ananias laid his hands on Saul who was immediately healed and filled with the Holy Spirit. Saul was then baptized in water. After he had eaten and regained his strength, Saul spent several days with the disciples in Damascus.

Commentary

The story of Saul's conversion and Spirit baptism is an important episode in Acts. It sets the stage for the final sixteen chapters of the book, where Paul's ministry takes center stage. Later in Acts, Paul will, on two occasions, refer back to this incident (22:4-21; 26:12-23). Saul's being filled with the Spirit is unique among the seven key outpourings of the Spirit in Acts in that, in this instance, only one person is filled with the Spirit. We should not, however, underestimate its importance. Saul's being filled with the Spirit is a key event in his preparation as the apostle of Christ to the Gentiles and in fulfilling the Gentile Mission (see Figure 2.1, page 30.)

9:10 a disciple named Ananias. Literally, "a certain disciple" (NASB). Ananias was not an apostle, and there is no indication that he was even a local church officer in Damascus. He was simply a Spirit-filled believer in Christ. He was, nevertheless, a man of high character and good reputation (22:12). We also know that he was full of the Spirit since he heard the voice of the Lord, and since he prayed with Saul to be healed and filled with the Spirit.

9:11 Saul ... he is praying. Luke again emphasizes the role of prayer in receiving the Spirit. According to Luke, prayer is the context in which Spirit baptism in received (cf. Luke 11:9-13; Acts 1:14; 4:24; 8:15; 10:2-4, 9, 30-31; 13:1-3; 19:6).

9:15 *This man is my chosen instrument.* Saul is God's chosen instrument to carry the gospel to the Gentiles and the children of Israel. Beyond prayer, commitment to the mission of God is the proper context for receiving the Spirit in Acts. In Luke's view Spirit baptism is received, not for salvation or personal blessing, but for empowerment for mission (1:8; cf. 5:29-32).

9:17 *Placing his hands on Saul.* In context it is reasonable to assume that one purpose for which Ananias laid hands on Saul was to commission him for missionary service (cf. vv. 15-16; 22:14-15; 26:16-18). (See note on 8:17.)

Brother Saul. Ananias' calling Saul "brother" is another indication that Saul was a Christian before Ananias prayed for him to receive the Spirit. Ananias, who knew why Saul had come to Damascus, would never have called him brother had he not believed that he had truly become a brother in Christ.

so that you may see again and be filled with the Holy Spirit. Ananias' twofold commission from Christ was to pray with Saul to be healed and to be filled with the Spirit. We can assume that both occurred when he laid hands on him. As was the case with Peter (2:4; 4:8, 31) John (2:4), Stephen (6:3, 8), Philip (6:3), and Barnabas (11:24) Luke wants his readers to know that Saul had been filled with the Spirit before he describes his involvement in ministry. He wants the reader to understand that Spirit baptism is an essential prerequisite for any effective ministry (cf. Luke 24:49; Acts 1:8).

Life Application

The example of Ananias teaches us two important lessons: First, it teaches us that God can use anyone who will be filled with the Spirit and will remain open and obedient to His instructions. Although Ananias was just a layman, God used him to pray for a future apostle to receive the Spirit and be healed. This story also helps us to understand the great significance of even one person being filled with the Holy Spirit. We should not be discouraged on those occasions when we pray with people, and only one, or just a few, are filled. One or more of those few may, like Saul of Tarsus, become a powerful witnesses for Christ.

Chapter 6: Continued Expansion

SAUL'S WITNESS IN DAMASCUS AND JERUSALEM

Reading Assignment: Acts 9:20-30

The Story

When Saul was filled with the Holy Spirit he immediately began to preach the gospel in the synagogues of Damascus, Because of the great change in his life, the people wondered if he was the same man they had heard about in Jerusalem. As the days went by, Saul became ever more powerful in his witness for Christ. After some time the Jews in Damascus hatched a plot to assassinate Saul. However, he was able to escape.

Saul then went to Jerusalem where he sought fellowship with the believers there. They too were afraid of him, unsure that he had really become a Christian. Barnabas interceded for him and brought him to the apostles in Jerusalem. He told them the story of Saul's conversion and powerful witness for Christ in Damascus. In Jerusalem, Saul became a mighty witness for Christ, moving about freely and speaking boldly in the name of the Lord Jesus. He also spent time debating with the Grecian Jews, who plotted to kill him. When the brothers learned about this plot, they took him to Caesarea. From there he sailed to Tarsus, his hometown.

Commentary

9:20 At once he began to preach. As a result of his being filled with the Spirit, Saul "at once" began to preach the gospel. Here is another example of how Luke purposefully combines the two ideas of empowerment and witness throughout Acts. The pattern is consistent: every time the Spirit is poured out, witness results. As previously stated, we call this pattern Luke's *empowerment–witness motif.* It helps us to understand Luke's primary intent in writing Acts. Note that the content of Saul's preaching is the message of Christ, for He went about "proving that Jesus is the Christ" (v. 22).

9:22 Saul grew more and more powerful. This phrase is an indication that Saul remained full of the Holy Spirit. As he daily yielded to the Spirit's influence in his life, he grew ever more powerful in ministry.

9:28 in Jerusalem, speaking boldly in the name of the Lord. Being full of the Holy Spirit, Paul's bold witness continued even after he left Damascus and went to Jerusalem.

Life Application

The primary purpose of Spirit baptism is empowerment for witness. Christ does not pour His Spirit out on us primarily for our own personal blessing—though many blessings may come from our being filled with the Spirit—but to impart into us the desire, boldness, and ability to effectively proclaim Christ to the lost. This is why it is essential that every believer be baptized in the Holy Spirit. As we daily yield ourselves to the Spirit, our usefulness for Christ becomes greater and greater.

THE CHURCH IS STRENGTHENED AND GROWS

Reading Assignment: Acts 9:31

The Story

After Saul was converted, the churches in Judea, Galilee, and Samaria enjoyed a time of peace. As the Spirit continued to work in the lives of the disciples in these regions, the church was strengthened and grew in numbers. Believers lived in the fear of the Lord.

Commentary

9:31 encouraged by the Holy Spirit. Believers throughout Judea, Galilee, and Samaria continued to move under the Spirit's guidance and direction. As they did, they received help and strength from the Spirit. This is the only passage in Acts where the Greek word *parakleesei* is used in relationship to the Holy Spirit. It reminds us of Jesus' words in John 14-16 concerning the Counselor (*Parakletos,* also translated "Comforter" or "Helper"). There, Jesus promised His disciples that when the *Parakletos* came, He would dwell in them (14:17), empower them to do "greater works" (v. 12), teach them all things (v. 26), testify concerning Christ (15:26), aid them in evangelism (16:6-11), guide them into all truth (v. 13), and bring glory to Christ (v. 14).

grew in numbers, living in the fear of the Lord. As at the beginning, the church continued to experience both quantitative ("grew in numbers") and qualitative ("living in the fear of the Lord") growth (cf. 2:41-47; 4:31-35).

Life Application

As we move in the Spirit, we can expect Him to come to us to encourage and enable us in our Christian lives and ministries. As we follow His leading, the church will grow in number and in its relationship with the Lord.

PETER'S SPIRIT-EMPOWERED MINISTRY IN JUDEA

Reading Assignment: Acts 9:32–43

The Story

The storyline of Acts turns again to Peter, recounting his itinerant ministry in northwestern Judea. He traveled to the town of Lydda where he healed Aeneas, a Christian brother who had been paralyzed for a long time. Because of this miracle, everyone living in Lydda and in the nearby village of Sharon turned to the Lord.

In the coastal town of Joppa there lived a disciple by the name of Tabitha (or Dorcas). She was known and loved for her good works. She became ill and died, so the believers sent to Lydda for Peter. When he arrived in Joppa, Peter entered the upper room where they had laid her, and said to her, "Tabitha, get up." The dead woman opened her eyes and sat up. Upon hearing about this miracle, many people in Joppa believed in the Lord. Peter remained in Joppa for some time, staying at the house of Simon the tanner.

Commentary

Months after the initial outpouring of the Spirit on the Day of Pentecost, Peter continued to minister in the power of the Spirit. His charismatic ministry in northwestern Judea gives us insight into how the apostles engaged in pastoral care.

9:34 Jesus Christ heals you. As Jesus often did, Peter speaks a healing word to the sick man. His words show that Jesus, even after His ascension, continued His healing ministry (cf. Heb. 13:8). As at the Beautiful Gate, Peter was again ministering under the Spirit's direction. The Spirit must have revealed to him the fact that Christ was, at that moment, healing Aeneas. Peter simply stated the fact that it was happening.

9:35 All those who lived in Lydda and Sharon saw him and turned to the Lord. Peter's Spirit-empowered healing ministry in word and deed opened the hearts of the residents of Lydda and Sharon to receive the gospel and turn to the Lord.

9:40 Tabitha, get up. Peter healed Tabitha through the spoken word. This method of healing the sick has been called a "command of faith." Jesus often used this method in healing the sick (cf. Luke 6:8, 10; 7:11-15; 8:53-54; 18:40-43; John 5:8-9). (See comment on

14:10.)

9:42 many people believed in the Lord. Again, as with Aeneas, the result of the miracle is witness, for many believed in the Lord. The purpose of signs and wonders is not to attract attention to themselves, or to the one being used by God to work the miracles. The purpose of signs and wonders is to demonstrate the power of the kingdom of God and to point people to the Lord.

Life Application

We, as ministers of the gospel, should, like Peter, seek to imitate the ministry of Jesus, both in word and in action. Further, we must always direct people toward Christ. The purpose of miracles is not to attract attention to ourselves, but rather to point people to the Savior. Only He can meet their deepest spiritual needs. Like Peter, we must, at all times, remain full of the Spirit and open to His directions.

CONCLUSION

As the days went by, the early disciples continued to move in the power of the Holy Spirit. They also remained committed to fulfilling Christ's mission of preaching the gospel to the lost. Jesus had told them that they would be His witnesses "in Jerusalem, and in all Judea and Samaria, and to the ends of the earth." They had preached the gospel and established churches throughout Jerusalem, Judea, Galilee, and Samaria. The Holy Spirit was now preparing them to preach the gospel to the ends of the earth.

A third and final outpouring of the Spirit is about to occur during the Transitional Period. This outpouring, which we call the Caesarean Outpouring, will open wide the door of faith to the Gentiles. We will discuss this key outpouring of the Spirit and its far-reaching implications for the church in the next chapter.

QUESTIONS FOR REFLECTION AND REVIEW

1. Why did Saul of Tarsus go to Damascus?
2. Jesus asked Saul, "Why do you persecute me?" How was Saul persecuting Jesus?
3. What indications do we have in this account that Saul was truly converted on the Damascus Road?
4. What did the Lord tell Ananias about Saul before he had him pray for Saul?

5. Why do you think Luke includes the story of Saul's Spirit baptism in his narrative?
6. What were the immediate and ongoing results of Saul's being filled with the Spirit?
7. How does the Damascene Outpouring contribute to Luke's *empowerment–witness motif* first introduced in Acts 1:8?
8. Describe Peter's charismatic ministry in northwestern Judea. What were the results of the miracles he performed at this time?

QUESTIONS FOR CLASSROOM DISCUSSION

1. After Saul (Paul) had been filled with the Spirit, he "at once he began to preach in the synagogues that Jesus is the Son of God" (9:20). What important lessons can we learn from his experience with the Holy Spirit?
2. The context of Paul's being filled with the Spirit was his call and commissioning as a missionary. What are the implications of this fact concerning the proper context and purpose of Spirit baptism today?
3. According to 9:31, there seems to have been a spontaneous multiplication of churches in Judea, Galilee, and Samaria. What accounted for such a multiplication? What should we do today to see a similar multiplication of churches?
4. Peter's charismatic ministry in northwestern Judea resulted in many people coming to the Lord? What lessons can we learn from this ministry?

– Chapter 7 –

The Door Is Opened for the Gentiles

(Including the Caesarean Outpouring)

PRE-LESSON READING ASSIGNMENT

Acts 10:1—12:25

INTRODUCTION

Before Jesus returned to heaven He left His church with a commission, a command, and a promise. He commissioned them to be His witnesses in all the earth. Today we call this commission the Great Commission. It is found in all four gospels and Acts (Matt. 28:18-20; Mk16:15-18; Luke 24:46-49; John 20:21-22; Acts 1:8). Jesus further commanded His disciples to stay in Jerusalem until they had been clothed with power from heaven (Luke 24:49; Acts 1:4-5). And, finally, He promised them that they would receive power when the Holy Spirit came upon them, thus enabling them to be effective witnesses for Him in all the earth (Acts 1:8). The disciples obeyed His command, received His promise, and immediately began to fulfill His commission.

Jesus' promise of power was first fulfilled on the Day of Pentecost when Christ poured out the Spirit on His disciples, empowering them to be His witnesses (2:1-4). A few weeks later,

God poured out His Spirit a second time in Jerusalem, again empowering the church for its missionary task (4:31). These two outpourings enabled the church to fulfill the first part of Jesus' mandate—to be his witnesses in Jerusalem (1:8). We call this witness in Jerusalem the Jewish Mission.

Christ's desire for His church, however, was that it be an omni-ethnic international community of believers. Before this could happen, however, it needed to be prepared for its mission to the nations. This preparation came through a series of providential events and key outpourings of the Holy Spirit. We call this period in Acts the Transitional Period. It is during this period that we now find ourselves in our study. We have already examined some of the providential events that helped to prepare the church for its coming Gentile Mission. These events included the persecution and scattering of the Jerusalem believers. We have also examined two key outpourings of the Spirit that took place during this same period, the Samaritan Outpouring and the Damascene Outpouring. These helped to prepare the church for its coming Gentile Mission.

In this chapter we will examine a third key outpouring of the Spirit that took place during the Transitional Period, the Caesarean Outpouring (see Figure 2.1, page 30). This outpouring of the Holy Spirit opened the door wide to Gentile inclusion into the body of Christ. It further opened the door to full Gentile participation in the mission of God. It all began with God supernaturally arranging a divine appointment between a Gentile soldier and a Jewish apostle.

A DIVINE APPOINTMENT

Reading Assignment: Acts 10:1-26

The Story

A God-fearing Gentile man by the name of Cornelius lived with his family in the city of Caesarea. He was a Roman centurion of the Italian Regiment. He prayed often and gave generously to the poor. One day an angel of God appeared to him in a vision. The angel informed him that God had taken note of his prayers and gifts to the poor. He told Cornelius to send men to Joppa and bring back a man named Simon Peter. In obedience Cornelius sent three men to Joppa to get Peter, who was staying in the home of Simon the tanner.

The next day, as the men were approaching Joppa, Peter went upon the roof to pray. There he fell into a trance and saw a vision. In the vision heaven opened, and a large sheet was let down by four

Chapter 7: The Door Is Opened for the Gentiles

corners. It was filled with all sorts of unclean animals, reptiles, and birds. A voice commanded Peter to "kill and eat." Peter refused, saying, "I have never eaten anything impure or unclean." The voice challenged him, "Do not call anything impure that God has made clean." This scene was repeated three times, and the sheet was taken back to heaven.

As Peter pondered these things, the three men from Caesarea arrived at the door to Simon's house. The Spirit then spoke to Peter, telling him that three men were looking for him, and that he should not hesitate to go with them, for God had sent them.

The men told Peter the story of Cornelius and of how he had sent them to bring him to Caesarea. The next day Peter took six Jewish brothers with him and went with the three men to Caesarea. When they arrived at the house of Cornelius the following day, they found that Cornelius had called together a large number his relatives and close friends. They were ready to hear what Peter had to say.

Commentary

The meeting of Peter and Cornelius is an example of what has been called a "divine appointment," which occurs when God Himself sets up a meeting. He then arranges the circumstances and moves on the hearts of individuals to ensure that the meeting takes place. This is what happened with Peter and Cornelius.

God had a great purpose and plan for this meeting. His purpose was to show that His kingdom was open to all who would seek Him, whether Jew or Gentile. It was also to demonstrate that any people of any nation can become full participants in His mission if they will be filled with His Spirit. His plan was to bring a group of Palestinian Jewish believers together with a group of Roman Gentiles, and then move powerfully by His Spirit upon them all. In this story we again see the Holy Spirit acting as Superintendent of the Harvest. It is He who is directing the work of missions.

10:1 Caesarea. Caesarea was an important seaport city built by Herod the Great between 25 and 13 B.C. It was located about fifty miles (eighty kilometers) northwest of Jerusalem, and served as the residence of the Roman procurator of Palestine. Caesarea had a mixed Jewish and Gentile population.

a man named Cornelius. Along with Peter, Cornelius is the chief player in this story. Luke describes him as a God-fearer, that is, a Gentile who sincerely sought to serve and follow the God of Israel. He was a prayerful man, godly, generous, and deeply reverent. To the Jewish mind, nevertheless, he remained an unclean Gentile. Even more, he was a Roman soldier, and thus a living symbol of Gentile oppression over the Jews.

10:3 a vision. An angel of God appeared to Cornelius in a vision. The Spirit moved on this yet-to-be-converted man, directing him to the truth. One work of the Holy Spirit is to point men to the truth (John 6:44; John 16:8-11). Many ex-Muslims can testify today of how Christ appeared to them in a vision, beginning their quest for Him.

10:9 Peter went up on the roof to pray. Cornelius and Peter are both noted for their prayer in this story (vv. 2, 4, 9, 30-31, 11:5). Prayer is a central prerequisite for an outpouring of the Holy Spirit. (Concerning the relationship of prayer to receiving the Holy Spirit, see comments on 1:14.)

10:10 he fell into a trance. Peter's falling into a trance was an act of the Holy Spirit. It was while he was in this state that the Lord gave him a vision. Believers should not seek after visions; however, when they come, they should welcome and cherish them.

10:15 Do not call anything impure that God has made clean. God was teaching Peter that Jewish Christians should no longer look at Gentiles as impure or unclean. Christ died for them just as He died for the Jews. Neither should Gentiles be required to become Jewish proselytes before becoming Christians. Because of what Christ has done, they have the same right as the Jews to approach God for salvation and blessing. This represents a major shift in thinking for the Jewish Christians. It opened the door for Gentile inclusion in the blessing of Abraham (Gen. 22:18; cf. Gal. 3:16).

10:19 the Spirit said to him. Because Peter had been filled with the Spirit (2:4) and he remained full of the Spirit through prayer (2:42; 3:1; 6:4) and repeated fillings of the Spirit (4:8, 31), he was able to hear and clearly discern the voice of the Spirit.

Life Application

We should not consider anyone unworthy of hearing and responding to the message of Christ. We should gladly carry the gospel to all people. When we do, we can expect the Holy Spirit to guide us. When such guidance comes, we can be sure that the Spirit is working on both ends of the situation. Not only does He guide us into witnessing situations, but also prepares the hearts of the ones to whom He is directing us. If we, like Peter, will be filled with the Spirit and remain prayerful, we too can expect the Lord to speak to us and to guide us.

Chapter 7: The Door Is Opened for the Gentiles

PETER GOES TO THE GENTILES

Reading Assignment: Acts 10:27-33

The Story

When Peter and his companions entered Cornelius' house they found a large gathering of people ready to hear what Peter had to say. After expressing his misgivings about entering into a Gentile home, Peter assured the residents that "God has shown me that I should not call any man impure or unclean." He then asked them why they had sent for him. Cornelius told of his vision and how an angel had told him to send for Peter. He concluded, "Now we are all here in the presence of God to listen to everything the Lord has commanded you to tell us."

Commentary

10:28 God has shown me. Peter's newfound understanding of God's ways did not come to him by intellectual endeavor, but rather by a direct action of the Holy Spirit. What the Holy Spirit showed him, however, was nothing new. It was what the Scriptures had taught from the beginning, that God is the God of all creation, and that He loves all nations and wants them all to know and serve Him (i.e., Gen. 12:3; Ps. 2:8; Matt. 12:18).

10:33 we are all here in the presence of God. Cornelius understood that when people prayerfully gather in the Lord's name, He joins them (Matt. 18:20). God's presence is manifested when His people pray and call upon His name. In such an atmosphere the Holy Spirit is easily received.

Life Application

We should not hesitate to follow the leadership of the Holy Spirit, even when He leads us into unfamiliar and uncomfortable situations. When we do follow His leading, we can be assured that His presence will go with us.

PETER'S SPIRIT-INSPIRED MESSAGE

Reading Assignment: Acts 10:34-43

The Story

Peter began his message to Cornelius' household with an admission: "I now realize," he said, "how true it is that God does not show favoritism but accepts men from every nation who fear him and do what is right." He then launched into a recital of the gospel message, declaring that Jesus is Lord of all. He told how God had anointed Jesus with the Holy Spirit and power, and how He had gone about doing good and healing all who were oppressed by the devil, for God was with Him.

Peter then addressed the theme of Spirit-empowered witness, stating that God had raised up the apostles to be witnesses of all that Jesus did. They testified about Him and how He was crucified and how God had raised Him from the dead. After His resurrection, Jesus was not seen by everyone, but by witnesses whom God chose. He sent those same witnesses to testify that Jesus is the one whom God has appointed as the judge of all people. Not only that, the prophets also bore witness to Christ, saying that everyone who believes in Him receives forgiveness of sins.

Commentary

While presenting the actual words and essence of Peter's sermon to the household of Cornelius, Luke carefully constructed the sermon to help his readers understand exactly what was taking place on that day, and what God was trying to accomplish. The sermon has three major themes: The first was Peter's newfound realization that he should call no man common our unclean. This represented a seismic shift in Peter's thinking concerning the Gentiles. It was also a direct challenge to the Judaizers within the Jerusalem church. It was, however, absolutely essential that this shift in thinking take place if the church was to become all that Jesus intended.

The second major theme in Peter's sermon is the gospel, the message of Christ. This message was the core of all apostolic witness. Peter thus declared that Jesus was the Messiah and Lord of all. He spoke of His death, His resurrection, and His post-resurrection appearances (cf. 1 Cor. 15:1-8).

Peter's third and most developed theme was Spirit-anointed vocational witness. He told of how Jesus was anointed by the Holy Spirit to perform His ministry. The same applied to the apostles who were eye witnesses of everything Jesus did, including His death and resurrection. These same apostles saw Him alive after His resurrection. He commanded them to preach and testify to the people that He was the judge of the living and the dead. Finally, the prophets testified about God's universal salvation for all who would believe. This witness theme is important, for it sets the stage for the outpouring of the Spirit about to take place.

10:34 I now realize ... God does not show favoritism. Here Peter repeated the lesson he learned on the rooftop in Joppa. Before the gospel could advance beyond parochial Judaism the church had to come to the understanding that God accepts people from every nation who will fear Him and do what is right.

10:36 Jesus Christ, who is Lord of all. Jesus is not only the promised Jewish Messiah, He is Lord (Gk. *Kurios*) over all people and nations. Jesus is referred to as "Lord" nearly one hundred times in Acts. The title identifies Him both as deity and supreme ruler in God's kingdom.

10:38 God anointed Jesus of Nazareth with the Holy Spirit and power ... God was with him. Although Jesus was truly God, in His incarnation He emptied Himself of the use of His divine attributes and ministered as a man full of the Holy Spirit (cf. Phil. 2:6-7). Jesus' ministry was thus performed, not in His own power as the second Person of the Trinity, but in the power of the Holy Spirit. This is a key theme in Luke, beginning with Jesus' announcement that "The Spirit of the Lord is on me, because he has anointed me to preach good news to the poor" (4:18, cf. 3:21-23), and continuing throughout His ministry (4:1, 14; 5:16; 9:1; 11:20; 24:45, 49; Acts 1:2). It is for this reason that Jesus could say to His disciples that they would be able to do the same, and even greater, works than He (John 14:12). It is because they would be anointed by the same Spirit who anointed Him.

10:39 We are witnesses. As previously mentioned, Spirit-anointed vocational witness is the major theme in Peter's sermon to Cornelius' household and is a major theme in Acts. The word "witness" is used twice in this passage (vv. 39, 41), and implied two other times, using the cognate word "testify" (vv. 42-43). Witness first appears in 1:8 where Jesus tells His disciples that they will be His "witnesses ... to the ends of the earth." (See comments on 2:32.)

10:39-40 They killed him ... but God raised him from the dead. The core of the gospel message is the vicarious death and glorious resurrection of Christ (cf. 1 Cor. 15:1-8). (See comments on 1:3.)

Life Application

If Jesus ministered in the power of the Spirit, then we too must seek to minister in that same power. Just as He was anointed by the Spirit (Luke 3:21-22 with 4:18-19), we too must be anointed by the Spirit. This anointing comes as a result of one's being baptized in the Holy Spirit as were the 120 on the Day of Pentecost and as were the

Gentile seekers in Caesarea. The anointing remains as we daily live and walk in the Spirit. We must keep the message of Jesus' death, burial, and resurrection at the center of all our preaching and teaching.

THE HOLY SPIRIT IS POURED OUT ON GENTILES

Reading Assignment: Acts 10:44-48

The Story
Before Peter had finished his message, the Holy Spirit came powerfully upon all who were listening. The Jews who accompanied Peter to Caesarea were amazed that the gift of the Holy Spirit had been poured out *even* on the Gentiles. They knew it was so because they heard them speaking in tongues and magnifying God. Peter then called for these new believers to be baptized in water, saying, "They have received the Holy Spirit just as we have." After this he stayed with Cornelius and his companions for a few days.

Commentary
Again the Holy Spirit is poured out. The Caesarean Outpouring is the fifth of seven key outpourings of the Spirit in Acts. It is also the third and final outpouring during the Transitional Period. This outpouring opened wide the door for the upcoming Gentile Mission (see Figure 2.1, page 30). The purpose of the Caesarean Outpouring was the same as for every other outpouring of the Spirit in Acts: to empower the church for missional witness (cf. 1:8; 10:46; 11:15)

10:44 While Peter was still speaking these words. The "words" Luke is referring to are Peter's words concerning Spirit-empowered vocational witness (vv. 38-43). It was at that precise moment in Peter's sermon that the Holy Spirit fell on all those who were present. This "divine coincidence" helps us to understand the reason the Holy Spirit was given on this occasion. He was given so that the Gentile household of Cornelius could be empowered for vocational witness, just as Christ Himself had been (v. 38).

the Holy Spirit came on all. Empowerment for mission is an experience for all Christians. The word "all" often occurs in Scripture in relation to people's experiencing the Spirit. Moses wished "that *all* the Lord's people were prophets and that the Lord would put his Spirit on them!" (Num. 11:29). Joel prophesied of a time when God would pour out His Spirit on "*all* people" (Joel 2:28). On the Day of Pentecost "they were *all* filled with the Holy

Spirit" (Acts 2:4). On that same occasion Peter announced that the gift of the Holy Spirit was "for *all* who are far off—for *all* whom the Lord our God will call" (Acts 2:39). Now, here at the household of Cornelius, "the Holy Spirit came upon them *all*." (Emphases added in the above quotes.)

10:45 the gift of the Holy Spirit had been poured out even on the Gentiles. Joel had prophesied that God would pour out His Spirit on all people (2:28-29). God continued to fulfill that promise by giving the Spirit to uncircumcised Gentiles.

10:46 For they heard them speaking in tongues and praising God. The Greek word translated "for" (*gar*) in this verse is often translated "because." The Jewish brethren knew that the Gentiles had received the Holy Spirit because they heard them speak in tongues and magnify God. Speaking in tongues and prophetic witness thus serve as evidence that one has received the Holy Spirit. This is the second instance in Acts where tongues are specifically mentioned as occurring immediately upon one's receiving the Holy Spirit (cf. 2:4). Tongues is again specifically mentioned in Acts 19, when the Ephesian disciples receive the Spirit (v. 6).[24]

While the NIV translates *megaloono* as "praising," better translations are "magnify" (NKJV) or "exalting" (NASB). These newly-Spirit-baptized Gentiles were likely exalting God by declaring His mighty works to others, as did the 120 disciples and Peter at Pentecost (2:11, 14ff), rather than by praising Him as the NIV indicates. The Caesarean Outpouring is another example of Luke's *empowerment–witness motif* first introduced in 1:8.[25]

10:47 They have received the Holy Spirit just as we have. The Gentiles in Caesarea received the Spirit just as the 120 Jews in Jerusalem at Pentecost, and for the same purpose, Spirit-empowered witness.

Life Application

We too can expect to receive the Holy Spirit today just as He was received by these Gentile believers in Caesarea—and just as the disciples did on the Day of Pentecost. When we receive the Holy

---

[24] In the two other instances in Acts of individuals initially receiving the Holy Spirit, speaking tongues is consistent with the data (8:17-18; 9:17-18 with 1 Cor. 14:18).

[25] For a fuller explanation of this theme see the author's book *Empowered for Global Mission*, pp.190-194.

Spirit, we can expect the same results; we will speak in tongues and receive power to be effective witnesses for Him.

THE DOOR IS OPENED

Reading Assignment: Acts 11:1-18

The Story

Soon the news of what had happened at Caesarea spread throughout all Judea. Everyone was saying that the Gentiles had also received the word of God. Some Jewish believers, however, were not happy about what Peter had done. So, when Peter returned to Jerusalem, they began to criticize him, charging him with the offense of going into the house of uncircumcised Gentiles and eating with them.

Peter defended his actions by explaining exactly what had happened to him, including his vision and the Spirit's injunction to him: "Do not call anything impure that God has made clean." He further told them how the Spirit had spoken to him and told him to have no hesitation about going to Caesarea. Peter then told them about Cornelius' vision, and how he had sent for him to bring to them a message from God. The message would show them how they could be saved.

Peter finally told them of how the Holy Spirit fell on the Gentiles, noting that He "came on them as He had come on us at the beginning." Peter was then reminded of the final speech of Jesus, how He had said to His disciples, "John baptized with water, but you will be baptized with the Holy Spirit." He concluded, "If God gave them the same gift as He gave us ... who was I to think that I could oppose God?" When the assembly heard this, they held their peace and confessed that God has granted the Gentiles repentance unto life.

Commentary

The outpouring of the Spirit on the Gentiles in Caesarea was a pivotal moment in the history of the church. On that occasion, God gave to those Gentile seekers two dynamic, almost simultaneous, experiences. First, He granted to them "repentance unto life" (cf. 11:18). He then, almost immediately, empowered them for witness by pouring out the Holy Spirit on them, just as He had done with the 120 "at the beginning" (v. 15). God was indeed pouring the new wine of the Spirit into the old wineskins of Jewish religious tradition, and the old wineskins could not contain it. God thus used the Caesarean Outpouring to help prepare the church for its mission to "the ends of the earth" as Jesus had outlined in 1:8.

This outpouring is yet another key example of Luke's *empowerment–witness motif* in Acts. The Caesarean Outpouring resulted in powerful witness in two directions. First, it resulted in witness to the inhabitants of Caesarea. It did this through immediate prophetic proclamation of the gospel (see notes on 10:46), and by creating a new center of Spirit-empowered witness in an important Roman seaport (cf. 18:22, 21:8, 16). Second, the Caesarean Outpouring witnessed back to the church in Jerusalem. It said to the Jewish Christians there that they should not place unnecessary requirements on Gentiles—other than faith and repentance—before they could become Christians. Uncircumcised Gentiles should be allowed into the church, not only as full-fledged members, but also as full participants in God's mission.

11:12 The Spirit told me. When explaining his actions to the apostles and elders in Jerusalem, Peter answered that the Spirit had spoken to him, directing him to do what he did. Again, the Spirit is actively involved in directing and fulfilling the mission of Christ. Because Peter was open and obedient to the voice of the Spirit, God was able to use him.

11:15 the Holy Spirit came on them. This phrase reminds us of Jesus' promise in 1:8: "But you will receive power when the Holy Spirit *comes on you*..." (emphasis added). Luke's use of the same terminology in both instances helps us to understand how we are to interpret the Caesarean Outpouring. Here at Caesarea God was fulfilling His promise of Acts 1:8 that He would empower believers for missional witness when the Holy Spirit "came upon" them. Peter further testified that the Holy Spirit came upon the Caesareans "as he had come on us at the beginning." They received the Spirit in the same way and for the same purpose as the disciples at Pentecost—empowerment for witness.

11:16 you will be baptized with the Holy Spirit. When the Spirit fell on the Caesareans, Peter remembered these words of Jesus spoken just before His ascension into heaven (1:4-8). They were spoken in the context of Jesus' preparing His disciples for the Day of Pentecost, when they would be empowered by the Spirit to take the gospel to all nations (v. 8). The implication is again clear: the Caesareans' baptism in the Holy Spirit was for the same purpose as the believers at Pentecost, empowerment for mission.

11:17 God gave them the same gift as he gave us. God gave the new Caesarean believers the same gift (the baptism in the Holy

Spirit) for the same purpose (empowerment for witness) as He gave to the apostles and other believers on the Day of Pentecost. Today God baptizes believers in the Spirit for the same purpose.

11:18 So then, God has granted even the Gentiles repentance unto life. Peter's reasoning is seamless. If God has empowered Gentiles to be his witnesses to the nations, and He has given them the same divine evidence as He gave to the 120 at Pentecost (speaking in tongues), then it cannot be denied, He must have first granted them repentance unto life.

Life Application

As we minister for Christ, we should expect the same divine guidance that the Spirit gave to Peter and other New Testament believers. When He does give us direction, we should be willing to go without hesitation to any place or to any people. As we go, we should bear in mind that, not only will God use us to spread His word, but also He will use those to whom we take the gospel. It is therefore essential that we ensure that those who receive the gospel are immediately empowered by the Spirit to take the gospel to others.

THE CHURCH STRENGTHENS AND EXPANDS

Scripture Reading: Acts 11:19–12:25

The Story

Luke now takes his readers back to the scattering of the Jewish believers in Acts 8. He tells how some of those who were scattered by the persecution traveled as far as Phoenicia, Cyprus, Cyrene, and Syrian Antioch. Those who first arrived in Antioch preached the gospel to fellow Jews only. Some, however, who came to Antioch by way of Cyprus and Cyrene, preached gospel to the Greeks (non-Jews) also. The Lord's hand was with them, and a great number of people turned to the Lord.

When news of what was happening in Antioch reached the church at Jerusalem, they sent Barnabas to check on the work. Barnabas was full of the Holy Spirit and faith, and when he arrived in Antioch, he was glad when he saw "evidence of the grace of God." He encouraged the disciples there to remain true to the Lord. As a result of his ministry, many people came to Christ.

Barnabas then went to Tarsus, where he found Saul. He brought him back to Antioch, where he and Saul worked together teaching many people. It was after a year of such teaching that the disciples in Antioch first came to be known as Christians.

About that time a group of prophets came down from Jerusalem. One of their number, named Agabus, prophesied through the Spirit that a great famine was coming. In response to this prophecy, the disciples in Antioch decided to help their brothers living in Judea by sending a gift to them by Barnabas and Saul.

Soon after this, King Herod began persecuting the church in Jerusalem. He killed James and then seized Peter and put him into prison to be held for trial. The church, when it heard what happened, began to intercede for his release. The night before his trial, an angel of the Lord appeared in Peter's cell, awoke him, and told him to get up. As he did, the chains fell from his wrists. The angel then led him out of the prison. Dazed, Peter thought he had seen a vision. When he finally came to himself, he understood that the Lord had sent His angel to deliver him. He then went to the house of Mary, the mother of John Mark, where a large group of believers had gathered to pray for him. At first the believers did not believe that it was he. When they finally recognized him, they were astonished.

The next morning confusion filled the prison. No one knew what had happened to Peter. In anger, Herod had the guards executed. He later moved to Caesarea. Because he refused to acknowledge God, an angel of the Lord struck him down, and he was eaten by worms and died.

Even in the midst of such persecution "the word of God continued to increase and spread." When Barnabas and Saul had finished their mission of delivering the relief money from the saints in Antioch to those in Jerusalem, they returned to Antioch, taking with them John Mark.

COMMENTARY

As the months passed, the church continued to strengthen and expand. Seven years after Pentecost the church had spread throughout all Judea, Samaria, and Galilee, southward into Gaza and North Africa, westward into Cyprus in the Mediterranean Sea, and northward into Phoenicia, Syria, and Cilicia. (It had also likely spread to many places not mentioned in Acts.) In the remainder of chapter 11 and in chapter 12, Luke tells about the planting of the church in Antioch and of further developments affecting the church in Jerusalem.

Missionary Witness in Antioch (11:19-30)

When does evangelism become missions? Evangelism becomes missions when believers begin to minister across cultures. We see this happening in the church in Antioch. The first wave of Jewish Christians to arrive in Antioch told the message only to Jews. The second wave, however, preached the gospel to Greeks also. Although the first wave had traveled many miles from their home in Jerusalem, and had crossed national borders, they were still doing evangelism because they were only reaching their own people. However, when the second wave began to reach out to those of different cultural and ethnic backgrounds, they were doing missions!

The church founded in Antioch was to become the second great center of Christian missions, after Jerusalem. It will be from this church that Paul will launch his three missionary journeys. Luke, therefore, tells us about the founding of this great church.

11:20 the good news about the Lord Jesus. As in every other instance in Acts, wherever the believers went, their central message remained the good news about the Lord Jesus. This message must also remain the centerpiece of our preaching today, for only the message of Jesus is able to save people from their sins and give them eternal life (Acts 4:12; 16:31).

11:21 The Lord's hand was with them. This is another way of saying that the manifest presence and power of the Holy Spirit accompanied them. In Scripture the Spirit is often pictured as the hand (arm or finger) of the Lord (Eze. 3:14; 37:1; Luke 11:20. See comments on 4:30).

11:23 evidence of the grace of God. The evidence of the grace of God that Barnabas saw was the changed lives of the people who had become disciples of Jesus. We should expect this same evidence in our ministries today.

11:24 a good man, full of the Holy Spirit and faith. Barnabas is mentioned thirty times in Acts and five times in the Pauline epistles. Because of his generous nature, he earned the title, "Son of Encouragement" (4:36). In the church in Antioch he lived up to his name, for there "he encouraged them all" (v. 23). Barnabas was also an apostle and traveling companion on Paul's first missionary journey (13:3–14:26). Here he is called "a good man, full of the Holy Spirit and faith." He was also a preacher (15:35), a teacher (11:26; 13:1; 15:35), a prophet (13:1), and a worker of miracles (14:3; 15:12).

a great number of people were brought to the Lord. As a result of Barnabas' Spirit-filled ministry, many people came to know the Lord. Here Luke draws a direct relationship between the preacher's character, his being full of the Holy Spirit, his faith, and church growth.

11:26 The disciples were called Christians first at Antioch. Note that it was disciples (i.e., committed learners) who were called Christians (Gk. *Christianous*) at Antioch. It was only after an entire year of intensive discipleship training that these disciples began to display the character of Christ to such an extent that they were called Christians.

11:28 Agabus ... through the Spirit predicted ... a severe famine. Agabus was one of a group of prophets who came from Jerusalem to strengthen the work in Antioch (v. 27). This is the first of two mentions of this prophet in Acts (cf. 21:10). He seemed to have had a special gift of predictive prophecy. Not all prophecy in Scripture, however, is predictive. Even with the Old Testament prophets most of their ministry was not predicting the future, but rather a declaration of the word of the Lord to their contemporary audiences. In the church the threefold purpose of prophecy is strengthening, encouraging, and comforting believers (1 Cor. 14:3. See comments on 21:10).

Persecution, Prayer, Deliverance, and Witness (12:1-25)

Persecution now came to the Jerusalem church from a second source. The first wave of persecution had come from the Jewish authorities. This wave comes from Herod. Persecution is an oft repeated theme in Acts. (For an explanation of the role of persecution in Acts, see comments on 8:1.)

12:5 the church was earnestly praying to God. Again Luke emphasizes the power of prayer and the central role that it played in the life of the early church. Throughout Acts we see the believers constantly in prayer, both individually and corporately. Prayer is a powerful weapon at the disposal of the church.

12:24 the word of God continued to increase and spread. In spite of constant harassment, and even martyrdom, the church stayed focused on its mission and continued to proclaim the gospel.

Life Application

If we are to have truly missional churches, we must gladly minister to people of different ethnic and cultural backgrounds. We cannot allow people of different tribes and religions who live in our areas, cities, or neighborhoods to go unevangelized. We must find ways to reach them with the gospel. In this way we can be true missionaries, without ever leaving our own home towns. Further, it is important that we ensure that the Lord's hand is with us as we minister. We must have the Spirit's presence and power upon us. Just as Barnabas was good man, full of the Holy Spirit and faith, we too should seek to live holy lives, be filled with the Spirit, and act in faith in all that we do for Christ.

When we face difficulties in fulfilling the Great Commission, we should turn to God in earnest prayer. Through prayer we can tap into the miracle-working power of God. It is also through prayer that we receive strength and guidance for the work ahead. If we will seek God's face and remain committed to His mission, we too can expect to see the word of God increase and spread wherever we are ministering.

CONCLUSION

With the story of Peter's deliverance from prison, we come to the end of the second section of Acts, the Transitional Period. The church is now ready to launch into its Gentile Mission. This it will do with a powerful move of the Holy Spirit in the church in Antioch. We will discuss this move of the Spirit in the next chapter.

QUESTIONS FOR REFLECTION AND REVIEW

1. Describe the way that the Holy Spirit worked as Superintendent of the Harvest to bring about a "divine appointment" between Cornelius and Peter in Caesarea.
2. Explain how prayer plays a prominent role in the Caesarean Outpouring.
3. What was the meaning of the vision that the Spirit gave to Peter on the rooftop?
4. Why is it important to understand that Jesus ministered in the power and anointing of the Holy Spirit? (cf. 10:38). What are the implications for our ministries today?
5. What subject was Peter presenting when the Holy Spirit was poured out in Caesarea? What is the significance of this "divine coincidence?"
6. The Holy Spirit was again poured out on all who are present. What is the significance of this?
7. How did the Jewish brothers who accompanied Peter to Caesarea know that the Gentiles had received the Holy Spirit?
8. How does the author interpret the Gentiles' "magnifying God" in 10:46? How is this interpretation consistent with Luke's empowerment–witness motif?
9. According to 10:47, for what purpose did the Gentiles receive the Holy Spirit?
10. How is Luke's *empowerment–witness motif* demonstrated in the Caesarean Outpouring?

11. How, according to 11:15-17, do we know that the Gentiles in Caesarea were given the Holy Spirit to empower them as witnesses?
12. Describe how the church in Antioch, Syria, was started.
13. How does Luke describe Barnabas in 11:24? Why does he want us to know that he was full of the Holy Spirit?

QUESTIONS FOR CLASSROOM DISCUSSION

1. The Holy Spirit arranged a "divine appointment" between Peter and Cornelius? Can we expect Him to do the same thing for us today? How can we ensure that we do not miss such appointments?
2. The Holy Spirit showed Peter that he "should not call any man impure or unclean" (10:28). What present-day missional lessons can we learn from this powerful truth?
3. According to Acts 10:38, Jesus ministered in the power and anointing of the Holy Spirit (cf. Lk 4:18-19). What are some implications for our ministries today?
4. The Jewish believers with Peter knew that the Caesareans had received the Holy Spirit because the heard them speaking in tongues and magnifying God. Can we know for sure when people have been similarly baptized in the Holy Spirit today? Explain your answer.
5. Acts 11:19-20 (cf. 13:1-3) describes the church in Antioch. What lessons can we learn from this great missionary church about establishing an effective missionary church today?

Chapter 7: The Door Is Opened for the Gentiles

– Part IV –
The Gentile Mission

– Chapter 8 –

Paul's First Missionary Journey

(Including the Antiochian "Outpouring")

PRE-LESSON READING ASSIGNMENT

Acts 13:1-14:28

INTRODUCTION

We now progress in our study to the period of the Gentile Mission. This is the third part of Jesus' missionary agenda as outlined in Acts 1:8. The church has already extended into Jerusalem, Judea, and Samaria. The time has now come for it to expand to the "ends of the earth," which in Acts 1:8 corresponds to the Gentile Mission (see Figure 2.1, page 30).

The Gentile Mission begins with a powerful move of the Holy Spirit in the church in Antioch. We call this move of the Spirit the Antiochian "Outpouring." It is the fifth of seven key outpourings of the Holy Spirit in Acts and the first outpouring during the Gentile Mission.

Chapter 8: Paul's First Missionary Journey

THE ANTIOCHIAN "OUTPOURING"

Reading Assignment: Acts 13:1-3

The Story

There were prophets and teachers in the church at Antioch. These included Barnabas, Simeon (also called Niger—or the Black Man), Lucius (from Cyrene), Manaen (the foster brother of King Herod the tetrarch), and Saul. Once, during a time of worship and fasting, a prophetic word was given. The Holy Spirit instructed the church to set apart Barnabas and Saul for the missionary ministry to which He had called them. After more fasting and prayer, they laid their hands on the two missionaries and sent them on their way.

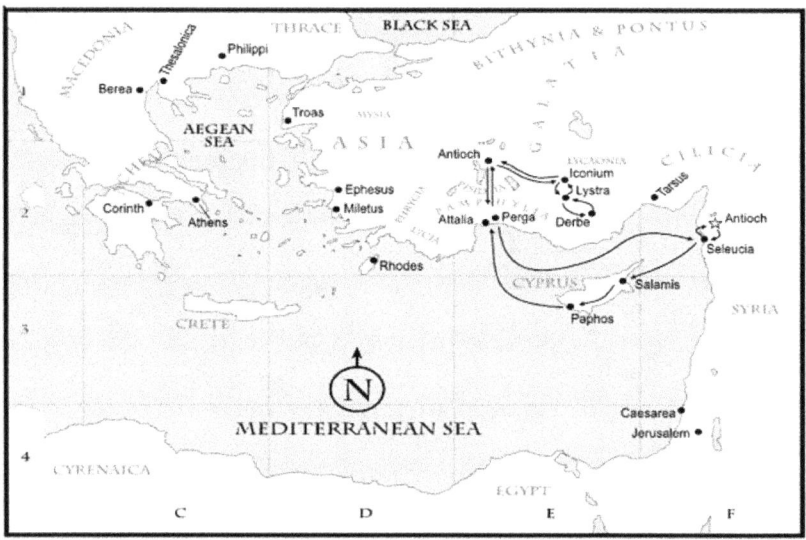

Figure 8.1 Paul's First Missionary Journey ©2005 Biblical Studies Press

Commentary

The church's Gentile Mission was launched by a powerful move of the Spirit in the church of Antioch, which we are calling the Antiochian "Outpouring." Note that we have put the word "Outpouring" in quotation marks. This is because what happened in Antioch cannot be technically termed an outpouring of the Spirit, as are the other six key outpourings in Acts. It could more accurately be termed an *action* or *move* of the Spirit. We are calling it an outpouring, however, to maintain continuity in our terminology. It must be noted, nevertheless, that this powerful move of the Spirit presupposes one or more outpourings of the Spirit in the church in

Antioch.

Luke has already described the beginning of the church in Antioch in 11:19-26. The church was started by Christian refugees who fled Jerusalem during the persecution that broke out after Stephen's martyrdom. It quickly grew into a powerful multiethnic church. Under the guidance and care of Saul and Barnabas it became a truly Spirit-anointed missional church. It was from this congregation that the church's first ever intentional missionary effort was launched, and the Gentile Mission officially began. And it began, as we have stated, with a powerful move of the Holy Spirit in the church.

It is significant that Luke locates a *pneuma event* (i.e., a direct intervention of the Holy Spirit) near the beginning of each of Paul's three missionary journeys. These interventions of the Holy Spirit are, more specifically, located at the launching of new missionary initiatives as indicated in Figure 8.2, below. These pneuma events are significant because they let us know that all of Paul's missionary ministry was empowered and directed by the Holy Spirit.

"Pneuma Events" and Paul's Missionary Journeys

Missionary Journey	Reference	Pneuma Event	New Initiative
First Journey	13:1-4	The Spirit moves in the Antioch church	Launching the Gentile Mission
Second Journey	16:6-10	The Spirit directs Paul's missionary team westward into Macedonia	Launching the mission into Western Europe
Third Journey	19:1-7	The Spirit is poured out on the Ephesian disciples	Launching the mission into Asia Minor

Figure 8.2

The Antiochian Outpouring is yet another key example of Luke's *empowerment–witness motif* first presented in 1:8: "You will receive power ... you will be my witnesses." By repeating this pattern over and over, Luke shows his readers that any believer or church filled with the Holy Spirit and committed to fulfilling Christ's mission can be used mightily by God.

13:1 Antioch. Antioch, Syria, was called the "queen of the East," and was the third city in the Roman Empire, after Rome and Alexandria. It was a cosmopolitan city and a commercial trading center. Its population was made up mainly of Syrians, Greeks, Jews, and Romans. Antioch was an ideal location for the emergence of a thriving missionary church and as a base for Paul's three missionary journeys.

prophets and teachers. Every healthy church should have prophets and teachers in its membership. Paul describes both ministries as grace gifts given by Christ to the church (Eph. 4:7-11). Both are also charismatic giftings, and, according to Luke, both speak by inspiration of the Spirit (Luke 5:17; Acts 2:17-18, 11:28). Jesus himself was a prophet and a teacher (Luke 24:19; John 3:2; 13:13), as were Paul and Barnabas (Acts 11:26; 13:1). Both ministries are needed today.

13:2 worshiping the Lord and fasting. Luke sees the church as a worshiping body. Before Pentecost, the disciples "stayed continually at the temple, praising God" (Luke 24:53). After Pentecost, the newly-Spirit-baptized believers spent much time together "praising God" (Acts 2:47). The Jerusalem believers praised God after Peter's report that the Gentiles had received the Spirit at Caesarea (11:18). Also, in Jerusalem the brothers praised God for what He had done among the Gentiles through Paul's ministry (21:20). Now, in Antioch, Luke pictures the church "worshiping the Lord." Prayer with fasting was also a common practice of the New Testament church (Luke 5:35; Acts 13:3; 14:23).

the Holy Spirit said. Luke included this move of the Spirit in Antioch because he wanted his readers to know that Paul's missionary journeys were an initiative of the Holy Spirit. On this occasion the Spirit spoke to the church through a prophetic gift. The message could have come through tongues and interpretation or, more likely, through the gift of prophecy (cf. 1 Cor. 14:1-5).

the work to which I have called them. True apostles and missionaries are not self-appointed; they are called by God. Paul and Barnabas already knew their calling, and they knew where they had been sent. The issue here seems to be timing. The Spirit was saying, "Now is the time to begin the mission."

13:3 after they had fasted and prayed. The church fasted and prayed after hearing the prophetic word concerning Barnabas and Saul. It seems that the church was "testing" the prophecy. Paul later wrote that prophecies must be tested. He said that "two or three prophets should speak, and the others should weigh carefully what is said" (1 Cor. 14:29). Prophecies are weighed by the word of God and through prayer and fasting. No prophecy given in an assembly should be received until it is first tested and approved. The believers in Antioch could also have been seeking God's further insight and direction. Also, they could have been interceding for the safety and success of the two missionaries.

they placed their hands on them. Just as apostles and missionaries are not self-appointed, neither are they self-sent. Barnabas and Saul were sent out by the church and by the Holy Spirit (cf. 13:4). Paul himself later asked concerning missionaries, "How can they preach unless they are sent?" (Rom. 10:15).

Life Application

If we are to have powerful missionary churches, we must be ever open to the moving of the Holy Spirit in our midst. We must ensure that our members have been baptized in the Holy Spirit and that they thoroughly understand their responsibility of remaining full of the Spirit and focused on the mission of God. A truly missional church, like the church in Antioch, will reach out aggressively in evangelism and church planting. At the same time, it will remain focused on the nations that need to hear the gospel. Such a church will be strong in pastoral care and discipleship training. The gifts of the Spirit will be in operation, and the people will be taught to give generously and sacrificially to the work of missions. The truly missional church will gather often for Spirit-anointed worship and times of intensive prayer and fasting. It is God's will for every local congregation to be a Spirit-empowered missional church.

CYPRUS: SPIRIT-EMPOWERED MINISTRY

Reading Assignment: Acts 13:4-12

The Story

Barnabas and Saul were sent on their way by the church in Antioch and by the Holy Spirit. With them was John Mark, Barnabas' nephew. The men traveled southwestward from Antioch to the nearby coastal town of Seleucia. From there they sailed to the island of Cyprus in the eastern Mediterranean Sea. Disembarking at Salamis, they began to preach the gospel in the local synagogue. They then traveled westward across the island, preaching from town to town. Eventually, they reached Paphos on the western coast of Cyprus.

In Paphos Barnabas and Saul met two men, the proconsul of the island, Sergius Paulus, and a Jewish sorcerer and false prophet Bar-

Jesus. The proconsul sent for Barnabas and Saul so he could hear the word God. However, Bar-Jesus (also known as Elymas) opposed them and tried to turn Sergius Paulus from the faith.

As this was happening, Paul was again filled with the Holy Spirit and given divine insight into what God was about to do. He looked straight at the sorcerer and announced that the hand of the Lord was against him, and that he would go blind for a season. Immediately it happened: Elymas began to grope about in darkness, begging for someone to take him by the hand. When the proconsul saw this, he was astonished and believed the apostles' teaching about the Lord.

Commentary

Being sent on their way by the church and by the Holy Spirit, Paul and Barnabas arrived at Cyprus and began the primary work of missions, proclaiming the message of Christ. They moved systematically across the island preaching the gospel—and likely establishing congregations—wherever they went. It is also likely that there already existed on the island congregations of believers, which had been started by Christian refugees who fled because of the persecution of Acts 8 (11:19-20).

The meeting of Paul and Elymas is a classic power encounter[26]—a an occasion arising in ministry when the power of Satan must be directly confronted by a demonstration of God's greater power. Here, the sorcerer, Elymas, opposed Paul and Barnabas and tried to turn Sergius Paulus from the faith. Likely he did not do this by using rational arguments against the Christian faith, for, being a sorcerer, reason was not his stock-in-trade. He more likely tried to turn the proconsul from the faith by using his occultic arts. Paul, however, was filled with the Holy Spirit and boldly challenged him.

Through a word of knowledge the Spirit revealed to Paul what God was about to do. Acting in faith, Paul announced to Elymas that the hand of the Lord was against him, and that he would be blinded for a season. When Paul's prediction immediately came true, Sergius Paulus' heart was opened to the gospel, and he believed in Christ.

13:4 sent on their way by the Holy Spirit. Again the Holy Spirit is presented as the Superintendent of the Harvest. He is the primary strategist, equipper, sender, director, encourager, and sustainer of

---

[26] For a fuller discussion of power encounter in ministry, see the author's book, *Power Encounter: How To Minister in the Power and Anointing of the Holy Spirit,* Revised Edition (also published under the title *Power Ministry: A Handbook for Pentecostal Preachers*).

missions.

Cyprus. The residents of Cyprus were notorious for their licentious worship of Venus and the Assyrian goddess, Astarte. The island was the birthplace and home of Barnabas. There was already a Christian presence on the island when Barnabas and Saul arrived (11:19).

13:5 proclaimed the word of God. The apostles' message was the word of God, or the gospel. This phrase is often used in Acts to mean the preaching of the gospel. In missions our message is the "full counsel of God" (20:27, NKJV), and the heart of that message is the message of Jesus (4:2; 5:42; 8:5; 9:20; 17:3). (See comments on 8:25 and 17:13.)

13:9 filled with the Holy Spirit. This phrase is not describing Paul's initial filling with the Holy Spirit, for that happened several years earlier when Ananias laid hands on him in Damascus (9:17-18). This experience of Paul's can more properly be termed a refilling or an anointing with the Holy Spirit. Like Peter in 4:8, Paul is being anointed by the Spirit for charismatic ministry.

13:12 the proconsul ... believed, for he was amazed at the teaching about the Lord. Power ministry is not an end in itself. The ultimate goal of power ministry is to bring people to faith in Christ. Power encounter (a demonstration of God's power) must always be accompanied by truth encounter (the proclamation of the gospel). In this verse "the teaching of the Lord" seems to include both proclamation and demonstration.

Life Application

When involved in ministry, we must trust the Lord to anoint us to proclaim the gospel with power. We must also trust Him to manifest His power through us in the release of spiritual gifts. When we face opposition from Satan, we can be confident that the Spirit of God is more powerful than that of the enemy (1 John 4:4). If we are full of the Spirit, we can boldly challenge demonic forces in the name of Jesus and in the power of the Holy Spirit. In all that we do, our goal must be to point people to Christ as their Lord and Savior.

ANTIOCH: THE GOSPEL IS PROCLAIMED

Reading Assignment: Acts 13:13-52

The Story

From Paphos, Paul, Barnabas, and John Mark sailed northward until they arrived at Perga in Pamphylia. There John left the group and returned to Jerusalem. Paul and Barnabas, however, continued northward through Pamphylia as far as Pisidian Antioch. The next Sabbath Paul was invited to speak in the Jewish synagogue there.

Paul began his message by reminding those present of how God had blessed Israel in many ways. He especially blessed Israel by sending to them the message of salvation through Jesus, the Savior and descendent of David. Though the people of Jerusalem and their rulers rejected Jesus and asked Pilate to execute Him, God vindicated Him by raising him from the dead. This was all foretold by the prophets. Now, through this same Jesus, they could have forgiveness of sins, and through faith in Him, they could be justified before God. This was something that the Law of Moses could never do. They, therefore, must not reject Jesus. If they do, God will judge them, as the prophets have solemnly warned.

After the meeting, some asked Paul and Barnabas to come and speak again on these topics. Many Jews and God-fearing proselytes followed Paul and Barnabas, and the apostles urged them to continue in God's grace. The next Sabbath almost the entire city gathered to hear the word of the Lord. This caused some Jews to become jealous, so they began to contradict what Paul was saying. Paul and Barnabus then turned to the Gentiles. As they did, they applied to themselves the words of Isaiah the prophet: "I have made you a light for the Gentiles." When the Gentiles heard this, they rejoiced and glorified the Lord.

The word of the Lord then spread through the whole region. In response, the Jews stirred up some high-ranking officials of the city, who in turn instigated persecution against Paul and Barnabas, expelling them from their region. Paul and Barnabas therefore shook the dust from their feet against them and went to Iconium. The disciples in Pisidian Antioch, nevertheless, were filled with joy and with the Holy Spirit.

Commentary

Paul's sermon in Pisidian Antioch is another example of apostolic preaching, sometimes called the apostolic kerygma.[27] As in every other case in Acts, Jesus, especially His death and resurrection, is the central theme. Paul appeals to Scripture to prove his case. Finally, he calls his hearers to repentance and faith in Christ. These elements should be a part of all gospel preaching.

Some commentators have pointed out that verses 38 and 39 are a summary of Paul's letter to the Galatians that he would later write to

---

[27] For a discussion on the apostolic kerygma see comments on 2:22-36.

these same people: "Therefore, my brothers, I want you to know that through Jesus the forgiveness of sins is proclaimed to you. Through him everyone who believes is justified from everything you could not be justified from by the law of Moses."

13:30 God raised him from the dead. In this short sermon Paul mentions Christ's resurrection five times (vv. 30, 33, 34, 35, 37), thus demonstrating its importance to the message of the gospel. (See comments on 1:3.)

13:38 through Jesus the forgiveness of sins is proclaimed to you. We do not preach the gospel simply to transfer information. The purpose of gospel preaching is to call people to make a decision to follow Jesus and receive forgiveness of sins and eternal life in Him.

13:47 a light for the Gentiles ... to the ends of the earth. Jesus is Savior of the world (John 4:42; 1 John 4:14). He is a light, not only to the Jews, but to the Gentiles also. The phrase "ends of the earth" (Gk. *eschatos tees gees*) reminds us of Jesus' promise in 1:8: "You will be my witnesses ... to the ends of the earth." Our mission is to preach the gospel in Pentecostal power to all nations before Jesus returns (Matt. 24:14).

13:50 They stirred up persecution. Although persecution came again and again, the apostles persisted in proclaiming the gospel.

13:52 the disciples were filled with joy and with the Holy Spirit. This verse reveals that Paul led the new converts in Pisidian Antioch into Spirit baptism, for they were "filled ... with the Holy Spirit." This fact is borne out in Paul's own words in Galatians 3:2-5 and 3:14. As a result of these people being filled with the Spirit, "the word of the Lord spread through the whole region" (v. 49). Joy is one natural by-product of being filled with the Spirit (Luke 10:21; Rom. 14:17; Gal. 5:22; 1 Thess. 1:6).

Life Application

We must be faithful to preach the gospel wherever we go. As we preach, the cross must remain our central message. We must clearly teach people of Christ's saving work on the cross and His glorious resurrection from the dead. We must tell them that through faith in Him they can have the forgiveness of their sins and eternal life. Further, we must let them know that He has ascended to the right hand of God where He has poured out the Holy Spirit to fill us with His joy and to empower us to reach others with the message of the cross. And, in all that we do, we must never forget that the gospel is not for our people only, it is for all people everywhere on earth.

ICONIUM: SIGNS AND WONDERS

Reading Assignment: Acts 14:1-7

The Story

Upon arriving in Iconium, Paul and Barnabas went into the Jewish synagogue, as was their usual practice. There they preached with such power and clarity that a great number of Jews and Gentiles believed. However, as in Pisidian Antioch, several Jews rejected the message of Christ and began to poison the minds of the Gentiles against the apostles, saying evil things about them. Paul and Barnabas, however, were undaunted, and stayed a long time in Iconium, preaching boldly. The Lord confirmed their message by performing mighty signs and wonders among the people.

The people of the city were, nevertheless, divided in their opinion concerning the apostles. Some supported them; some opposed them. When Paul and Barnabas learned of a plot to incite a mixed mob of Gentiles and Jews to capture and stone them, they fled from the city. They then went to the Lycaonian cities of Lystra and Derbe and the surrounding area. Everywhere they went, they preached the gospel.

Commentary

In Iconium, as in Antioch, Paul and Barnabas encountered the hostility of the Jews. Their preaching of the gospel resulted in division in the city. The root cause of this division, however, was not their preaching; it was rather the reaction of those who opposed the message.

14:1 they spoke so effectively that a great number of Jews and Gentiles believed. It is important that we learn to effectively proclaim the word of the Lord. Effectiveness in preaching comes from the preacher's thorough knowledge of Scripture, his personal character, and the anointing of the Holy Spirit on his or her ministry.

14:3 confirmed the message of his grace by enabling them to do miraculous signs and wonders. Again God confirmed the word they preached with miraculous signs and wonders, a favorite expression of Luke. He uses it in various forms eleven times in Acts (2:19, 22, 43; 4:30; 5:12; 6:8; 7:36; 8:6, 13; 14:3; 15:12). Jesus promised that He would confirm the preaching of the gospel with accompanying signs (Mark 16:15-18). That promise has never been rescinded. As we faithfully go and preach the gospel to those who have never heard, we can expect God to confirm the message in the same way today. Signs and wonders are manifestations of the

Spirit's power (Rom. 15:19).

14:4 the apostles. Here both Paul and Barnabas are called apostles. Apostolic ministry is broader than the original Twelve. Apostles exist today. However, nowhere in Scripture is the word, "apostle," used as a title (i.e., the Apostle Paul); it is always used to describe a function or ministry. We have no scriptural warrant for calling any person by the title Apostle. We do, however, have plenty of scriptural warrant for those who function in a truly apostolic fashion. Apostolic ministry involves pioneer church planting done in the power of the Spirit in formerly un-penetrated areas and among unreached peoples (Rom. 15:17-21; 2 Cor. 12:12).

14:6-7 they continued to preach the good news. Even after being chased out of the city, Paul and Barnabas continued to preach the gospel. We cannot let opposition keep us from preaching Christ to all who will listen.

Life Application

When we go out to preach the gospel, we must not expect everyone to gladly receive our message. Some, however, will. Whatever the case, we must continue to preach the good news as long as God wants us to remain in an area. If we will live holy lives, remain full of the Holy Spirit, and faithfully proclaim the gospel, we can expect God to confirm His word by performing signs and wonders.

LYSTRA: GIFTS IN OPERATION

Reading Assignment: Acts 14:8-20a

The Story

One day, as Paul was preaching in Lystra, a crippled man, lame from birth, was present. He had been crippled from birth. During his message, Paul looked directly at the man and through the Holy Spirit saw that he had faith to be healed. He commanded the man, "Stand up on your feet!" The man immediately jumped up and began to walk.

The crowd went wild with excitement and began to shout that Paul and Barnabas were the Greek gods Zeus and Hermes come down to earth in human form. When the two apostles saw a pagan priest bringing two bulls to sacrifice to them, they ripped their clothes in dismay and cried out, telling the people to stop. "We bring you good news," they shouted to the people, "telling you to turn from these worthless things to the living God, who made heaven and earth and sea and everything in them." They told them that He was the same God who had revealed himself to them with rain and crops, and had given them joy to fills their hearts. Even so, Paul and Barnabas could scarcely restrain the people from sacrificing to them.

About that time a delegation of Jews arrived from Antioch and Iconium, and, as they had done before, they began to poison the people's minds against Paul and Barnabas. An angry crowd then seized Paul, stoned him, and dragged him outside the city, leaving him for dead. But when the disciples gathered around him, he was healed and emboldened, and went back into the city.

Commentary

As a result of a wonderful miracle, Paul and Barnabas gained great credibility among the people of Lystra. They then seized the opportunity to present the gospel to a more receptive audience.

14:9 Paul ... saw that he had faith to be healed. Only God can see into a man's heart and determine if he has faith. Paul could have known this only by divine revelation.

14:10 Stand up on your feet. Like Peter, Paul uses a command of faith to heal the sick man (see comment on 9:40). Speaking (or commanding) was the method Jesus used most often in healing the sick (Mark 7:34; Luke 4:39; 6:10; 7:14; 8:48; 13:12; 17:14; 18:42; John 5:8; 9:7; 11:43). Paul could have been exercising the gift of faith on this occasion (1 Cor. 12:9). If the man had not stood up, Paul would have been shamed, and his ministry in Lystra would have been greatly hindered. However, since the man did stand, a wonderful opportunity to preach the gospel resulted. Paul had to act with great faith to perform this miracle.

14:15 We are bringing you good news. The primary purpose of all missionary ministry is to present the good news and call people to faith in Christ.

14:20 the disciples ... gathered around him. These disciples gathered around Paul to pray. They probably prayed for him to receive healing, which he did. They may also have prayed for him to receive a fresh infilling of the Holy Spirit. He must have received strength and boldness from the Lord, for after they had prayed, he went back into the city!

Life Application

To be truly effective missionaries and ministers of the gospel, we must know how to respond to the promptings of the Holy Spirit and to be used by Him to minister spiritual gifts. Ministry is more than simply talking (1 Cor. 4:20); it also involves hearing the voice of the Spirit and obeying. It involves preaching and teaching the gospel under an anointing of the Spirit (1 Cor. 2:1-5). It further involves acting in faith and allowing the Spirit to minister through us through prophetic words, and miracles of healing and deliverance. If this is to happen in our lives and ministries, we must learn to daily walk in the Spirit. We must live lives of prayer and holiness before the Lord.

FURTHER INSIGHT: SPIRITUAL GIFTS IN MISSIONARY WORK

We learn from the book of Acts that the operation of spiritual gifts is an important part of missionary work. In Paul's ministry in Lystra the manifestation of spiritual gifts opened the way for effective evangelism. This was true in many other instances in Acts.[28] Unlike Paul in his epistles, who focuses on the operation of spiritual gifts in the church gathered together for worship (1 Cor. 12-14), in Acts Luke focuses on the operation of spiritual gifts in front-line evangelism and missions.

As we read through Acts, we discover that these gifts often worked together in groups to bring about the desired result of people coming to Christ. This happened in Lystra. As Paul was preaching a Spirit-anointed message (prophetic gift), he was enabled by the Spirit to look into a man's heart and see that he had faith to be healed (revelation gift). Then, acting in extraordinary faith, Paul commanded the cripple man to stand on his feet. The man obeyed, and a miracle occurred (power gift).

We see a similar thing taking place when Peter and John healed the lame man at the Beautiful Gate (3:1–4:4). Gifts were manifested from all three categories. Through a word of knowledge (revelation) Peter knew that it was God's time to heal the lame man. Through a gift of healing (power), the man was miraculously healed. And through a manifestation of the gift of prophecy (prophetic), Peter stood and powerfully addressed the crowd. Because of this tandem release of spiritual gifts, many were added to the kingdom (4:4).

Can anyone legitimately deny the importance of spiritual gifts in missionary work today? Every missionary and minister of the gospel must ensure that spiritual gifts are in operation in his or her life and

---

[28] According to the author's count, there are sixty-six instances of spiritual gifts in operation in Acts. This includes gifts from all three categories: prophetic gifts, revelation gifts, and power gifts (cf. 1 Cor. 12:8-10). See Appendix 2.

ministry. Missionaries should also ensure that the churches they plant understand how to operate in the gifts of the Spirit.[29]

DERBE: SOUL HARVEST

Reading Assignment: Acts 14:20b-23

The Story
The following day Paul and Barnabas went to Derbe. While there, they preached the gospel and won many new disciples to the Lord. They then returned to Lystra, Iconium, and Antioch, where they strengthened the new believers, encouraging them to remain true to the Lord in spite of persecution. They also appointed elders in each church and committed them to the Lord with a time of prayer and fasting.

Commentary
Few details are given concerning Paul and Barnabas' missionary ministry in Derbe. What we are told, however, is exciting. As a result of their preaching the gospel there, the apostles experienced a great soul harvest!

14:21 They preached the good news ... and won a large number of disciples. True to their commission from Christ, the apostles preached the gospel in Derbe, as they had done in every other place (Mark 16:15; Luke 24:46-48; Acts 1:8). As a result, they won many people to the Lord.

14:22 strengthening the disciples and encouraging them. The missionary's role goes beyond preaching the gospel and bringing people to salvation. Jesus told us that we are to make disciples of them (Matt. 28:19). A disciple is more than a convert; a disciple is a follower and learner of Christ. The missionary's role thus includes encouraging Christ's followers to remain true to Him. This can be done through fellowship (Rom. 1:12; Eph. 6:21-22; Phm. 7; Heb. 10:25), teaching (Acts 20:2; Rom. 15:4; 1 Thess. 4:18; 2 Tim. 4:2), and prophetic words (Acts 9:31; 15:32; 27:33-36; 1 Cor. 14:3).

the kingdom of God. The kingdom of God is mentioned eight times in Acts (1:3, 6; 8:12; 14:22; 19:8; 20:25; 28:23, 31). It can be defined as God's sovereign reign over His creation. Christ has been declared king over the kingdom of God (Eph. 5:5; 2 Pet. 1:11; Rev.

---

[29] For a fuller discussion of the role of spiritual gifts in missionary work, see the author's book *Empowered for Global Mission: A Missionary Look at the Book of Acts,* Chapter 12, "The Role of Spiritual Gifts in Missions," pp. 273-298.

11:15). To preach the gospel of the kingdom is, therefore, to preach Christ (Acts 8:12; 28:23, 31). We are to preach this gospel in all the world before Jesus comes again (Matt. 24:14). (See comments on 1:3, including the footnote.)

Life Application

In Derbe the preaching of the gospel resulted in a great harvest of souls. Because Paul had great confidence in the gospel he preached, he did not hesitate to proclaim it wherever he went (v. 15). He knew that it contained the power of God to bring people to salvation (Rom. 1:16). We, too, should have great confidence in the gospel, and we should be faithful to preach it often, calling people to faith and repentance. We must never forget that the message of Jesus is the only message that will get people to heaven (John 14:6; Acts 4:12; 1 Tim. 2:5).

ANTIOCH: THE FIRST MISSIONS CONVENTION

Reading Assignment: Acts 14:24-28

The Story

Leaving Lycaonia, Paul and Barnabas returned through Pisidia into Pamphylia. After they had preached in Perga, they went down to Attalia. From there they sailed back to Antioch, where the church had first committed them to the work they had now completed. When the church had gathered, the apostles gave a report of all that God had done through them in opening the door of faith to the Gentiles. They then remained in Antioch with the disciples for a long time.

Commentary

This passage tells us of the world's first ever missions convention. After Paul and Barnabas returned to Antioch from their missionary journey into Cyprus and southern Galatia, the church gathered to hear their report. It was a report of how God's grace had reached out to the Gentiles. The apostles, no doubt, told of how God had sustained them in the work and how the Spirit had moved in power among the Gentiles, bringing healing, deliverance, hope, and salvation to those who had never before heard the gospel of Jesus Christ.

14:26 the work they had now completed. The two apostles did not just begin their mission, they completed it. They were able to endure the hardships and complete their mission because they were truly called of God (13:2), because they remained focused on their mission (14:21, 25), and because they stayed full of the Holy Spirit (13:9). We too can complete the work that God has given us, even under trying circumstances, if we will do the same.

14:27 they gathered the church together. The church was excited and anxious to hear what God had accomplished through their missionaries. They therefore called a special missionary meeting to hear the apostles' report.

reported all that God had done through them. The believers in Antioch must have rejoiced when they heard how God had worked through Paul and Barnabas to bring Christ to the Galatians, both Jews and Gentiles. The essence of missions is God working through Spirit-filled missionaries to bring the good news of Jesus Christ to the lost and to demonstrate the power and superiority of His kingdom through mighty signs and wonders.

God ... opened the door of faith to the Gentiles. When Paul was saved and filled with the Spirit, God had informed him that he would be His "chosen instrument to carry [His] name before the Gentiles" (Acts 9:15; 22:21; 26:17-18). Now Paul's apostleship and missionary calling to the Gentiles has been firmly established. God used him and Barnabas to open to them "the door of faith."

Life Application

Like the church in Antioch, churches today should also have missionary meetings. In these meetings, missionaries can share with the church about their calling and burden for the lost. They can also share news about what God is doing among the people to whom they have been sent. Such meetings will encourage the people to participate in missions through prayer, giving, and maybe even going themselves. They will also encourage the missionaries, knowing that the church stands behind them in their work. Every church must be involved in missions in this way.

FURTHER INSIGHT: PLANTING INDIGENOUS CHURCHES

Paul and Barnabas' first missionary journey gives us our first insight into Paul's missionary methods. An analysis of his methods reveals the following:

1) Paul planted churches. Paul did not just "get people saved." Rather, he planted indigenous churches, meaning that the churches were able to support themselves, govern themselves, and extend themselves. The methods he used to plant such churches were

- the proclamation of the gospel (Acts 13:5; 23-43; 14:3, 7, 14-18; 14:21),
- a demonstration of God's power through signs and wonders (13:9-12; 14:3, 8-10),
- ensuring that those who were saved were also filled with the Holy Spirit (13:52),
- teaching and encouraging new disciples to remain true to the faith (13:43), and
- mobilizing believers to reach out to others (13:49).

2) Paul appointed leaders over the churches. According to Acts 14:23, "Paul and Barnabas appointed elders for them in each church." These men would lead the church in Paul's absence. Church leaders should be filled with the Holy Spirit and wisdom (Acts 6:3). They should also be people of mature character and respected in the community (1 Tim. 3:1-13).

3) Paul trusted the Holy Spirit. The last part of Acts 14:23 says, "With prayer and fasting, [Paul and Barnabas] committed them to the Lord, in whom they had put their trust." Paul and Barnabas could commit these new disciples to the Lord because they knew that they had been truly converted and filled with the Spirit (13:52; 14:1). If we make sure that the people have been truly born of the Spirit, and that they have been filled with the Spirit, then we can trust the Holy Spirit to teach and guide them, just as He has taught and guided us (cf. John 14:25-26; 16:13; 1 John 2:27).

CONCLUSION

God had opened the door to the Gentiles; however, not all of the church was convinced. Certain Jewish Christians in Jerusalem felt strongly that one must first become a good Jew before he can become a Christian. This meant that, before the Gentiles could follow Christ, they must first accept and adopt a Jewish lifestyle, which included keeping the Jewish laws, including circumcision. If this policy were adopted by the church, then the church's mission to the Gentiles would be greatly hindered. The question needed to be settled once and for all. In the next chapter we will see how the church addressed this critical question.

QUESTIONS FOR REFLECTION AND REVIEW

1. Describe the powerful move of the Holy Spirit that took place in the church in Antioch?

Chapter 8: Paul's First Missionary Journey

2. Why does the author say that when talking about the Antiochian "Outpouring" he puts the word outpouring in quotation marks?
3. How does the move of the Spirit in Antioch presuppose one or more previous outpourings of the Spirit in the church?
4. Carefully study Figure 8.2. Why do you suppose that Luke placed a move of the Holy Spirit at the beginning of each of Paul's three missionary journeys?
5. What was the result of the powerful move of the Spirit in the church in Antioch? How does this "outpouring" of the Spirit help to confirm Luke's *empowerment–witness motif*?
6. Why did the church pray and fast after they had received the prophecy? Why did they lay their hands on Barnabas and Paul?
7. According to verses 3-4, who cooperated in sending the missionaries to the field?
8. Describe Paul and Barnabas' ministry in word and deed on the island of Cyprus.
9. What part did the release of spiritual gifts play in the conversion of Sergius Paulus to Christ?
10. What is the central message of Paul's sermon in Antioch, Pisidia?
11. What indication from the text do we have that Paul taught on Spirit baptism in Antioch? (cf. v. 52).
12. What methods of presenting the gospel did the missionaries employ in Iconium?
13. How was Paul able to "see" that the lame man in Lystra had faith to be healed? How was he used in the healing of the man? What was the result of the healing?
14. Why did the disciples gather around Paul in 14:20? What resulted?
15. What is the role of spiritual gifts in missionary work?
16. Describe Paul and Barnabas' ministry in Derbe. What was the result?

17. What did Paul and Barnabas do when they returned to the church in Antioch at the end of their first missionary journey?
18. What three important indigenous church-planting principles can we learn from Paul's first missionary journey?

QUESTIONS FOR CLASSROOM DISCUSSION

1. Each of Paul's three missionary journeys began with a move of the Holy Spirit. What is the role of the Holy Spirit in the missionary advance of the church today?
2. In 13:9, Paul is again described as being "filled with the Spirit." How important is it that a missionary or minister of the gospel remain full of the Holy Spirit? How will a lack of the Spirit's presence affect his or her ministry?
3. The central theme of Paul's message in Antioch was Christ's death and resurrection. What is the central message of most preaching we hear today? What should it be?

4. In Lystra the Lord used Paul to heal a lame man (14:9-10). Describe the healing. What gifts of the Holy Spirit could have been in operation on this occasion? What lessons can we learn from this story about the operation of spiritual gifts in our own evangelistic and missionary ministries today?
5. Paul deliberately planted Spirit-empowered indigenous missionary churches. What deliberate steps can we take today to plant such churches?

Chapter 8: Paul's First Missionary Journey

– Chapter 9 –

Missionary Council in Jerusalem

PRE-LESSON READING ASSIGNMENT

Acts 15:1-21

INTRODUCTION

After the Caesarean and Antiochian Outpourings, the church continued to grow and extend itself. By now, it had ranged as far north as Galatia in eastern Asia Minor. There, Paul and Barnabas had been sent as the church's first intentional missionaries to the Gentiles. They had experienced great success and several indigenous churches had been planted, resulting in many new believers being added to the Lord. These new believers came from four classes of people: Jews, Jewish proselytes, God-fearers, and Gentiles. The last two classes that created controversy in the church. Certain Jewish believers contended that, before these two groups could be saved, they must first submit to the Jewish rite of circumcision. This debate has been called the "Gentile Question." Acts 15 records the story of how the controversy was resolved.

In this chapter we will discuss the church council in Jerusalem where the issue was addressed head on. It occurred soon after Paul and Barnabas' First Missionary Journey. We call it the Missionary Council in Jerusalem, for indeed, that is what it was. It was a highly significant event in the church's missionary development. Luke included it in his narrative because of its significance in the church's missionary development. At this council the church officially determined that Gentiles did not have to submit to the Law of Moses, necessitating circumcision, to be saved. Salvation for both Jews and Gentiles is by faith in Christ alone. This decision freed the church to be the global missionary force Christ intended it to be, rather than a mere Jewish sub-sect.

DISSENSION IN ANTIOCH

Reading Assignment: Acts 15:1-5

The Story
Some Jewish brothers arrived in Antioch from Judea and began teaching the Christians there that believers must be circumcised before they could be saved. Paul and Barnabus stoutly opposed this teaching and entered into a sharp dispute with them. The leaders in the church in Antioch, therefore, appointed Paul and Barnabas, along with some other believers from the church, to go to Jerusalem and discuss the matter with the apostles and elders there. On their journey to Jerusalem the delegation traveled through Phoenicia and Samaria, where they gave reports about how the Gentiles had come to Christ. This news made the believers in those places glad. When Paul and Barnabas arrived in Jerusalem, they were received warmly by the leadership of the church.

They then gave a report of all that God had done through them among the Gentiles. However, some of the Pharisees who had become believers objected, saying that the Gentiles Christians must be required to be circumcised and obey the Law of Moses.

Commentary
Must a Gentile first become a good Jew before he or she can become a Christian? As simple as that question may seem to us today, it was not so simple for the early church. Christianity had been born into the cradle of Judaism. However, in order for it to grow into a worldwide movement, it had to break free from the binding legalism of the Jewish religion. Some Jewish Christians resisted the call for liberation. Others, like Paul and Barnabas, knew that it must take place if Christianity were to prosper among the nations. That is why they decided to travel all the way to Jerusalem to settle the matter once and for all.

15:2 sharp dispute. That some would teach that a person must keep the Law of Moses before becoming a Christian was no small issue. It struck at the very heart of the gospel of grace. Paul and Barnabas had no choice but to oppose this teaching, even if it meant sharp dispute. Some issues are so important that they cannot be ignored. They must be addressed and resolved.

this question. The "question" referred to is the Gentile question. After God had poured out His Spirit on the Gentile believers in Caesarea, the apostles and brothers in Jerusalem praised God and said that "God has granted even the Gentiles repentance unto life" (11:18). It was an historic occasion. It did not, however, finally settle the Gentile question. The question was this: How could those who, according to the Law of Moses, were ritually unclean, be accepted by God? How could uncircumcised Gentiles, who ate non-kosher foods and defiled themselves by participating in pagan practices, be true followers of Jehovah God without first becoming good Jews? And yet, had not Jesus himself commanded the church to take the gospel to these very people? Had He not commissioned His church to be His witnesses to the "remotest parts of the earth"? How, then, were they to reconcile these two seemingly contradictory issues? This was the question that needed to be resolved.

15:5 the party of the Pharisees. These legalistic Jewish Christians are sometimes called Judaizers. They were true believers in Christ. In fact, they were probably the most biblically conservative members of the church. They were, however, wrong in their belief that the Gentiles had to be circumcised and keep the Law of Moses before they could be saved.

Life Application

We must stand firm in our conviction that people can be saved by faith in Christ alone. While we must never be arrogant or contentious in our dealings with others, neither can we allow anyone to change the gospel. Paul was so firm on this position that he wrote, "Even if we or an angel from heaven should preach a gospel other than the one we preached to you, let him be eternally condemned!" (Gal. 1:8).

PETER, BARNABAS, AND PAUL TESTIFY

Reading Assignment: Acts 15:6-12

Chapter 9: Missionary Council in Jerusalem

The Story

Soon after Paul and Barnabas arrived in Jerusalem, the apostles and elders met to consider the Gentile question. After much discussion, Peter stood up and reminded the delegates of how God had used him to bring the message of the gospel to the Gentiles in Caesarea. He told them of how God had seen into the Gentiles' hearts and had accepted their faith in Him. God proved this by giving them the Holy Spirit, just as he had given to the Jewish believers at Pentecost. He made no distinction between them and the Jews, cleansing their hearts by faith. Peter concluded his address with a challenge: "Why do you want to test God?" he asked. "You are putting on the necks of these Gentile disciples a yoke that even we Jews have not been able to bear." "No!" he retorted, "we are all saved through the grace of the Lord Jesus." After Peter had concluded, the whole assembly sat in rapt attention and listened to Paul and Barnabas tell how, through them, God had worked many signs and wonders among the Gentiles.

Commentary

At the Jerusalem Council Peter, Paul, and Barnabas stood as witnesses to the fact that God had chosen to include the Gentiles in His plan of salvation. They testified of how God, through the power of the Spirit, had extended His hand to uncircumcised Gentiles. God himself had chosen to include them in His plan of salvation. This salvation does not come through keeping the law, but through faith in Christ.

15:7 God made a choice. God sovereignly planned that Peter would first preach the gospel to the Gentile believers in Caesarea. It is not our choice who should and who should not hear the gospel and be saved. The choice to include all people in His plan of salvation was God's alone.

15:8 by giving the Holy Spirit to them. God proved that He had accepted the Gentiles into His family by giving them the Holy Spirit. The baptism in the Holy Spirit is an experience for believers only. Jesus taught that the gift of the Holy Spirit is given to God's children (Luke 11:13). He further taught that the world (unbelievers) cannot receive the Spirit (John 14:17).

just as he did to us. God gave the Spirit to the Gentiles at Cornelius' house just as He did to the Jews at Pentecost. He gave them the same Spirit, in the same way, with the same accompanying sign (2:4; 10:46), and for the same purpose, empowerment for witness (Acts 1:8).

15:9 he purified their hearts by faith. It is through faith that all people are saved, whether Jew or Gentile. Salvation does not come by the works of the Law but "through the grace of our Lord Jesus" (v. 11). Paul would later write, "For it is by grace you have been saved, through faith—and this not from yourselves, it is the gift of God—not by works, so that no one can boast" (Eph. 2:8-9).

15:12 miraculous signs and wonders. The fact that God had done miraculous signs and wonders among (and on behalf of) the Gentiles is another strong indication that He wants to bless them and include them in His family.

Life Application

We should not put any unnecessary requirement on people that the gospel does not. Our job is to lead people to Christ, and then to help them grow into Christian maturity. This cannot be done by just giving them a set of rules by which to live. They must be brought into a living relationship with Christ and then taught to follow Him fully. In the words of Paul to the believers in Galatia, "A man is not justified by observing the law, but by faith in Jesus Christ. So we, too, have put our faith in Christ Jesus that we may be justified by faith in Christ and not by observing the law, because by observing the law no one will be justified" (Gal. 2:16; cf. Acts 13:38-39).

A WORD FROM THE LORD

Reading Assignment: Acts 15:13-21

The Story

After Peter, Paul, and Barnabas had finished their speeches, James spoke up and reinforced what Peter had said. He noted how in Caesarea God had visited the Gentiles and had taken from them a people for himself. This was in agreement with the words of the Hebrew prophets: "After this I will return and rebuild David's fallen tent. Its ruins I will rebuild, and I will restore it, that the remnant of men may seek the Lord, and all the Gentiles who bear my name, says the Lord, who does these things that have been known for ages" (vv. 16-17; Amos 9:11-12; Isa. 45:21-22).

James then delivered his judgment on the matter, stating that the leaders of the church should not make it difficult for the Gentiles who are turning to God. Instead, he said, they should write a letter to them telling them not to eat food sacrificed to idols, to abstain from all sexual immorality, from the meat of strangled animals, and from blood. He noted that these are some of the very things that Moses taught and have been preached against in Jewish synagogues for many generations.

Commentary

Paul and Barnabas, who had opposed the Judaizers in Antioch, were now joined by Peter. All three spoke in favor of including the Gentiles into the church without requiring them to first submit to the Law of Moses. James also joined them saying that the church should not make it difficult for the Gentiles to turn to God.

15:13 James spoke up. This is James, the half-brother of Jesus. He pastored the church in Jerusalem and wrote the New Testament epistle of James. Another James, the apostle and brother of John, was martyred by Herod in 12:2.

15:15 The words of the prophets are in agreement. God's intention to include the Gentiles in His redemptive plan was nothing new. His had always intended to take out "from the Gentiles a people for himself" (v. 14). God told Abraham that through his Seed (i.e., Jesus) all the nations of earth would be blessed (Gen. 22:18; cf. Gal. 3:16). The Hebrew prophets consistently testified to the same thing (i.e., Isa. 45:6, 22; 49:6; 51:4-5; 52:10; 56:7; Amos 9:11-12; Zeph. 2:11; Zech. 2:10-13). As a result, the Gentiles may also bear the Lord's name (v. 17).

15:16 I will return and rebuild David's fallen tent. This prophecy of Amos said that God would include the Gentiles in His redemptive plan after the restoration of the throne of David. Jesus is the king who now sits on the throne of David's restored kingdom. It is thus God's appointed time for full Gentile inclusion into the kingdom of God. Note how James appealed to Scripture to settle the Gentile question.

Life Application

At the Jerusalem Council the delegates listened to the testimonies of Peter, Paul, and Barnabas; however, their final decision was based on Scripture. We must ensure that all of our decisions concerning the work of God are based solidly on the word of God.

AN ENCOURAGING LETTER

Reading Assignment: Acts 15:22-35

The Story

After James' speech, the apostles and elders, with the consent of the whole assembly, chose two men from among them, Judas (also called Barsabbas) and Silas, to send to Antioch with Paul and Barnabas. With them they sent aetter addressed to "the Gentile believers in Antioch, Syria and Cilicia." The letter assured the Gentile believers that the men from Judea who had been troubling them did not have the authorization of the leadership of the church in Jerusalem. They were, therefore, sending Judas and Silas to accompany Paul and Barnabas to confirm that the letter had come from them. The letter called Paul and Barnabas "dear friends" and "men who have risked their lives for the name of our Lord Jesus Christ." The apostles further informed its recipients that the decision they had reached "seemed good to the Holy Spirit and to us," indicating that the Holy Spirit had inspired the decision. They assured the Gentile believers that they did not want to place any unnecessary burden upon them; however, they would be required to abstain from food sacrificed to idols, from blood, from the meat of strangled animals, and from sexual immorality.

As soon as the four men arrived in Antioch, they called a meeting of the church and read the letter aloud. When the Gentile believers heard it, they rejoiced. Afterward, Judas and Silas, who were prophets, encouraged and strengthened the believers there. After a while, Judas returned to Jerusalem with the blessing of the church. Paul, Barnabas, and Silas, however, remained in Antioch, where they and others taught and preached the word of the Lord.

Commentary

The decision reached by the Jerusalem Council was momentous. Because the delegates were open to the Spirit and the teachings of Scripture, they reached the correct decision. It resulted in great joy among the new Gentile believers in the church. More importantly, this opened the door for the church to continue to expand among the Gentiles unabated.

15:22 apostles and elders, with the whole church. Not only were the top leaders of the church brought into the decision-making process, but the whole church was involved. This seems to indicate that some primitive form of democracy may have been used in the early church.

15:23 believers in Antioch, Syria and Cilicia. Led by the Spirit, the church continued to expand into new regions. What accounted for these believers in Syria and Antioch? The believers in Syria possibly resulted from church-planting efforts of the church in Antioch. The believers in Cilicia possibly resulted from Paul's ministry there. He had spent time in Tarsus, Cilicia, and was probably involved in planting churches in that city and in the surrounding region, as was his custom (11:25). Luke did not record all of the church planting efforts of the early church, only those that helped to further his intent in writing. Hundreds of other churches were, no doubt, being planted by the apostles and other Spirit-filled disciples in the Middle East, North Africa, and Asia Minor. Because these early disciples were empowered by the Spirit, and totally committed to fulfilling the mandate of Christ, there was a spontaneous multiplication of churches.

15:28 *It seemed good to the Holy Spirit and to us.* The Holy Spirit actively guided the council's deliberations. The issue was too important to trust to human reason. Again, we observe the Holy Spirit acting as the Superintendent of the Harvest. We are not told exactly how the Holy Spirit helped them to reach their decision. Possibly a word of prophecy was given, as in Antioch on two earlier occasions (11:28; 13:2); possibly a word of knowledge was given to James or another delegate; or possibly there was a strong inner witness of the Spirit in their hearts. However the leading came, the Holy Spirit played an active and significant role in their decision making process.

15:31 *The people read it and were glad.* The Spirit-directed decision of the Jerusalem Council brought great joy to the Gentile believers. They could now focus their energy on truly serving Christ and advancing His kingdom, rather than on keeping nonessential legalistic rules.

Life Application

Throughout life we are required to make many decisions concerning our personal lives and ministries. We should never forget that God has a plan for each of us. That plan includes our participation in advancing the gospel to the ends of the earth. Therefore, every important decision should be made in consultation with other committed believers and with God. We should seek the guidance of the Spirit so that, when we make our decisions, we can also say, "It seemed good to the Holy Spirit and to us." When we make such decisions, great blessing comes to our lives and to the work of God.

CONCLUSION

Having settled the Gentile question, the church was now prepared to continue its Gentile mission unhindered by doctrinal disputes. After an extended time of teaching and preaching in the church in Antioch, Paul and Barnabas prepared for their second missionary journey. This journey, however, was to begin with a dispute of another sort. In the next chapter we will look at that dispute and Paul's missionary journey that followed it.

QUESTIONS FOR REFLECTION AND REVIEW

1. What was the nature of the dispute that arose in the church in Antioch?
2. Describe the "Gentile question" that was prominent in the early church.
3. Why was it so important that this issue be settled satisfactorily?
4. What evidences do Peter, Paul, and Barnabas give that God had accepted the Gentiles without their first becoming Jewish proselytes?
5. What would make one think that James' decision during the meeting came as a world from the Lord?
6. What was the result of the Spirit-guided decision of the church in Antioch?

QUESTIONS FOR CLASSROOM DISCUSSION

1. Paul reminded the delegates at the Jerusalem Council that God have given the Gentiles the Holy Spirit just as He did to the Jews. What are the missional implications of this fact?
2. James appealed to Scripture (15:15-16) and to the Spirit (v. 28) in making his decision at the Jerusalem council. What lessons can we learn from James' example when we are seeking to make important decisions concerning the mission of the church?

– Chapter 10 –
Paul's Second Missionary Journey
(Part 1)

PRE-LESSON READING ASSIGNMENT

Acts 15:36-16:40

INTRODUCTION

The Gentile Question had at last been settled. Gentiles did not have to first become converts to Judaism before they could become Christians. The door was now opened for uncontested outreach to the nations.

In this chapter we will examine how that outreach continued with Paul's Second Missionary Journey. It is the most extensive of his three journeys. During this journey, after revisiting the churches in Galatia, Paul and his missionary team were directed by the Spirit to venture westward into Europe. There they planted churches in the provinces of Macedonia and Achaia (Greece). After a brief stopover in Ephesus, they returned to Antioch where their journey began.

PAUL'S SECOND JOURNEY BEGINS

Reading Assignment: Acts 15:36-39a

Chapter 10: Paul's Second Missionary Journey (Part 1)

The Story

After a long stay in Antioch, Paul proposed to Barnabas that they visit all of the places where they had preached the gospel during their First Missionary Journey to see how the believers were faring. Barnabas wanted to take John Mark with them again. Paul, however, was strongly opposed to the idea, noting how, during their first journey, Mark had deserted the work and returned home. Their disagreement became so heated that Paul and Barnabas parted company and went their separate ways.

Commentary

Paul's second journey began with controversy. The controversy this time was not between Paul and the Judaizers, but between Paul and his close missionary associate and friend, Barnabas. Paul felt that John Mark, because of his unreliability, should not accompany them on their upcoming journey. Barnabas, however, thought that the younger man deserved a second chance. The controversy became so intense that the missionaries separated, with Barnabas revisiting the work on Cyprus, and Paul journeying northward through Syria and Cilicia into Galatia, and eventually into Western Europe. This controversy candidly reveals the humanity of these early Christian missionaries.

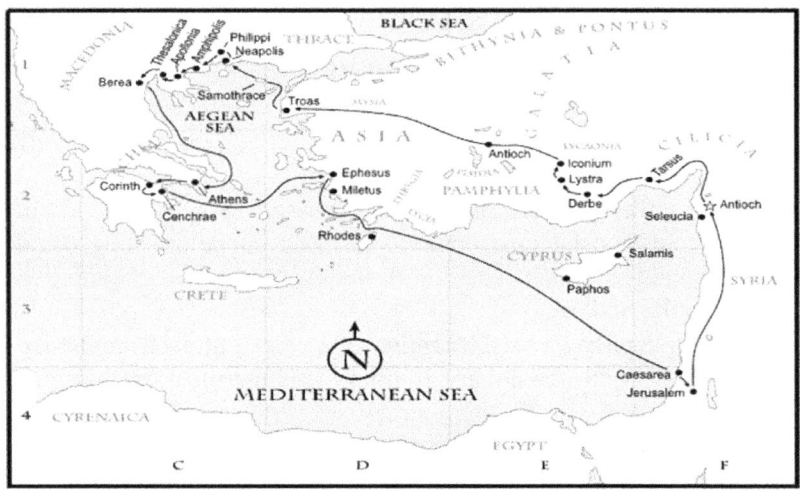

Figure 10.1 Paul's Second Missionary Journey ©2005 Biblical Studies Press

15:36 Let us go back and visit the brothers. This statement shows Paul and Barnabas' pastoral concern for the churches they had planted in Cyprus and southern Galatia. Their purpose in returning was to find out how the churches were getting along, encourage the believers, and strengthen the churches. It was Paul's desire to see every church he planted emerge as a Spirit-empowered missional church, one that could extend itself into the surrounding region.

15:39 They parted company. After a heated debate over John Mark, Paul and Barnabas went their separate ways. It is significant that neither man left the work, but both continued as active missionaries. It seems that, even after their disagreement, Paul and Barnabas came to a strategic agreement about who would go where.

Life Application

Missionaries and other Christian workers are human, and sometimes disagreements arise between colleagues. Unfortunately, on occasion, these disagreements can be sharp. At such times we should not be tempted to abandon the work that God has given us. We must be mature enough to come to strategic agreements about how each will continue in the work, even if we may, at times, have to work separately. If we remain kindhearted and mature in our attitudes, then, in time, even greater unity and agreement can come. Such was the case with Paul and Barnabas. In later years Paul requested that Mark join him in the work (2 Tim. 4:11; cf. Col. 4:10; Phm. 24). Mark even went on to write one of the four gospels in the New Testament.

GALATIA: PASTORAL VISITS

Reading Assignment: Acts 15:39b–16:5

The Story

Barnabas sailed with Mark to Cyprus. Paul chose Silas as his missionary partner and, commended by the brothers, traveled northward by land into Syria and Cilicia. As Paul and Silas traveled, they took time to strengthen the churches in these regions. Passing through Cilicia, they went to Derbe in southern Galatia, and then on to Lystra. There they met a well-respected young man named Timothy, whose mother was a Jewish believer, and whose father was Greek. Since Paul wanted Timothy to join their missionary team, he circumcised him, so that Timothy's presence would not bring offense to the Jews living in the area. As the missionaries moved from place to place, they read the letter from the Jerusalem Council containing the apostles' decisions and orders concerning the Gentile believers (15:23-29). Because of their visits, the churches were strengthened in the faith and grew in numbers daily.

Commentary

Paul's first order of business during his Second Missionary Journey was to return to the churches he and Barnabas had planted in southern Galatia during their first journey. His purpose was pastoral, to encourage the believers and strengthen the emerging churches. He took Silas with him.

15:40 Paul chose Silas. Silas, along with Judas Barsabbas, had come to Antioch from Jerusalem with Paul and Barnabas to deliver the decree from the Jerusalem Council concerning Gentile believers. Judging from his name, Silas was probably a Hellenized Jew. He also served as a prophet and former leader of the church in Jerusalem (15:22, 32). After delivering the decree, he remained in Antioch and ministered in the church through his prophetic and teaching ministry (15:30-32). Paul referred to him in his epistles (2 Cor. 1:19; 1 Thess. 1:1; 2 Thess. 1:1). Peter called him a "faithful brother" (1 Pet. 5:12).

commended by the brothers to the grace of the Lord. As at the beginning of the first journey, the Antiochian church is again actively involved in sending the missionaries to the field (cf. 13:3). Even though Paul had a divine call to the Gentiles (Acts 26:17-18; Gal. 2:2), and the clear direction of the Spirit (Acts 13:2-4), he did not proceed to the field on his own initiative. He went with the blessing and commendation of the church.

16:1 *a disciple named Timothy.* Timothy had probably been converted during Paul's First Missionary Journey or at some later time through the evangelistic efforts of the church in Lystra. He became a faithful coworker with Paul. Paul called him his "true son in the faith" (1 Tim. 1:2).

16:3 *he circumcised him because of the Jews.* Paul's requiring Timothy to be circumcised was not a compromise of his principles nor a violation of the Jerusalem Decree (Acts 15:23-29). It was rather an application of Paul's missionary strategy of becoming "all things to all men" in order to win as many as possible to Christ (1 Cor. 9:19-23). It thus serves as an example of incarnational missionary ministry. Since Titus was a Gentile, Paul did not require him to be circumcised (cf. Acts 15:1-2).

16:5 *the churches were strengthened in the faith.* One important role of missionary ministry is to strengthen churches and believers in the faith. Jesus' command was not to make converts but disciples (Matt. 28:19). Paul would later write that the ministry of apostles (i.e., himself) and prophets (i.e., Silas)—as well as evangelists, pastors, and teachers—was "to prepare God's people for works of service, so that the body of Christ may be built up" (Eph. 4:12).

grew daily in numbers. Because Paul and Barnabas had intentionally planted Spirit-empowered missional churches, the churches continued to grow in strength and number. In his letter to the Ephesians Paul wrote that a healthy, well-trained church "grows and builds itself up in love, as each part does its work" (4:16).

Life Application

Our work is not completed when the church planting campaign ends. We have the ongoing responsibility of giving pastoral oversight to the new work. Our goals must be to ensure that the new church is filled with the Spirit, strong in the word, and focused on the mission of God. Our methods should include fellowship, prayer, teaching, and godly counsel.

THE SPIRIT GUIDES THE MISSIONARIES

Reading Assignment: Acts 16:6-10

The Story

Leaving Lystra, Paul and his missionary colleagues traveled to the northwest through Galatia into Phrygia. They intended to go west into Asia Minor (and possibly Ephesus) but were kept from going there by the Holy Spirit. Arriving at the border of Mysia, they decided to venture further north into Bithynia on the Black Sea, but the Spirit of Jesus would not allow them to go that way either. As a result, they decided to travel westward through Mysia until they arrived in Troas on the Aegean coast. There they were joined by Luke. In a night vision in Troas, Paul saw a Macedonian man standing and entreating him, "Come over to Macedonia and help us." The missionary party concluded that God wanted them to preach the gospel in Macedonia. At once, they prepared to leave for that region.

Commentary

As with his First Missionary Journey, Paul's second journey began with a move of the Holy Spirit. Luke strategically places such a move of the Spirit near the beginning of each of Paul's missionary journeys. He does this so that the reader will know that everything done during the journeys was done in the power of the Spirit (Acts 13:1-4; 16:6-10; 19:1-7; see Figure 8.2, p. 119). Although this is the only mention of the Spirit's active role during Paul's second journey, we know by statements he made in his epistles that he ministered in the Spirit's power in Macedonia and Achaia (1 Cor. 2:4; 2 Cor. 12:12; 1 Thess. 1:5).

16:6-7 kept by the Holy Spirit ... the Spirit of Jesus would not allow them. The Holy Spirit again acts as the Superintendent of the Harvest. By keeping the missionaries from entering Asia and Bithynia, He was directing them to the specific fields He had prepared for them. The title "Spirit of Jesus" is another name for the Holy Spirit. He is the one whom Christ sent in His place (John 15:26; 16:7; Acts 2:33), and who reveals the things of Christ to us (John 16:15). Peter calls the Holy Spirit the Spirit of Christ (1 Pet. 1:11, cf. v. 12), and Paul calls Him the Spirit of Jesus Christ (Phil. 1:19).

16:9 a vision of a man of Macedonia. The Spirit directed Paul's missionary team into Western Europe through a vision. According to Luke's teaching in Acts, visions are one way that God actively guides Christ's messengers (Acts 9:10-12; 10:9-16; 16:9-10; 18:9-10: 23:11; 26:19). Other ways include speaking directly to their spirits by His Spirit (10:19-20; 11:12; 15:28: 20:22), providential circumstances (8:1-4), angelic appearances (5:19-20; 8:26; 10:3-7; 12:7-15; 27:23-24), and prophetic utterances (2:17-18; 11:28-30; 13:1-2; 15:32; 20:23; 21:10-11).

16:10 we got ready at once. When the Spirit directed, the missionaries responded quickly and decisively. By this and other "we" references, we know that Luke joined Paul's missionary team in Macedonia. He accompanied Paul as far as Philippi, where he remained behind.

Life Application

We should seek and expect the Holy Spirit to guide us when we are actively engaged in the Lord's work. This guidance may come in various ways, including dreams, visions, angelic appearances, and providential circumstances. The most usual way God leads us is by speaking directly to our spirits by His Spirit. To experience such guidance it is essential that we be prayerful and remain full of the Holy Spirit. What the Lord speaks to us by the His Spirit will always be in harmony with His written word, the Bible.

PHILIPPI: THE GOSPEL GOES TO EUROPE

Reading Assignment: Acts 16:11-15

The Story

Paul and his band of missionaries (Silas, Timothy, and Luke) sailed from Troas to Macedonia. They arrived at the Roman colony of Philippi, the leading city of the district. One Sabbath day the missionaries went down to the river and found a group of Jewish women who had gathered for prayer. They sat down and began to speak to the women. While they spoke, the Lord opened the heart of a woman named Lydia, a seller of purple from Thyatira and a Gentile proselyte. She accepted the gospel, and she and the members of her household were baptized. After this, she persuaded the missionaries to lodge at her home, saying, "If you consider me a believer in the Lord come and stay at my house."

Commentary

Because there seems to have been no synagogue in Philippi, Paul and Silas went down to the river to seek out Jews. When there was no synagogue in a place, the Jews would often meet by the riverside, since it provided a convenient place to find water for their rituals.

16:13 began to speak to the women. Lydia, a woman, was the first Christian convert in Europe. By telling her story, Luke again demonstrates his concern for women. For him women, because they too can be empowered by the Holy Spirit, can be full participants in the mission of God (cf. Acts 1:8, 14; 2:17-18).

16:14 The Lord opened her heart. The Holy Spirit works to open people's hearts to the gospel. A combination of the power of the gospel (Rom. 1:16) and the power of the Spirit (Acts 1:8) is needed to effectively lead people to Christ. Even though God opens people's hearts, they must each personally respond to the gospel in faith and repentance (Acts 20:21; cf. Mark 1:15).

Life Application

Throughout the history of the church, women have played a prominent role. Women were the first to proclaim the resurrection of Jesus (Matt. 28:5-8; Luke 24:9-10; John 20:16-18). They were present at Pentecost when the Spirit was poured out (Acts 1:14). The first convert in Europe was a woman (16:14). We should never treat women as second-class citizens in the kingdom of God. We should release them and encourage them to be full participants in gospel work.

A SLAVE GIRL IS DELIVERED

Reading Assignment: Acts 16:16-18

The Story

One day in Philippi, as the missionaries were on their way to a prayer meeting, they met a slave girl who was possessed by a spirit of divination. Her owners used her fortune-telling abilities to earn a lot of money for themselves. Day after day the girl followed the missionaries, shouting, "These men are servants of the Most High God, who are telling you the way to be saved." Finally, Paul became so troubled in his spirit that he turned to her and commanded the spirit in the name of Jesus to come out of her. Immediately the spirit left her, and she was set free.

Commentary

The story of the deliverance of the Philippian slave girl is yet another example of how Paul and the other ministers in Acts ministered in the power of the Holy Spirit. Through the manifestation of spiritual gifts Paul brought deliverance to a demon possessed slave girl.

16:18 Paul became so troubled. Though the slave girl was speaking the truth, the source and motivation of her message was demonic. Her activity may have been a demonically-inspired tactic, aimed at undermining the ministry of Paul and Silas in Philippi. Through the gift of discerning of spirits, Paul detected the source of her inspiration, and through the gift of miraculous powers—along with the name of Jesus—he drove out the demons (cf. 1 Cor. 12:10).

In the name of Jesus Christ I command you to come out of her! Jesus drove out the demon by the finger (or Spirit) of God (Luke 11:20; cf. Matt. 12:28). Today, believers are given this same power when they are baptized in the Holy Spirit. Those who faithfully follow Jesus and obey His commands have also been given the right to use His name in combating evil and advancing His kingdom on the earth (Mark 16:17; John 14:12-14; 16:23-24; Acts 3:6, 16: 4:10, 30; 1 Cor. 5:4). To use the name of Jesus is to act under His authority.

Life Application

We as Christ's ministers should be filled with the Spirit, and we should learn to operate in the gifts of the Holy Spirit. Had Paul not been able to do this, the slave girl would have remained in bondage and his and Silas' ministry in Philippi would have been much less effective. The Bible commands us to be filled with the Spirit (Acts 1:4-5; Eph. 5:18). It also commands us to earnestly seek after spiritual gifts (1 Cor. 12:31: 14:1). Those who ignore these commands can never be the effective ministers of the gospel that God intends for them to be.

Chapter 10: Paul's Second Missionary Journey (Part 1)

OPPOSITION AND DELIVERANCE

Reading Assignment: Acts 16:19-28

The Story

The owners of the slave girl became angry at Paul because they could no longer use the girl to make money. They grabbed Paul and Silas and dragged them before the authorities in the city's marketplace. There, they accused the missionaries of causing confusion among the people by advocating practices contrary to Roman law. The gathered crowd joined in the attack against Paul and Silas. The magistrates, therefore, ordered Paul and Silas to be stripped, flogged, and cast into prison where they placed them in an inner cell with their feet fastened in stocks.

That night around midnight, as the other prisoners listened, Paul and Silas began singing hymns to God. Suddenly a great earthquake shook the prison. The prison doors flew open, and the chains fell from all the prisoners. Waking up, the jailer saw what had happened and started to kill himself, believing that all of the prisoners had escaped. Seeing this, Paul shouted, "Don't harm yourself! We are all here!"

Commentary

Even in the severest trials the apostles stayed close to God and focused on their work. As a result, their hearts were filled with joy, and they became powerful witnesses to those around them.

16:25 About midnight Paul and Silas were praying and singing hymns to God. The church experienced constant opposition and persecution. In spite of this, as the gospel advanced, the missionaries remained full of the Holy Spirit and joy (Acts 13:52; Rom. 14:17; Gal. 5:22; Col. 1:11-12; 1 Thess. 1:6; Heb. 1:9). In their joy they prayed and sang hymns to God.

the other prisoners were listening. The apostles' Spirit-inspired praying and singing resulted in witness. This is a major theme in Acts: the infilling of the Spirit empowers Christians to be effective witnesses to the lost (cf. Acts 1:8). The other prisoners must have been very impressed when they heard Paul and Silas, who had been falsely accused, beaten, and thrown into prison, joyfully singing praises to God!

16:26 Suddenly ... a violent earthquake. The violent earthquake is yet another powerful theophany in Acts. The word "suddenly" reminds us of the outpouring of the Spirit at Pentecost (2:1), and the earthquake reminds us of the shaking at the Second

Jerusalem Outpouring (4:31). Both speak of the power and work of the Spirit. Characteristically, this move of the Spirit followed a time of prayer and praise (cf. Luke 24:53; Acts 1:14; 4:31).

Life Application
Joy during times of trial is an evidence of one's being full of the Spirit. Our being filled with the Spirit should be evidenced by more than speaking in tongues. As we abide in Christ, walk in the Spirit, and obey the Lord's commands, our lives will be filled with the joy of the

Lord. Such joyful lives will be a witness to those who observe us, and, as a result, they too will be encouraged to turn to Christ.

THE JAILER'S HOUSEHOLD IS SAVED

Reading Assignment: Acts 16:29-34

The Story
The jailer fell trembling before Paul and Silas. He implored them, "Sirs, what must I do to be saved?" They answered, "Believe in the Lord Jesus, and you will be saved—you and your household." The apostles then shared the gospel with him and his family. Afterward, the jailer took them and washed their wounds, and he and his family were baptized in water. He then took the apostles to his house and prepared a meal for them. He and his family were filled with joy.

Commentary
At the heart of Paul's ministry was the message of salvation. When the Philippian jailer inquired about how to be saved, Paul and Silas were ready with an answer. They told him that salvation comes through faith in Christ.

16:30 what must I do to be saved? This is the most important question in the Bible. All are lost, therefore, all must be saved (Rom. 3:23-24). This salvation has been provided through Christ's atoning work on the cross. The primary mission of the church is to proclaim the message of salvation to all nations (Mark 16:15-16; Luke 24:46-47).

16:31 Believe in the Lord Jesus, and you will be saved. People are saved through faith in Christ. Two essential elements of true saving faith are repentance toward God and faith toward the Lord Jesus (Matt. 21:323; Mark 1:15; Acts 19:4; 20:21; Heb. 6:1).

Repentance toward God involves acknowledging one's sins, asking forgiveness, and turning from sin to walk in newness of life. Faith toward the Lord Jesus involves believing in His death and resurrection, inviting Him into one's life as Lord and Savior, and trusting Him alone for salvation (cf. Rom. 10:9-10).

16:32 they spoke the word of the Lord. The phrase "word of the Lord" occurs ten times in Acts. In each instance it indicates the preaching of the gospel (8:25; 11:16; 13:44, 48-49; 15:35-36; 16:32; 19:10, 20). The only other place in the New Testament where the phrase is used is in 1 Peter 1:25, where the context indicates the same. (See comments on 8:25.)

16:33 immediately he and all his family were baptized. Although water baptism is not a requirement for salvation, Luke presents it as the new believers' first step of obedience. According to Peter, it is "the pledge of a good conscience toward God" (1 Pet. 3:21). It was the practice of the early church in Acts to baptize believers in water immediately after they put their faith in Christ (Acts 2:41; 8:12; 36-39; 9:18; 10:47-48; 16:15, 33; 18:8).

16:34 filled with joy. The joy of the apostles, demonstrated by their singing to God at midnight, now filled the heart of the jailer. This newfound joy was an evidence that he had been born of the Spirit, and possibly even filled with the Spirit, on this occasion.

Life Application

Every Christian should at all times be prepared to answer the question, "What must I do to be saved?" It is the responsibility of pastors and other church leaders to train everyone in the church how to lead others to Christ.

APOLOGIES AND DEPARTURE

Reading Assignment: Acts 16:35-40

The Story

The next morning the city officials sent orders to the jailer to release Paul and Silas, telling them that they could go in peace. Paul, however, refused, saying, "They beat us publicly without a trial, even though we are Roman citizens, and threw us into prison. And now do they want to get rid of us quietly? No! Let them come themselves and escort us out." Upon hearing this, the magistrates were distressed, realizing that they had mistreated Roman citizens. They, therefore, came in person to apologize to Paul and Silas, and to ask them to leave the city. After this, the missionaries went to the house of Lydia and encouraged the brothers there. They then left for Thessalonica.

Commentary

In demanding an apology from the magistrates, Paul's concern was not to preserve his own dignity or status; his concern was for the safety and blessing of the new church in Philippi. He, therefore, used his Roman citizenship as a means of ensuring fair treatment of Christians in the city.

16:37 Let them come themselves and escort us out. Paul wanted to leave Philippi with a good name. He did this so that the work of the church would not be hindered, and so that it could carry out its work without unnecessary interference. He, therefore, demanded that the city officials come and apologize before he left Philippi.

16:40 they met with the brothers and encouraged them. Paul and Silas were not only concerned with getting people saved, as important as that work is. Their concern went further: to the establishment of strong indigenous churches. Therefore, before departing for Thessalonica, the gathered the brothers together to encourage them in the work of the Lord.

Life Application

It is important how a missionary or Christian worker begins a work. It is also important how he or she departs the same work. Our departure must never result in weakening the church. Every pastor or church planter should insure that the church is strong enough to carry on the work, or that the church is left in able hands. He or she should also leave with a good name, so that the work will not be hindered.

CONCLUSION

During Paul's Second Missionary Journey he and his companions were led by the Spirit to enter Europe and, for the first time, preach the gospel there. As we have studied in this chapter, his ministry in Europe began in Philippi in eastern Macedonia. There, Paul and Silas established a strong indigenous missional church. He would later write a letter to this church and tell them how he thanked God for them, and how he carried them in his heart. They became partners with him in the gospel by helping to support his missionary work (Phil. 1:3-7).

In the next chapter we will examine the remainder of Paul's Second Missionary Journey, which will take him to Thessalonica, Berea, Athens, and Corinth. Paul will also make a brief visit to

Ephesus on his way back to Antioch. In each of these locales we can learn much from Paul about how to conduct an effective missionary and church planting ministry.

QUESTIONS FOR REFLECTION AND REVIEW

1. Describe Silas, Paul's companion on his Second Missionary Journey.
2. What was Paul's purpose in returning to Cilicia and Galatia at the beginning of his second journey? What was the result of their visits?
3. Who joined Paul and Silas in Derbe?
4. How did the Holy Spirit again work as the Superintendent of the Harvest in guiding Paul's missionary band to Macedonia and then into Europe?
5. What was the missionaries' response to the Spirit's direction?
6. What other means of divine guidance do we find in the book of Acts?
7. Who was the first Christian convert in Europe? Why is this significant?
8. How did Paul deal with the demonized slave girl in Philippi? How did he know that her words were demonically inspired?
9. How did Paul and Silas' singing in the prison at night serve as a witness to the other prisoners? What other kinds of witness are present in this story? What was the result?
10. What instructions did Paul give to the Philippian jailer on how to be saved?
11. What indication do we have of the Spirit's working in the jailer's heart?

QUESTIONS FOR CLASSROOM DISCUSSION

1. Paul and Silas began Paul's Second Missionary Journey by returning to the churches in Syria, Cilicia, and Galatia to strengthen them. What important church-planting lessons can we learn from this action of the apostles?
2. In 16:6-10 the Holy Spirit directed Paul and his missionary band eastward into Europe. What important lessons concerning divine guidance can we learn from this story?
3. Throughout Luke-Acts, Luke shows women as being filled with the Spirit and actively involved in the ministry. What should be the attitude of the Pentecostal church toward Spirit-filled women in ministry today?
4. What gave Paul and Silas the joy and courage to sing songs in the night, even after they had been beaten and thrown into prison? How can we have that same joy today?
5. Paul and Silas led the Philippian jailer to Christ. Are we consistently leading others to Christ? If now, why not? How can this unacceptable situation be remedied?

Chapter 10: Paul's Second Missionary Journey (Part 1)

– Chapter 11 –

Paul's Second Missionary Journey (Part 2)

PRE-LESSON READING ASSIGNMENT

Acts 17:1–18:22

INTRODUCTION

During Paul's Second Missionary Journey he and his missionary companions were led by the Spirit to preach the gospel in Europe. They began their European ministry in Macedonia on the northern shores of the Aegean Sea. In the last chapter we discussed Paul's missionary ministry in Philippi. In this chapter we will look at the remainder of Paul's Second Missionary Journey. This will include his continuing missionary work in Macedonia, his missionary ministry in Greece, and his brief stop in Ephesus. As was his ministry in Philippi, Paul's ministry in Thessalonica, Berea, Athens, Corinth, and Ephesus is filled with exciting stories of commitment and courage.

THESSALONICA: SUCCESS AND TURMOIL

Reading Assignment: Acts 17:1-9

The Story

Leaving Luke at Philippi, Paul, Silas, and Timothy traveled westward to Thessalonica. For the next three Sabbaths Paul went into the synagogue and reasoned with the local Jews and God-fearers. Using the Scriptures he showed how Christ had to suffer and rise from the dead. He boldly declared, "This Jesus I am proclaiming to you is the Christ." Many believed and joined the missionaries, including some Jews, many God-fearing Greeks, and several prominent women.

Some Jews became jealous, so they rounded up some hoodlums from the marketplace and incited a riot. They then led the mob to Jason's house, looking for the missionaries. When they did not find them there, they lashed out at Jason, and dragged him and some other brothers before the council. They shouted, "These men who have caused trouble all over the world have now come here." They accused the missionaries of ignoring Caesar's decrees by claiming that Jesus was king. After hearing this, the council members were greatly troubled, so they made the missionaries post bond, and released them.

Commentary

Paul and Silas' reception in the city of Thessalonica was less than hospitable. Nevertheless, they were able to plant a strong Spirit-empowered missional church there. We discover this from reading Paul's first letter to the Thessalonians. There he reminds the believers how he had preached the gospel to them "with power, with the Holy Spirit and with deep conviction," and how they had "welcomed the message with the joy given by the Holy Spirit." As a result, the church in Thessalonica became "a model to all the believers in Macedonia and Achaia," and from there "the Lord's message rang out ... not only in Macedonia and Achaia," but their "faith in God [became] known everywhere" (1 Thess. 1:5-8).

17:3 explaining and proving that the Christ had to suffer and rise from the dead. As he did in every place, in Thessalonica Paul faithfully proclaimed the message of Jesus' death and resurrection. The gospel alone contains the power to transform people's lives and bring them into a saving knowledge of Christ (cf. Rom. 1:16). Paul further informed the Jews in Thessalonica that "this Jesus I am proclaiming to you is the Christ," their long-awaited Messiah. (See comments on 1:3.)

17:7 saying that there is another king, one called Jesus. Jesus is, in truth, a king. He is the seed of David (Luke 1:32; Rev. 22:16), the King of kings and Lord of lords (1 Tim. 6:15; Rev. 19:16).

Life Application

Sometimes we are called upon to witness for Christ in the midst of opposition, and even hostility. In such cases we should ensure that we remain full of the Spirit and faithful in proclaiming the message of the gospel. We can do this by staying in close communion with Christ through prayer. If we will remain faithful to God's mission, He will use us to advance His kingdom and establish a strong work for Him.

Further, we should strive to plant churches like the one Paul planted in Thessalonica, churches full of joy and the Holy Spirit. These churches can become models for other churches in the area. From them the message of Christ can ring out to other places. Such churches can only come into being if the missionaries and church planters take intentional steps to insure that they do. These steps include the establishing of clear goals and focused teaching on the mission of the church. The new disciples in these churches must be instructed about how they too can be filled with the Spirit and become active participants in Christ's mission.

BEREA: THE MESSAGE IS RECEIVED

Reading Assignment: Acts 17:10-15

The Story

That night the brothers spirited Paul and Silas away to Berea. When they arrived in Berea they went to the Jewish synagogue and began teaching and preaching about Christ. Being of more noble character than the Thessalonians, the Bereans gladly received the word and eagerly examined the Scriptures to determine if Paul was teaching the truth. Many came to Christ, including some Jews, prominent Greek women, and Greek men. When certain Jews from Thessalonica heard that Paul was preaching the word of God in Berea, they came there and poisoned the people against Paul. So, Paul was again whisked away by the brothers and taken down to the coast. From there he was escorted to Athens, some one hundred miles south in Achaia. Silas and Timothy, however, remained in Berea. When Paul arrived in Athens, he sent word for Silas and Timothy to join him there as soon as possible.

Commentary

In Berea Paul and Silas found Jews of more noble character than those in Thessalonica. They were more open to the things of the Lord and eager to know the truth. Many received the message and came to Christ. However, because of the agitation of a delegation of Jews from Thessalonica, Paul had to leave for Athens.

17:12 Many of the Jews believed, as did also a number of prominent Greek women and many Greek men. The gospel is inclusive. Anyone can be saved and follow Christ, as is demonstrated by
the response in Berea where Jews, Gentiles, men, and women believed and followed Christ.

17:13 preaching the word of God. Again, we see Paul and his colleagues remaining true to the mission of Christ: they preached the gospel. The phrase "word of God" is used eleven times in Acts (Acts 4:31; 6:2, 7: 8:14; 11:1; 12:24; 13:5, 7, 46; 17:13; 18:11). It is often used synonymously with the gospel (i.e., 11:1). (See comment on 8:25 and 13:4).

Life Application

We should be faithful to preach the message of Christ wherever we go. And we should preach it to all classes of people, expecting a harvest of souls. Some will agitate and oppose the gospel; however, we must not be discouraged, for some will be "more noble" and will gladly accept Christ as Savior.

ATHENS: A FEW BELIEVE

Reading Assignment: Acts 17:16-34

The Story

In Athens Paul was deeply troubled by the city's gross idolatry. Day by day he taught in the synagogue and in the marketplace, teaching the people about the gospel and the resurrection of Jesus. One day he entered into a debate with some Greek philosophers. These philosophers always wanted to hear about some new idea, so they took him to the Areopagus (Mars Hill) and asked him to explain more fully his new teaching.

Taking his opportunity, Paul stood and declared the gospel to them. He began by noting how religious the Athenians were, and how he had seen their many objects of worship throughout the city. "I even found an altar with this inscription: 'To an Unknown God,'" he said, "I am going to tell you who this God is." He then launched into his message.

He told them that the one true God, who created everything in heaven and on earth, does not live in man-made temples. Neither does He need humans to take care of Him, since He is the one who gives life and breath—and everything else—to all people. This God has created from one blood all nations of people, and He has determined their times and the places where they should live. He did this so that they could seek Him, and perhaps find Him—although He is not far from anyone—for, Paul explained, "In Him we live and move and have our being." It is as some of their own poets had stated, "We are God's offspring."

And, if we are His offspring, then how could God be an image made of gold, or silver, or stone, no matter how beautiful it is? In times past God overlooked such conduct, but no more; He now commands everyone everywhere to repent. Those who do not repent will one day be judged by the man He has appointed, that is, Christ. This is the very man He raised from the dead!

When the people heard Paul talk about the resurrection of the dead, they began to mock. Some, however, said, "We want to hear about this again." A few people believed Paul and became his followers, including Dionysius, a member of Mars Hill, and a woman named Damaris. A few others also believed and followed Paul.

Commentary

Paul's ministry in Athens has been cited as a good example of cross-cultural adaption in preaching the gospel. In his message on Mars Hill, Paul called attention to the Athenian's worship, noting that they were very religious people. He also he referred to their monument to the Unknown God and quoted their pagan poets. He did these things to more closely identify with the culture of Athens. At the same time, however, he remained true to his mission and never compromised the gospel message.

17:16. Athens. Athens was the capital of Greece (Achaia) and the center of Grecian culture, art, philosophy, and architecture. About 250,000 people lived in Athens in the first century A.D.

he was greatly distressed. Rather than being impressed by the Athenian architectural wonders and the city's classical works of art, Paul was distressed in his spirit, realizing that they were symbols of the people's idolatry and lostness (cf. 1 Cor. 10:18-21). While we rejoice in the cultural achievements of mankind, we are not blinded to man's desperate need of Christ.

17:17 he reasoned in the synagogue ... as well as in the marketplace. Paul did not limit his preaching and teaching to the "church." He rather took the gospel into the marketplace where the lost people were. We should never limit our preaching to the church building; we must take the message of Christ to the streets. We must proclaim Christ both "publicly and from house to house" (20:20).

17:18 preaching the good news about Jesus and the resurrection. As always, Paul centered his preaching on the gospel of Christ, including His death and resurrection. (See comments on 1:3.)

17:26 From one man he made every nation of men. Although there are cultural differences between nations and peoples, there is only one race of people on the earth, the human race. All are descendants of Adam and Eve and are equally precious before God, who created them. All fell through Adam's transgression, and redemption was provided for all through Christ's death on the cross. All must therefore hear and believe the message of the gospel.

17:27 God did this so that men would ... find him. God has providentially placed all peoples, tribes, and nations in their appointed locations on earth. He has also determined the times of their visitation. He has done all of this so that they might seek and find Him. It is our responsibility to follow the leading of His Spirit and take the gospel to them wherever they may be.

17:30 now he commands all people everywhere to repent. To be saved, people must turn to God, repent of their sins, and put their faith in Christ. There is no other means of salvation (cf. 4:12).

Life Application

We must know our message: It is the message of Christ (1 Cor. 2:1-5). The center of this message is His death, burial, and resurrection (1 Cor. 15:1-6). Further, we must faithfully call men to faith in Him. They must repent of their sins, believe in Christ, and follow Him. While doing this, we must be sensitive to the people's customs and culture, and, when possible, use our knowledge of their culture to more effectively present the gospel to them. All along, we must understand that God is at work through His providence and His Spirit to prepare people to receive Christ. He empowers His church to proclaim the message of Christ to them. We must, therefore, be faithful to take the message to all peoples, whether in the next village or in distant lands.

CORINTH: AN EXTENDED STAY

Reading Assignment: Acts 18:1-17

The Story

Paul traveled from Athens to Corinth, where he met Aquila and his wife Priscilla. They had recently fled from Italy to Corinth because the emperor Claudius had expelled all the Jews from Rome. Since they were tentmakers like Paul, he stayed and worked with them. Every Sabbath, however, Paul went to the synagogue and sought to persuade the Jews and Greeks there to turn to Christ.

When Silas and Timothy arrived from Macedonia, Paul was able to devote himself exclusively to preaching the gospel. In time, however, when the Jews became hardened in their opposition against the gospel, Paul turned from them saying, "Your blood be on your own heads! I am clear of my responsibility to you. I now turn to the Gentiles."

Paul then left the synagogue and began to teach in the house of Titius Justus, a Jewish proselyte. Soon after that Crispus, the ruler of the synagogue, turned to the Lord, along with his entire family. Hearing about this, many Corinthians believed the gospel and were baptized.

One night the Lord came to Paul in a vision and told him not to be afraid but to "keep on speaking, do not be silent." The Lord told Paul that He was with him, and no one would harm him. The Lord further assured him, "I have many people in this city." As a result, Paul was greatly encouraged and remained in Corinth for a year and a half teaching the word of God.

In time, when Gallio became the governor of Achaia, the Jews united against Paul and brought charges against him, accusing him of persuading people to worship God in ways contrary to Roman law. Gallio, however, dismissed their charges since, he said, he was not interested in matters of Jewish law and customs. In retaliation, the mob seized Sosthenes, the new leader of the synagogue, and beat him outside the courtroom. Gallio, however, showed no interest in the matter.

Commentary

When Paul arrived in Corinth, he came with a new plan. In Athens he had tried to convince the people to turn to Christ by using superior wisdom and philosophy, yet with little results. In Corinth, however, he had a new strategy. He resolved to know nothing while he was with them "except Jesus Christ and him crucified" (1 Cor. 2:2). When Paul later wrote to the Corinthian church, he recounted his ministry among them: "My message and my preaching were not with wise and persuasive words, but with a demonstration of the Spirit's power, so that your faith might not rest on men's wisdom, but on God's power" (vv. 4-5).

18:1 Corinth. Corinth was the capital and commercial center of Greece, and the seat of the Roman proconsul (Acts 18:12). The city was notorious for its immorality. It had about 500,000 residents when Paul visited the city.

18:4 trying to persuade Jews and Greeks. When Paul preached, he did not simply tell the story of Jesus. He tried to persuade people to follow Jesus as Lord and Savior. He called for a decisive response from his hearers. Our job is not simply to tell people about Jesus, we must seek to persuade them to turn to Him in faith and repentance. This can be best done by being full of the Spirit and by faithfully and clearly proclaiming the gospel.

18:5 Paul devoted himself exclusively to preaching. When Silas and Timothy arrived in Corinth, Paul could quit his tentmaking and devote himself entirely to preaching the gospel. As missionaries and pastors it should always be our goal to devote ourselves exclusively to the proclamation and teaching of the gospel.

18:8 many of the Corinthians who heard him believed and were baptized. As a result of Paul's missionary work in Corinth, many came to know the Lord. A large Spirit-empowered church was founded.

18:9 the Lord spoke to Paul in a vision. Paul is again guided by a vision. In the vision the Lord spoke to him telling him not to be afraid. The Spirit not only directs us in our work for God, He also comes to us to comfort and encourage us in our times of discouragement. On this occasion the Spirit gave Paul a vision of Christ. What an encouragement that must have been to the beleaguered apostle!

Life Application

When we go out to preach the gospel, we should go in the power of the Spirit. And we should focus our preaching and teaching on "Christ and him crucified" (1 Cor. 2:2). When difficult times come, if we will follow the Spirit's leading, we can expect the Lord to come to us with words of comfort and encouragement. Sometimes He may appear in a vision. At other times He will speak directly by His Spirit to our spirits. Such times of encouragement most often come when we are seeking the Lord's face in prayer.

EPHESUS: A BRIEF STOPOVER

Reading Assignment: Acts 18:18-22

The Story

After remaining in Corinth for some time, Paul left with Priscilla and Aquila and sailed for Syria. He had his hair cut off to fulfill a vow he had made. On his journey to Antioch he and his companions passed through Ephesus. While there, Paul went into the synagogue and reasoned with the Jews. They asked him to spend more time with them. However, he declined, promising to return to them if God willed. Leaving Priscilla and Aquila in Ephesus, he sailed to Caesarea, where he greeted the church. He then went northward to Antioch in Syria.

Commentary

While in Corinth, Paul decided to return to Antioch, where he had begun his journey. On the way there he made a brief stopover in Ephesus, where he evidently planted a small body of believers. He left Priscilla and Aquila there to care for them, while he journeyed on to Antioch.

18:19 went into the synagogue and reasoned with the Jews. Some of these Jews evidently believed on Christ since verse 27 speaks of "the brothers" in Ephesus who wrote to the disciples in Corinth concerning Apollos.

18:21 I will come back if it is God's will. Paul intended to return to Ephesus and make it his base of missionary operation to reach all of Asia Minor. This he did during his Third Missionary Journey.

Life Application

We should always witness for Christ, even when we are en route from one place of ministry to another. If we will remain focused on the mission of God and sensitive to the voice of the Spirit, He will direct us as to what we must do. As Paul wrote, we must "make the most of every opportunity" (Eph. 5:16).

CONCLUSION

Paul returned to his home base in Antioch, thus completing his Second Missionary Journey. During this journey he and Silas had planted churches in the European provinces of Macedonia and Achaia. They had also begun a small work in Ephesus. In his Third Missionary Journey, Paul will return to Ephesus to conduct his most successful campaign of all, the Ephesian Campaign. We will look at that campaign in the next chapter.

Chapter 11: Paul's Second Missionary Journey (Part 2)

QUESTIONS FOR REFLECTION AND REVIEW

1. Describe Paul and Silas' reception in the city of Thessalonica. In spite of this, what was the result of their work there?
2. What was Paul's message in Thessalonica?
3. Contrast the character of the residents of Berea with those of Thessalonica.
4. Paul preached the "word of God" in Berea. Explain what the phrase means in Acts.
5. What distressed Paul in Athens, the cultural center of the Greek world?
6. What was his message in Athens?
7. Describes the results of his ministry there.
8. How did Paul support himself when he first arrived in Corinth? With whom did he work? What changed when Silas and Timothy arrived?
9. What kind of church did Paul found in Corinth? What were his message and methods there? (cf. 1 Cor. 1:7; 2:1-5).
10. How did the Holy Spirit encourage Paul in Corinth? (18:9).

QUESTIONS FOR CLASSROOM DISCUSSION

1. In Thessalonica Paul experienced great opposition to his missionary work (Acts 17:5-9); nevertheless, a powerful missionary church was established there (1Thess. 1:5-8). How can one be successful in church planting even when experiencing opposition?
2. In Athens Paul was distressed when he saw all of the idolatry in the city. What action did he take? What should be our attitude toward sin and idolatry in our own societies? What actions should we take?
3. In Corinth the Lord came to Paul in a vision to comfort and encourage Him. Can we expect the same today? In what ways can we expect the Lord to come to us?

– CHAPTER 12 –

PAUL'S THIRD MISSIONARY JOURNEY

(INCLUDING THE EPHESIAN OUTPOURING)

PRE-LESSON READING ASSIGNMENT

Acts 18:23–20:38

INTRODUCTION

After an extended stay in Antioch, Paul launched out on his Third Missionary Journey. This was his final such journey in Acts. The journey began with a second pastoral visit to the regions of southern Galatia and Phrygia. Paul then returned to Ephesus, where he conducted the most successful evangelism and church-planting campaign of his career. In this chapter we will look at these and other activities of Paul during his Third Missionary Journey. In doing this, we will learn some valuable lessons about missions strategy.

PASTORAL VISITS TO GALATIA AND PHRYGIA

Reading Assignment: Acts 18:23

The Story
After spending time in Antioch, Paul set out again, returning to the regions of Phrygia and Galatia. In each place he traveled he

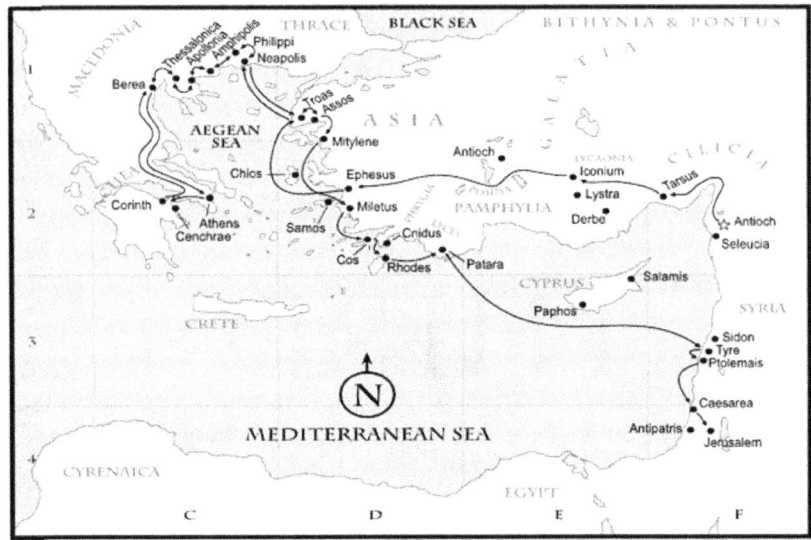

Figure 12.1 Paul's Third Missionary Journey ©2005 Biblical Studies Press

strengthened the disciples.

Commentary

18:23 After spending some time in Antioch, Paul set out. Unlike his first two journeys, on this one Paul did not take anyone with him.

strengthening all the disciples. Paul's concern for people did not end when he led them to the Lord, or even when he started a new church. He returned to strengthen those who had chosen to follow Christ. Although evangelism and church planting are major issues in missions, the role of the missionary is more than evangelistic; it is also pastoral. Not only must churches be planted, but also believers must be encouraged and strengthened in their faith. They must be taught the word of God and led into the Spirit-filled life. In this way they can grow into mature believers and effective witnesses for Christ.

Life Application

Sometimes in ministry we must "go it alone" as did Paul at the beginning of his Third Missionary Journey. At such times, we must not be tempted to withdraw or shirk our responsibilities to God. We must press forward to the work. If we will be faithful to do the work that the Lord assigns us, even when we have to do it alone, in His time He will bring companions to our side to help us. Although Paul began this journey alone, before it was completed he had a large team of workers with him (cf. 20:4).

APOLLOS, PRISCILLA, AND AQUILA

Reading Assignment: Acts 18:24-28

The Story

While Paul was ministering in Phrygia and Galatia, a brother by the name of Apollos from Alexandria, Egypt, arrived in Ephesus. Apollos was an educated man with a thorough knowledge of the Old Testament Scriptures. He had been taught the way of the Lord and preached with great fervor. Even though he had only received the baptism of John, he spoke accurately about Jesus. When Priscilla and Aquila heard him preaching boldly about Jesus in the synagogue, they took him aside and taught him about the ways of God more thoroughly.

Later, Apollos decided to go to Achaia. The brothers in Ephesus encouraged him and wrote a letter of recommendation for him addressed to the disciples in Achaia. When he arrived there, he was greatly used by God to strengthen the church. He powerfully refuted the Jews in public debates, proving from the Scriptures that Jesus was indeed the Christ.

Commentary

The story of Apollos illustrates the fact that men and women other than the twelve apostles were faithfully proclaiming the message of Christ in many parts of the ancient world. There seems to have been an active church in Apollos' hometown, Alexandria, Egypt, of which the book of Acts tells us nothing. Churches were being planted in many other places not mentioned in Acts or Paul's epistles. Luke only writes about those places that helped to further his purpose in writing Acts.

18:24-25 Apollos. Apollos is described as "a learned man, with a thorough knowledge of the Scriptures." This understanding obviously included what the Scriptures taught about the Christ, for Apollos had been "instructed in the way of the Lord" and he "taught about Jesus accurately." In 1 Corinthians Paul described Apollos as the one who watered the seed that he had planted, causing the church to grow (1 Cor. 3:5-6; cf. 1:12; 3:22; 4:6; 16:12).

18:25 he spoke with great fervor. These words of the NIV are an interpretation of the Greek text, rather than a translation. An accurate translation of the Greek text (*zeōn to pneumati*) is "fervent in spirit (or Spirit)" (cf. NASB, NKJV, RSV). The same expression is used in Romans 12:11, where the RSV translates it "aglow with the Spirit." This phrase seems to indicate that Apollos has been filled with the Spirit. That Apollos had been filled with the Spirit is also indicated by both his ministry in Ephesus (where he "spoke with great fervor," v. 25) and in Corinth (where he "vigorously refuted the Jews in public debate," v. 28, cf. 1:8).

18:27 the brothers ... wrote to the disciples there. The fact that there were brothers in Ephesus indicates that there was a church there. It was possibly started when Paul first visited Ephesus near the end of his second journey (18:18-21). The church had been nurtured through the ministries of Priscilla, Aquila, and Apollos (vv. 19, 24-26). It, or part of it, possibly met in the household of Priscilla and Aquila (v. 26).

18:28 proving from the Scriptures that Jesus was the Christ. Like Peter (4:12), Philip (8:5), and Paul (9:22), Apollos' ministry centered on Jesus and the proclamation of the gospel.

Life Application

There are times when public or classroom teaching is not sufficient. Sometimes we must do as Priscilla and Aquila did with Apollos. We must personally instruct certain individuals and mentor them in the faith and in ministry. We must do this so that they might more clearly understand the gospel and their responsibility in spreading it.

THE EPHESIAN OUTPOURING AND CAMPAIGN

Reading Assignment: Acts 19:1-10

The Story

While Apollos was ministering in Corinth, Paul set out from Phrygia and traveled westward through the interior of Asia, finally arriving at Ephesus. There he encountered twelve disciples. Without hesitation he asked them, "Did you receive the Holy Spirit when you believed?" They answered that they had not even heard about the Holy Spirit. Puzzled, Paul inquired further, "Into what then were you baptized?" They answered, "Into John's baptism."

Paul then explained to them that John's baptism was a baptism of repentance. People received it in anticipation of Jesus' coming. When the twelve disciples heard this, they were re-baptized, this time in the name of the Lord Jesus. Paul then laid his hands on them, and the Holy Spirit came upon them. They began to speak in tongues and prophesy.

Paul then took these men and went into the Jewish synagogue, where for three months he preached boldly and argued persuasively about the kingdom of God. After a while, however, some members of the synagogue became obstinate and refused to believe what Paul was preaching. Some even slandered the Christian way.

Paul then left the synagogue and began teaching daily in the lecture hall of Tyrannus. These lectures continued for two years. Amazingly, by the end of this time, everyone who lived in the entire province of Asia, both Jews and Greeks, had heard the word of the Lord!

COMMENTARY

Paul's Ephesian Campaign has been described as the chief achievement of his missionary career and the climax of his missionary work. Interestingly, Paul's ministry in Ephesus is the only recorded instance of his evangelistic and church-planting efforts during his Third Missionary Journey. It is as if Luke wanted to highlight this extraordinary work. In the Ephesian Campaign Luke sums up Paul's missionary strategy, a strategy he successfully employed throughout the Roman empire (cf. Rom. 15:17-21). This strategy can serve as a model for missionary strategy today. We will divide our comments on this passage into two parts: the "Ephesian Outpouring" and the "Ephesian Campaign." We will then analyze and apply Paul's missionary strategy under the heading, "Further Insight."

The Ephesian Outpouring (vv. 1-7)

Paul arrived in Ephesus with a well-thought-out goal and strategy which can be discovered through a thoughtful examination of his ministry there. Paul's goal was to evangelize and establish churches throughout the Roman province of Asia (cf. v. 10). His strategy involved three main elements, which we call "pillars" (see "Further Insight," below). The first pillar of Paul's strategy was to ensure that the Ephesian church was empowered by the Holy Spirit. This happened in the "Ephesian Outpouring" (19:1-7).

The Ephesian Outpouring is the seventh and last key outpouring of the Holy Spirit in Acts. As with the previous six, it resulted in powerful missional witness. Also, as with the previous six outpourings, it demonstrates Luke's *empowerment–witness motif,* first presented in Acts 1:8. Luke's primary intent in writing Acts was to call the church of his day (and ultimately the church of our day) back to its Pentecostal and missionary roots. The Ephesian Outpouring and Campaign clearly demonstrate that any church, if it will be empowered by the Spirit, and remain focused on the mission of God, can become a powerful witnessing community. And it can do this even in the midst of opposition and persecution.

19:1: *Ephesus.* Ephesus, the provincial capital of Asia, was a great city of about 750,000 inhabitants. It contained the famed temple of Artemis (Diana), one of the Seven Wonders of the Ancient World. For years Paul had wanted to go to Ephesus (cf. 16:6; 18:19-21). He knew that establishing a strong Spirit-empowered missional church in Ephesus was the key to evangelizing all of western Asia.

There he found some disciples. These men were true Christians. Without exception, when Luke uses the word "disciple" without any qualifying adjective, he is talking about disciples of Christ.[30] Although these twelve men had been born again, they had not yet been baptized in Holy Spirit, as were the disciples on the Day of Pentecost. They were probably members of the emerging church in Ephesus. (See comment on 18:27).

19:2 *Did you receive the Holy Spirit when you believed?* In asking this question, Paul was not inquiring as to the twelve disciples' salvation. He was rather inquiring as to their readiness to participate in the mission of reaching Ephesus and Asia with the gospel. A Spirit-empowered church was the first pillar of Paul's missionary strategy (as will be discussed below in "Further Insight"). When Paul asked this question, he could have had in mind the words of Jesus: "Stay in the city until you have been clothed with power from on high" (Luke 24:49; cf. Acts 1:4-5).

19:6 *Paul placed his hands on them.* Paul laid hands on the twelve disciples to help them be filled with the Spirit. He could also have been commissioning them for missional ministry. In Acts, the laying on of hands is often used in commissioning to ministry, as with the seven "deacons" (6:6) and Saul (9:17). (See note on 8:17.)

the Holy Spirit came on them. Here, Luke intentionally uses the same wording he used in Acts 1:8 ("when the Holy Spirit comes on you") so that his readers might understand that the Holy Spirit came upon these men just as He came on the disciples at Pentecost—not to bring about their new birth, but to empower them for witness. The Ephesian Outpouring occurred 25 years after the Day of Pentecost. It is an apt example of those whom Peter described as being "far off" (2:38-39). They, too, could receive the gift of the Holy Spirit. And

---

[30] cf. Luke 9:16, 18, 54; 10:23; 16:1; 17:22; 18:15; 19:29, 37; 20:45; 22:39, 45; Acts 6:1, 2, 7; 9:10, 19, 26, 38; 11:26, 29; 13:52; 14:20, 22, 28; 15:10; 16:1; 18:23, 27; 19:1, 9, 30; 20:1, 30; 21:4, 16.

so can we today!

they spoke in tongues and prophesied. These twelve men spoke in tongues and prophesied, just as the Jewish Christians had done at Pentecost and the Gentiles at Caesarea (2:4; 10:46). According to Luke's teaching in Acts, there are two results that one can expect when he or she is baptized in the Holy Spirit: The first is speaking in tongues as the Spirit gives utterance. This is the "initial physical evidence" or "normative sign" of one's being baptized in the Holy Spirit. The second is prophetic (i.e., Spirit-empowered) witness. Empowering is the first pillar in Paul's missionary strategy (see Figure 12.2, p. 177). This is the functional result of one's being baptized in the Holy Spirit. Both results should be considered normative. The disciples prophesying in this instance should be understood in Lukan terms of Spirit-empowered witness (Acts 1:8; 2:14-18) rather than in Pauline terms of Spirit-inspired edification (1 Cor. 14:3-5). It is a direct fulfillment of Jesus' statement in 1:8: "You will receive power ... and you will be my witnesses."

The Ephesian Campaign (vv. 8-10)

The Ephesian Campaign directly followed the Ephesian Outpouring. It took place over a period of about two years and resulted in "all the Jews and Greeks who lived in the province of Asia" hearing the gospel, and in probably hundreds of churches being planted. In executing the Ephesian Campaign, Paul was following a predetermined missionary strategy. (This strategy is discussed in more detail below in "Further Insight: Paul's Missionary Strategy.") Now that the church had been empowered by the Spirit, it had to give itself to the proclamation of the gospel and the mobilization of workers to reach out to Ephesus and all of the province of Asia.

19:8 Paul ... spoke boldly. Boldness is a characteristic of Spirit-empowered witness (cf. Acts 4:29-31; 9:28; 13:46; 14:3; 18:26; 28:31). The fact that Paul preached with great boldness, even in the midst of great opposition (cf. 1 Cor. 15:32; 16:9-10), is an indication that, many years after his initial infilling with the Spirit (9:17-18), he was still full of the Holy Spirit. Paul's ministering in the power of the Spirit is also indicated by the fact that he laid hands on others to receive the Spirit (19:6) and was used by God to work extraordinary miracles (v. 11). The proclamation of the gospel with signs following is the second pillar of Paul's missionary strategy (see Figure 12.2, p. 177).

about the kingdom of God. The kingdom of God is a key theme in Luke-Acts. It is mentioned 29 times in Luke and eight times in

Acts (Luke 1:33; 4:43; 6:20; 7:28; 8:1, 10; 9:2, 11, 27, 60, 62; 10:9, 11; 11:2; 20, 31; 12:32; 13:18, 20, 28-29; 14:15; 16:16; 17:20-21; 18:16-17, 24-25; 18:29; 19:11-12, 15; 21:31; 22:16, 18; 22:29-30; 23:42, 51; Acts 1:3, 6; 8:12; 14:22; 19:8; 20:25; 28:23, 31)

19:9 He took the disciples with him. This is a possible reference to the same twelve disciples mentioned in verse 1. Once these twelve men had been filled with the Holy Spirit, Paul immediately took them into the synagogue with him to preach the gospel. This is mentoring at its very best.

discussions daily in the lecture hall of Tyrannus. Once Paul had ensured that the church in Ephesus was empowered by the Spirit, and while he was yet proclaiming the gospel with signs following, he set up a training school for missionaries and church planters. This represents the third pillar of Paul's missionary strategy, mobilization, as discussed below (see Figure 12.2, p. 177).

19:10 two years ... all the Jews and Greeks ... of Asia heard the word of the Lord. What an amazing accomplishment! In just two years everyone in Asia—even those of various cultures and ethnic backgrounds—heard the gospel. Many churches were planted, including the seven churches of Asia mentioned in Revelation 2-3. Church history reveals that Asia became a center of Christian witness for many years. All these accomplishments testify to the effectiveness of Paul's strategy.

FURTHER INSIGHT:
PAUL'S MISSIONARY STRATEGY

Luke includes the story of Paul's ministry in Ephesus as his most comprehensive example of Paul's missionary strategy. It, in effect, sums up his missionary strategy demonstrated in his First and Second Missionary Journeys. Paul employed this strategy in reaching all of Roman Asia with the gospel of Christ in just two years. We will do well to understand and employ this strategy in our own missionary and church planting efforts today. In the Ephesian Campaign Paul's strategy included three key "pillars," as follows:

Pillar One: Empowering

The first pillar of Paul's missionary strategy was empowering (see Figure 12.2, page 177). This empowering was twofold: It first involved the empowering of the missionary himself. Every missionary and church planter must go to the work full of the Holy Spirit. It further involved the empowering of the churches to be planted. Let's look briefly at each of these essential elements:

Paul entered Ephesus full of the Holy Spirit (see comments on 19:8). He thus ministered as a Spirit-empowered witness in accordance with Jesus prescription in 1:8. Paul understood, however, that it was not enough for him alone to be full of the Spirit. He knew that, if the work was to prosper, any church he planted must also be Spirit-empowered. Therefore, upon arriving in Ephesus, his first order of business was to ensure that the believers in that city had been baptized in the Holy Spirit. That is why he asked the twelve disciples, "Did you receive the Holy Spirit when you believed?" And

---

THE NEW TESTAMENT "STRATEGY OF THE SPIRIT"
Acts 19:1-20

◉ Empowering	➡ ➡	of the missionary of the church
◉ Witness	➡ ➡	Proclamation Demonstration
◉ Mobilization	➡ ➡	Training Sending

Figure 12.2

that is why he immediately prayed with them to receive the Spirit. This concern of Paul's surely remained throughout his entire time in Ephesus. Also, Paul must have persisted in his insistence that all of those who were being added to the church were also baptized in the Holy Spirit, and thus empowered for witness. It is also likely that Paul instilled in his disciples this same passion to see their converts empowered by the Holy Spirit.

Thus, the two essential aspects of the first pillar of Paul's missionary strategy are the empowering of the missionary and the equally important empowering of disciples in the church being planted. This twofold empowering thus laid the spiritual groundwork for the emerging missionary work of the Ephesian church. Thus empowered, the church in Ephesus was to become a powerful center of missionary activity, reaching into every corner of the province.

Pillar Two: Witness

The second pillar of Paul's missionary strategy was witness. This is to be expected, since witness is the spontaneous result of one's being empowered by the Spirit (1:8). As with empowering, witness also has two aspects: proclamation and demonstration (see Figure 12.2 above). First, Paul bore witness to the gospel through powerful proclamation. This proclamation began in the synagogue in Ephesus, where Paul "spoke boldly there for three months, arguing persuasively about the kingdom of God" (19:8). He also taught "publicly and from house to house" declaring to both Jesus and Greeks that "they must turn to God in repentance and have faith in our Lord Jesus" (20:20-21). The second aspect of witness is demonstration. Paul's oral witness was accompanied by powerful demonstrations of kingdom power through mighty signs following (19:11-20; cf. Rom. 15:17-19). No doubt, the witness of Paul's newly Spirit-filled colleagues included the same two aspects.

Pillar Three: Mobilization

The third pillar of Paul's missionary strategy was mobilization. Once the church had been empowered by the Spirit, and while the gospel was yet being preached and its power demonstrated, Paul began mobilizing the church for regional missions. This mobilization is indicated in verse 10: "This went on for two years, so that all the Jews and Greeks who lived in the province of Asia heard the word of the Lord." Without ever leaving Ephesus, Paul was able to reach the entire province of Asia with the gospel in just two years. This could only have been done by effectively mobilizing the believers in Ephesus. As with the other two pillars, this pillar also has two aspects: training and sending (see Figure 12.2, page 177).

Paul trained workers and church planters in the school of Tyrannus. There seems to be a direct link between Paul's training and the fact that in the space of only two years everyone living in Asia heard the word of the Lord. The school's curriculum must have included a strong emphasis on church planting and evangelism, and the atmosphere of the school must have been saturated with the presence of the Spirit. While the disciples were being trained, Paul sent them into every corner of the province to preach the gospel and plant Spirit-filled churches. No doubt, Paul's disciples employed the same missionary strategy as did Paul. The application of this strategy resulted in a spontaneous multiplication of churches throughout the entire region "so that all the Jews and Greeks who lived in the province of Asia heard the word of the Lord" (19:10).

New Testament "Strategy of the Spirit"

Paul's strategy for Ephesus and Asia Minor was not original with him. It was part of a larger New Testament "Strategy of the Spirit." Paul was simply following the example of Jesus when He sent His church into the world. And Jesus Himself was following the plan that the Heavenly Father used in sending His Son into the world. When the Father sent Jesus into the world, He sent Him with a clear mission, to redeem mankind. First, however, Jesus had to be empowered by the Spirit. He then ministered in the Spirit's power preaching the gospel and demonstrating the power of God's kingdom through signs and wonders.

Jesus then used the same strategy in sending His church into the world. He mobilized His followers by training them and sending them out. As they went, they were to preach the gospel and to demonstrate its power with signs following. Before they did any of this, however, they were to wait in Jerusalem to be empowered by the Spirit. This occurred on the Day of Pentecost and on many other occasions in Acts.

Paul, in his Ephesian campaign, was simply "working the plan." He was following the example of the Father in sending Jesus into the world and of Jesus in sending His church into the world.

Life Application

We as missionaries and church planters must approach our work with a well-thought-out, biblically-based strategy. Everything we do must be focused and intentional. Our labors must be aimed at planting Spirit-empowered missional churches. To do this, we must make sure that we go to the work full of the Holy Spirit, and we must further ensure that the people we lead to Christ, and the churches we plant, have also been empowered by the Spirit. Only then will these believers and churches have the spiritual dynamic necessary to spread the gospel to the surrounding areas. Further, we must preach the gospel in the power of the Spirit, expecting Christ to confirm His word with signs following. Finally, we must carefully mobilize the churches we plant for further missional ministry. We can do this through focused intentional training and the effective sending and placement of those who have been trained.

FURTHER MINISTRY IN EPHESUS

Reading Assignment: Acts 19:11-41

Chapter 12: Paul's Third Missionary Journey

The Story

During Paul's time in Ephesus, God did extraordinary miracles through him. People would take cloths that had touched his body and place them on the sick, and they were healed as evil spirits left them.

One day some Jews, the seven sons of Sceva, tried to cast demons out of a man. They commanded the evil spirits to come out "in the name of Jesus, whom Paul preaches." To their surprise one of the evil spirits spoke back to them saying, "Jesus I know, and Paul I know, but who are you?" At that, the demon possessed man jumped on them and severely beat them. When word got out about what had happened, the people of Ephesus feared and held the name of the Lord Jesus in honor. Believers then began to come forward and publically confess their misdeeds. Several sorcerers brought their scrolls and had a public burning. In this way the message grew in power and spread throughout the region.

Paul then decided to return to Jerusalem, passing through Achaia and Macedonia on his way. After that he planned to visit Rome. He sent Timothy and Erastus into Macedonia to prepare the way; however, he remained in Ephesus for a while.

About that time, an idol maker named Demetrius incited a great disturbance in Ephesus. He did this because the growth of the church was beginning to hurt his business. He whipped up a large crowd by claiming that Paul was defaming the Ephesian goddess, Artemis. Soon the entire city was in an uproar, with a wild mob repeatedly shouting, "Great is Artemis of the Ephesians!"

The crowd then seized two of Paul's companions and dragged them into the theater. Paul himself would have followed them there, but the disciples and city officials restrained him. After about two more hours of confusion and shouting, the city clerk was able to quiet the crowd. He explained how Paul and his companions had neither robbed the temple nor blasphemed the Ephesian goddess. If Demetrius and his colleagues had a complaint against these men, he said, they could file it in the courts. He then dismissed the assembly.

COMMENTARY

Success in ministry does not always bring applause; sometimes it results in bitter opposition. In Ephesus so many people were coming to the Lord that the local idol-making industry was severely impaired. Because of this, the leaders of this industry stirred up a riot against the church.

Spirit-Empowered Ministry (vv. 11-20)

Paul's ministry in Ephesus was marked by power encounters. Luke cites two examples. The first was the overcoming of demons through "extraordinary" means (vv. 11-12). The second was the almost comic result of the seven sons of Sceva's misuse of the name of Jesus (vv. 13-19). As a result of seeing the power of God displayed, many people believed the gospel and turned to the Lord (v. 20).

19:11 God did extraordinary miracles. Paul's preaching in Ephesus was accompanied by powerful manifestations of divine power. Note that the subject of this sentence is "God" not Paul. Paul was simply the channel; the miracles, however, were wrought by the power of the Spirit. Though God can, and at times will, work such extraordinary miracles, they are not to be considered normative.

19:17 the name of the Lord Jesus was held in high honor. The Spirit-empowered activities of Paul and others in Ephesus resulted in powerful witness. This is the predominant theme of the book of Acts. Because of this witness "the word of the Lord spread widely and grew in power" (v. 20). Power encounter should be a part of our evangelistic ministries.

Riot and Vindication (vv. 21-41)

As in every other case in Acts where the apostles were brought before the governing authorities, they were found innocent of any charges of treason or sedition. The vindication of the gospel and of God's messengers is a recurring theme in Acts.

19:23 a great disturbance about the Way. In Ephesus the proclamation of Christ took place in the midst of great opposition. While there, Paul wrote his first letter to the Corinthians, where he said, "I fought wild beasts in Ephesus" (1 Cor. 15:32), and "there are many who oppose me" (16:9).

19:26 large numbers of people ... in Ephesus and in practically the whole province of Asia. In spite of strong opposition, Paul and those he discipled continued to preach the gospel throughout the entire city and region. Thousands came to the Lord, and many churches were planted. Among these churches were probably the seven churches mentioned in Revelation 2-3.

Life Application

When we enter new areas to preach Christ, we can expect opposition—especially if we are successful. Local religious and business leaders will often rise to oppose our efforts to establish the church in their area. In such cases we should not be deterred. We must stay full of the Spirit and remain focused on the task that God has given us. As we do, we can expect God to confirm the preaching of the gospel with miraculous signs.

FINAL MINISTRY IN EUROPE AND ASIA

Reading Assignment: Acts 20:1-38

The Story

After the riot, Paul took time to encourage the Ephesian believers. He had hoped to set off immediately for Syria; however, because of a Jewish plot against his life, he decided to go first to Macedonia. Everywhere he went along the way, he encouraged the brothers. From Macedonia he went to Greece, where he remained for three months. With him was an international team of missionaries, including Sopater, Aristarchus, and Secundus from Macedonia, Gaius and Timothy from Galatia, Tychicus and Trophimus from the province of Asia, and Luke. Except for Luke, these men took a different route than Paul. However, they eventually rejoined him and Luke in Troas.

On Sunday the believers in Troas met to receive the Lord's Supper and to hear Paul speak. Because he was going to leave the next day, Paul talked until midnight. As he spoke, a young man named Eutychus became so sleepy that he fell from the window of the third-story room where they were meeting. Rushing down, they found Eutychus dead. Paul, however, threw himself on the young man and put his arms around him. "Don't be alarmed," he said to the people, "he's alive!" Greatly encouraged, the disciples went back upstairs and continued their meeting until morning.

From Troas Paul went by foot to Assos where he met the missionary party who had gone ahead of him by ship. The group then proceeded to Miletus, where Paul sent for the elders of the Ephesian church to come and meet with him. Knowing that this was the last time he would see them, he spoke with great affection. He reminded them of his conduct and his trials when he was with them, and how he had gone about preaching the kingdom of God, and had not hesitated to teach them everything they needed to know about following Christ. He further told them that the Spirit was compelling him to go to Jerusalem. Though he had been warned through prophetic words that he would be captured and put in prison there, he knew that he had to obey the Spirit's voice. His chief desire in life was to complete the mission that the Lord Jesus had given to him, to testify concerning the gospel of God's grace. He further told the elders that he was innocent before man and God because he had not hesitated to proclaim to them the whole will of God.

Paul then instructed the Ephesian elders to remain true to God and to the calling the Spirit of God had given them. They were to be faithful shepherds of the church, which Christ had purchased with His own blood. He further warned them that "savage wolves" would soon come in and ravage the church. Some would even arise from their midst. They should, therefore, be vigilant to guard the flock of God.

Finally, Paul committed them to God and His grace. He exhorted them to follow his example of generosity, honesty, and hard work. They were not only to take care of themselves, but also they were to take care of the weak among them, remembering the words of Jesus, "It is more blessed to give than to receive." After Paul had finished speaking, everyone knelt down and prayed. They began to weep and embrace and kiss Paul. What caused them the most grief was Paul's statement that they would never see his face again. They then escorted him to the ship, where they bid him farewell.

COMMENTARY

Paul, during his two-year-plus stay in Ephesus, had established a strong church in the city and throughout the province of Asia. He had done this by applying his missionary "Strategy of the Spirit." In the process he had mentored and trained many leaders with whom he had formed strong bonds of affection. These bonds are seen in this story. Also seen is a glimpse of some important elements of Paul's teaching ministry. His pastoral concern for the Ephesian elders, and for those to whom they were called to minister, is evident. At the heart of all that he said and did was his unswerving commitment to the calling he received from Christ. Paul evidently transferred that same commitment to these elders. Jesus said, "Everyone who is fully trained will be like his teacher" (Luke 6:40). Paul continued to move under the Spirit's direction. It was the Spirit of God who was directing him to go to Jerusalem, and eventually to Rome (v. 22; cf. 19:21). Our discussion in this section is divided into three subsections, as follows:

International Missionary Team (vv. 1-6)

Paul often moved with others in missionary teams, and often those teams were international in makeup. We see a similar thing happening today. Missions has come full circle. It is now "from all nations to all nations." Twenty-first century missionaries are often called upon to work in international teams. This requires that today's missionaries know how to interrelate cross-culturally, not only with their host cultures, but with others on their missionary team.

20:2 speaking many words of encouragement. Again, we see Paul's pastoral heart. Everywhere Paul went, he encouraged the saints.

20:4 He was accompanied. Paul's missionary team included men of at least four different nationalities. These men were traveling with Paul to help deliver the relief funds to the church in Jerusalem. They also, no doubt, assisted Paul in his missionary ministry along the way.

Eutychus Raised from the Dead (vv. 7-12)

During Paul's short stay in Troas, where he had many years earlier received his Macedonian vision, the church met to receive the Lord's Supper and to hear the apostle's words of exhortation.

20:10-12 He's alive! The raising of Eutychus was indeed an outstanding miracle. As a result of this miracle "the people…were greatly comforted." Divine healing not only alerts sinners to the power of the gospel, it also brings blessing and comfort to believers.

Farewell to the Ephesian Elders (20:13-38)

Paul's farewell address to the Ephesian elders is one of the most moving speeches in Scripture. His words are full of emotion and concern for these fellow workers. They reveal Paul's great heart—a heart filled with love for Christ and His church—and his great commitment to the cause of Christ.

20:17 the elders of the church. These are men whom Paul had trained and mentored during his two-year stay in Ephesus. They were now leaders in the church who trained and shepherded others. One of the greatest ways a missionary or pastor can extend his ministry is through the training and mentoring of others.

20:20 publicly and from house to house. Paul did not limit his teaching and preaching to public settings. His passion to communicate Christ also took him from house to house preaching and teaching the message of Christ.

20:22 compelled by the Spirit. As he had been so many times before in his ministry, Paul is again directed by the Holy Spirit (cf. 11:28-30; 13:1-4; 16:6-10). He did not proceed to Jerusalem unaware of what was to come. The Holy Spirit had given him ample warning of how prison and hardships awaited there (v. 23; cf. 21:4, 11). Again, we see the Holy Spirit acting as the Superintendent of the Harvest.

20:24 if only I may finish the race. Paul was not moved by threat of hardship, or even death. He was moved by an intense desire to complete the task that the Lord Jesus had given him, to preach the gospel to those who had never heard (cf. Rom. 15:20).

20:27 the whole will of God. While we are to preach the gospel to the lost, we are required to teach "the whole counsel of God" (NKJV; i.e, the complete teachings of the Bible) to the church.

20:28 the Holy Spirit has made you overseers. Pastors and elders are to realize that it is the Holy Spirit who made them overseers and shepherds of the church, which Christ purchased with His own blood. They must, therefore, look to the Spirit and to the word of God for direction about how they should conduct their ministries. They must never forget that church leaders will be held accountable to God for how they do their work (Rom. 14:12; Heb. 13:17; James 3:1).

20:33 I have not coveted anyone's silver or gold or clothing. Those ministers of the gospel who love money have disqualified themselves from effective Christian service. Paul was not motivated by the love of money or fine clothes. He was motivated by the Spirit of God and by love for Christ and the ones for whom He died. Paul wrote to Timothy, his son in the faith: "Some people, eager for money, have wandered from the faith and pierced themselves with many griefs. But you, man of God, flee from all this, and pursue righteousness, godliness, faith, love, endurance and gentleness" (1 Tim. 6:10-11). This is the way for true ministers of Christ.

Life Application

As ministers of the gospel, our chief desire in life must be faithful pursuit of the calling we have received from Christ. We can do this only if we will keep our motives pure, live holy lives, remain full of the Spirit, and stay true to the word of God. Every minister of the gospel must be constant in prayer and always open to the voice of the Spirit.

CONCLUSION

So ends the story of Paul's three missionary journeys. It does not, however, end the apostle's passion to take the gospel "where Christ was not known" (Rom. 15:20). Paul still hopes to visit Jerusalem, and from there travel to Rome (Acts 19:21; Rom. 1:15). From Rome he hopes to take the gospel even farther westward into Spain (Rom. 15:24, 28). Paul would indeed visit Rome, but not as he had originally planned. He would visit as a prisoner. In the next two chapters we will look at Paul's visits and ministry in Jerusalem and Rome.

QUESTIONS FOR REFLECTION AND REVIEW

1. From where did Paul begin his Third Missionary Journey? Who went with him?
2. Upon leaving Antioch, where did Paul go first? Why?
3. Describe Apollos and his ministry in Ephesus and Corinth.
4. Why does the author say that a church existed in Ephesus before Paul's arrival in Acts 19? When was this church probably started?
5. How can a careful study of Paul's ministry in Ephesus be of benefit to ministers and missionaries today?
6. Why do we say that the twelve disciples Paul found when he arrived in Ephesus were true Christians?
7. What was Paul's first question to these men when he arrived in Ephesus? What was his purpose in asking the question?
8. According to the author, for what possible reason did Paul lay hands on these disciples when he prayed with them to receive the Holy Spirit?
9. Luke's terminology in 19:6 (i.e., "the Holy Spirit came on them") reminds us of what promise of Jesus? (cf. Acts 1:8).
10. How is this incident a verification of Jesus' promise that the gift of the Holy Spirit is also to those who are "far off" (2:38-39).
11. How does the immediate results of the Ephesian disciples' Spirit baptism compare with the immediate results of the disciples at Pentecost and the Gentiles at Caesarea?
12. How successful was Paul's work in Ephesus? What accounted for that success?
13. List and describe the three pillars of Paul's missionary strategy?
14. How did Paul's missionary strategy compare with the strategy used by Jesus?
15. Describe the role of spiritual gifts during Paul's missionary ministry in Ephesus.
16. Describe Paul's relationship and meeting with the Ephesian elders in 20:17-38.

QUESTIONS FOR CLASSROOM DISCUSSION

1. On arriving in Ephesus, Paul immediately asked the disciples if they had received the Holy Spirit? Why is it so important that we often ask this question of those to whom we are called to minister?
2. What was the immediate result of the Spirit coming on the Ephesian disciples? What was the ongoing result? What results can we expect when we see the Holy Spirit coming upon and filling believers?
3. Paul had a well-formulated strategy when he arrived in Ephesus. What is your strategy for reaching the area to which God has called you? Describe the role of the Holy Spirit in your strategy.

4. Paul reminded the Ephesian elders that he had taught them "the whole will of God" (20:27). What steps can we take to ensure that we teach the whole will of God in our ministries?

Chapter 12: Paul's Third Missionary Journey

– Part V –
Jerusalem and Rome

Chapter 12: Paul's Third Missionary Journey

– CHAPTER 13 –

JERUSALEM AND TRIALS

PRE-LESSON READING ASSIGNMENT

Acts 21:1–25:32

INTRODUCTION

The Spirit was leading Paul to go to Jerusalem. He wanted to meet with James and the other leaders of the church and report to them how the work of the Lord had progressed among the Gentiles. After that he wanted to go to Rome, where he would establish a new missionary base, from where he would range even further westward into Spain (cf. Rom. 15:24, 28).

TO JERUSALEM: JOURNEY, ARRIVAL, AND ARREST

Reading Assignment: Acts 21:1-36

The Story

Leaving the Ephesian elders in Miletus, Paul and his companions, including Luke, sailed to Tyre where they met some disciples. These disciples, speaking by the Spirit, urged Paul not to go to Jerusalem. Paul and his party, nevertheless, proceeded on to

Caesarea, where they stayed with Philip the evangelist and his four unmarried daughters who prophesied.

While in Caesarea, Agabus prophesied that in Jerusalem Paul would be bound and handed over to the Gentiles. Hearing this message, everyone pleaded with Paul not to go to Jerusalem. He, however, was determined, and told them, "I am ready not only to be bound, but also to die in Jerusalem for the name of the Lord Jesus."

When Paul and the other missionaries arrived in Jerusalem, the brothers greeted them warmly. The following day Paul reported to James and the elders of the church all that God had done among the Gentiles through his ministry. Hearing this, they glorified God. They then convinced Paul to take a purification vow and join four other Jewish Christians in the temple the next day. In this way, they surmised, those Jewish Christians who were zealous for keeping the law would have nothing of which to accuse Paul.

The next day Paul went into the temple. While he was there, some Jews from Asia saw him. Because they had seen him the day before with Trophimus, a Gentile, they assumed that Paul had taken him into the temple courts. They, therefore, seized Paul and began shouting, accusing him of defiling the temple. Word spread quickly, and an angry mob gathered. Soon the whole city was in an uproar. The Jews began beating Paul, and would have killed him, had not some Roman soldiers intervened. The Roman officer then seized Paul and took him to the barracks. All along, the crowd kept shouting, "Away with him."

COMMENTARY

Journey to Jerusalem (21:1-16)

As Paul moved steadily toward Jerusalem, he was repeatedly warned that danger and imprisonment awaited him there. Some of these warnings came by the Holy Spirit. Many of his colleagues interpreted this to mean that he was not to go to Jerusalem. Paul understood their fears; however, he also knew that he was moving in the will of the Lord. He was prepared to even die in Jerusalem if necessary. His greatest concern was to obey the voice of the Spirit and complete the ministry Christ had given him.

21:7 we greeted the brothers. Paul was greeted by a delegation of brothers in Ptolemais, a city in northern Galilee. This is the first time Luke mentions a church in this city. Luke does, however, talk about the growth of the church in Galilee (9:31). Ptolemais is one of hundreds of places where the church had been planted by many unnamed Christian brothers and sisters.

21:8 Caesarea. This city was the site of the Caesarean Outpouring some 20 years earlier (10:44-46). In this verse we discover that there is an active church there. Philip, formerly one of the seven "deacons" of Acts 6, and the evangelist of Acts 8, lived there.

21:9 four unmarried daughters who prophesied. Philip had four daughters who were prophetesses. This is in accordance with Joel's prophecy, quoted by Peter on the Day of Pentecost, "Your ... daughters shall prophesy" (Joel 2:28; Acts 2:17; cf. 1 Cor. 11:4-5). Women are given the Holy Spirit for the same reason men are given the Holy Spirit, that they might preach the gospel in the power of the Spirit (Acts 1:8, 14; 2:18).

21:10 a prophet named Agabus. Prophets played a vital role in the expansion of the early church (cf. Acts 2:17-18; 11:27; 13:1-2; 15:32; 19:6; 21:9-10). On this occasion Agabus graphically, and accurately, predicted Paul's arrest and imprisonment in Jerusalem. Although Agabus' prophecy was predictive, the primary function of prophecy, according to Paul, is the "strengthening, encouragement and comfort" of believers (1 Cor. 14:3). In Acts Luke portrays prophecy primarily as Spirit-empowered proclamation of the gospel to the lost.[31]

21:11 The Holy Spirit says. To speak as a prophet is to speak for God by the inspiration of the Holy Spirit. Prophecies, however, since they always contain a human element, must be tested (1 Cor. 14:29; 1 Thess. 5:19-21; see comment on 13:3). They are to be judged by other Spirit-filled believers in harmony with the word of God. While Paul accepted the truth of Agabus' prophecy, he did not accept the interpretation others placed on the prophecy. They tried to stop him from going to Jerusalem. He, however, knew that it was God's will for him to go there, even if it meant imprisonment or death (21:12-14).

Arrival (21:17-26)

Paul's meeting with James and the elders of the Jerusalem church is significant. Remember, it was James who led the Jerusalem Council (Acts 15), and who wrote the letter that Paul and Barnabas delivered to the Gentile churches. James now rejoiced with Paul over what God had accomplished among the Gentiles. There were, however, still some traditionalists in the Jerusalem church and elsewhere (sometimes called Judaizers) who thought that one must

---

[31] For more on predictive prophecy, see comment on 11:28. For more on Luke's definition of prophecy, see comments on 2:14 and 19:6.

keep the Law of Moses to truly serve Christ.

21:19 what God had done among the Gentiles. The Greek word for Gentiles is *ethne*. It means the nations of the world. God's salvation and blessings are for all peoples and all nations (Gen. 12:3; Rev. 5:9; 7:9). It is the church's primary task to take the message of Christ to all nations before the soon coming of Christ (Matt. 24:14; 28:18-20).

21:20 When they heard this, they praised God. James and the elders of the Jerusalem church rejoiced when they heard how the Gentiles had received the gospel. We too should rejoice when the gospel is taken to the unreached tribes of the world. We should do all that we can to ensure that those tribes are reached.

how many thousands of Jews have believed. Even as the word of the Lord was spreading among the Gentile nations, the work continued to prosper in Judea, for James reported that many thousands of Jews had believed.

Arrest (21:27-36)

Paul was arrested on trumped-up charges based on innuendo and false perceptions. Nevertheless, the repeated accusations of some Asian Jews incited an angry mob of Jews wanting to kill him.

21:27 Jews from the province of Asia. These Asian Jews had probably come to know Paul during his ministry in Ephesus, where Paul endured strong opposition and persecution from both the Jews and Gentiles (Acts 19:23; 20:19; 1 Cor. 15:32; 16:9).

21:31 they were trying to kill him. Again Paul's life is in danger. Throughout his ministry he faced the prospect of pain and death (1 Cor. 15:30-31; 2 Cor. 11:25-26). Paul, however, was not driven, nor paralyzed, by his fear. He was rather moved by the love of Christ and the power of the Holy Spirit (Acts 20:22; 2 Cor. 5:14).

Life Application

There are more than a million Pentecostal churches in the world today—along with many other evangelical churches. Most of these churches are faithfully preaching the gospel of Christ. However, much like the church in Ptolemais, few know the names of those who planted these churches, or of the believers there. But God knows, and on the Day of Judgment those who have labored faithfully for Him will be lavishly rewarded.

Like Paul, we should not be motivated by fear or any other selfish concern. We should be motivated by our love for Christ and the empowering presence of His Spirit within. We are further moved by a clear understanding of God's mission and our part in fulfilling that mission.

PAUL'S SPEECHES IN JERUSALEM

Reading Assignment: Acts 21:37-23:11

The Story

When the Roman commander heard Paul speaking in Greek, he allowed him to address the crowd. Switching to Aramaic, Paul reminded his hearers of how he, too, was once a zealous follower of the Law of Moses and a violent persecutor of the church. He told them the story of how he had met the resurrected Christ on the road to Damascus and how he was converted and commissioned to preach the gospel to the Gentiles. When the crowd heard him speak about the Gentiles, they became furious, and began throwing dust into the air, shouting, "Rid the earth of this man! He's not fit to live!" Seeing this, the commander ordered a centurion to flog and interrogate Paul. Paul, however, surprised the centurion by asking, "Is it legal for you to flog a Roman citizen who hasn't even been found guilty?" Upon hearing that Paul was a freeborn Roman citizen, the commander relented and released him.

The next day, the commander called for a meeting of the chief priests and all the Sanhedrin and brought Paul to stand before them. After a brief confrontation with Ananias, the high priest, Paul presented his defense. Knowing that the assembly was divided between Pharisees and Sadducees, he said, "My brothers, I am a Pharisee, the son of a Pharisee. I stand on trial because of my hope in the resurrection of the dead." When he said this, the Pharisees (who believe in the resurrection) and the Sadducees (who do not believe in the resurrection) began arguing with one another. Finally, some of the Pharisees concluded that Paul was innocent, and asked, "What if a spirit or an angel has spoken to him?"

The assembly then fell into such confusion that the commander had to order his soldiers to rescue Paul and take him back to the barracks. The next night, the Lord appeared to Paul and told him, "Take courage! As you have testified about me in Jerusalem, so you must also testify in Rome."

COMMENTARY

Paul Addresses the Crowd (21:37–22:21)
In his address to the angry crowd, Paul did not hesitate to

proclaim the gospel. Although his very life was at stake, he remained true to his calling. This is the first of Paul's five trials in Acts. They are as follows:

1. His trial before the Jewish mob in the temple (21:37–22:29)
2. His trial before the Sanhedrin in Jerusalem (22:30–23:10)
3. His trial before Felix (24:1-27)
4. His trial before Festus (25:1-12)
5. His trial before King Agrippa (25:13–26:32).

In each trial Paul was found innocent of all charges.

21:37-40 Do you speak Greek? ... he said to them in Aramaic. Paul was a highly educated man and spoke several different languages. This ability greatly aided him in his missionary work. Language learning is a very important part of missionary work. Those who feel that God is calling them into cross-cultural missions must be prepared to learn the language of their host culture.

22:4 I persecuted the followers of this Way to their death. Paul admitted that his persecution of Christians resulted in the death of some. Paul, however, did not let his past life hinder him. He knew that he had been completely forgiven by Christ. He, rather, allowed the memory of his past opposition to Christ to motivate him to even greater service for his Lord (cf. 1 Cor. 15:9-10; Gal 1:13-16).

22:21 Go; I will send you far away to the Gentiles. Paul received this direct command from Christ in a vision (cf. v. 17). It reminds us of Jesus' Great Commission to His church to "go into all the world and preach the good news to all creation" (Mark 16:15). Paul's specific command was to go "far away to the Gentiles."

Paul the Roman Citizen (22:22-29)

When the Roman soldiers discovered that Paul was a freeborn Roman citizen, they where alarmed at how he had been treated. They immediately began to treat him with more respect.

22:25 Is it legal for you to flog a Roman citizen. As a Roman citizen Paul had certain legal rights. When it suited his purposes, he did not hesitate to use those rights, especially when it resulted in the furtherance of the gospel (cf. 16:37-40; 23:27).

Before the Sanhedrin (22:30-23:11)

Upon discovering that Paul was a Roman citizen, the Roman commander proceeded with more caution. Because he wanted to know the exact charges against Paul, he called for a meeting of the Sanhedrin.

23:6 I stand on trial because of my hope in the resurrection of the dead. Paul again testifies concerning the resurrection of the dead. As we have discovered in our study of Acts, the message of Jesus' resurrection was a central component of the gospel Paul preached (Acts 17:18; Rom. 10:9-10). He wrote, "If there is no resurrection of the dead, then not even Christ has been raised. And if Christ has not been raised, our preaching is useless and so is your faith" (1 Cor. 15:13-14). The death, burial, and resurrection of Christ are key elements of true gospel preaching today (1 Cor. 15:1-6). (See comments on 1:3.)

23:11 The following night the Lord stood near Paul. In a night vision the Lord again appeared to Paul, telling him to take courage because he must also testify in Rome. What an encouragement this must have been to Paul at this difficult time in his life.

Life Application

In times of great stress and difficulty we must, like Paul, remain focused on our mission and our message. If we will seek His face, Christ will come to us to encourage us. He will not always come in a vision, as he did to Paul in this instance, but He will come nevertheless. Jesus promised, "Surely I am with you always, to the very end of the age" (Matt. 28:20), and "Never will I leave you; never will I forsake you" (Heb. 13:5). Christ will come to us through the Holy Spirit and be our divine Comforter (John 14:16-18, KJV).

FURTHER INSIGHT: HOW THE HOLY SPIRIT
ENABLES MISSION

In Acts the Holy Spirit is actively involved in fulfilling the *missio Dei*. As we have shown in our study, He is indeed the Superintendent of the Harvest! He enables the church to fulfill its mandate to preach the gospel to all nations before Jesus comes again. He does this in at least three essential ways:

The Holy Spirit inspires mission

It is the Holy Spirit who moves the church off dead center and motivates believers to participate in God's mission. When asked why he went to the Gentiles in Caesarea, Peter answered, "The Spirit told me to have no hesitation about going with them" (Acts 11:12). When it was time for the church in Antioch to send out missionaries to the nations, the Holy Spirit moved in the church, and spoke, saying, "Set apart for me Barnabas and Saul for the work to which I have called them" (13:2). If we will ensure that our church members are filled with the Spirit, and if we will allow Him to move freely in our churches, He will inspire our people to get involved in missions.

The Holy Spirit empowers mission

Jesus said that His disciples would receive power for missional witness when the Holy Spirit comes upon them (Acts 1:8). The Spirit empowers our witness in various ways: He inspires our teaching and preaching (2:14-41; 11:22-26; 18:25), giving us boldness and insight into the gospel and into the lives of the people to whom we are ministering (4:31-33; 14:9). As we preach the gospel, He manifests His presence through spiritual gifts, including confirming signs and wonders (2:43; 5:12; 15:12). We, like the disciples before the Day of Pentecost, must faithfully wait "until [we] have been clothed with power from on high" (Luke 24:49).

The Holy Spirit sustains mission

The Spirit comes to those who are involved in fulfilling God's mission and encourages them in the work. As He did with Stephen, Paul, and others, the Holy Spirit will come to us in our times of great trial and discouragement. He will comfort us through dreams, visions, and inner works of grace (Acts 7:55; 16:9; 18:9). Through it all, as we seek the Lord's face, the Spirit will keep us focused on the mission of God. We can build ourselves up and keep ourselves in the love of God by praying in the Holy Spirit (1 Cor. 14:4; Eph. 6:18; Jude 20-21).

PLOT AND ESCAPE

Reading Assignment: Acts 23:12-35

The Story

The next morning a group of about 40 Jews hatched a plot against Paul. They bound themselves together with an oath, saying that they would neither ear nor drink until Paul was killed. They told the Jewish rulers about their plan, asking for their help. As a ruse, the chief priests and elders were to ask that Paul be brought before the Sanhedrin for questioning. The conspirators would then kill him on his way to the meeting.

Paul's nephew heard about the plot and told Paul, who called for his guard and had him take the boy to Claudius Lysias, the commander of the barracks. The boy told Lysias about the plot. That night the commander had Paul transferred to Caesarea, escorted by a detachment of Roman soldiers. He wrote a letter to Felix, the governor of Judea, telling him of the situation and stating that he had examined Paul and had found no charge against him deserving death or imprisonment.

In Caesarea Paul was handed over to Felix. When the governor discovered that Paul was from Cilicia, he said, "I will hear your case when your accusers get here." He then ordered that Paul be kept under guard in the palace of Herod.

COMMENTARY

The Plot to Kill Paul (23:12-22)

Not satisfied that justice had been done in the matter concerning Paul, a group of radical Jews conceived a plot to murder him before he could be tried.

23:12 a conspiracy. The conspiracy to kill Paul was conceived in the hearts of evil men. Its origin, however, was demonic. Jesus taught that the "gates of Hades" (i.e., the conspiracies of the devil) will not prevail against the church (Matt. 16:18).

23:16 the son of Paul's sister heard of this plot. It was no accident that Paul's nephew discovered the plot to kill Paul. The hand of God providentially arranged it. God not only directs us by His Spirit, but He also directs us by His providence.

Paul Transferred to Caesarea (23:23-35)

Guarded by a large contingent of Roman soldiers, Paul was secretly transferred in the night to Caesarea.

23:29 there was no charge against him. Throughout all of his trials Paul was found innocent of all charges. Luke wanted to show the Roman officials throughout the empire that the church was not a subversive organization, but that Christians are law-abiding citizens. This would, hopefully, help to lessen the persecution they were enduring.

Life Application

Our lives are in God's hands. We can know that at all times God is at work for us. One way He does this is by providentially arranging the circumstances and the events of our lives so that we are blessed and His kingdom is advanced. Paul wrote, "And we know that in all things God works for the good of those who love him, who have been called according to his purpose" (Rom. 8:28). Our job is simply to remain true to Him and seek to walk in the center of His will.

Chapter 13: Jerusalem and Trials

PAUL'S TRIAL BEFORE FELIX

Reading Assignment: Acts 24:1-27

The Story

Five days later, Ananias, the high priest, took with him some elders and a lawyer named Tertullus and went to Caesarea. There before Felix they presented their case against Paul. Tertullus, after an transparent attempt to flatter the governor, made his charge against Paul. "We have found this man to be a troublemaker," he said, "stirring up riots among the Jews all over the world. He is a ringleader of the sect of the Nazarene. He even tried to desecrate the temple."

When Paul was given permission to speak, he calmly denied the charges against him. He did admit, however, that he worshiped God as a follower of "the Way, which they call a sect." He testified concerning his hope in God that there will be a resurrection of the dead. He further stated, "It is concerning the resurrection of the dead that I am on trial before you today." Felix, who was himself acquainted with Christianity, deferred his decision, claiming that he wanted to first hear from Lysias, the commander of the barracks in Jerusalem.

A few days later, Felix and his Jewish wife Drusilla sent for Paul. This time Paul spoke to them about faith in Christ. He talked about righteousness, self-control, and the coming judgment. As Felix listened, he became fearful and demanded that Paul stop. "I will send for you when I can find a more convenient time," he said. Because he was hoping that Paul would offer him a bribe, he sent for him often and talked with him.

After two years Felix was succeeded by Porcius Festus. However, because Felix wanted to curry the favor of the Jewish leaders, he left Paul in prison.

Commentary

24:14 I worship the God of our fathers as a follower of the Way. Christianity is called "the Way" five times in Acts (9:2; 19:9, 23; 24:14, 22). The name reminds us of Jesus' words, "I am the way and the truth and the life. No one comes to the Father except through me" (John 14:6).

24:24 he spoke about faith in Christ Jesus. Faith in Christ is the essence of true Christianity. By this time, Paul had already written his letter to the Romans, penned while in Corinth during his Third Missionary Journey. Paul, no doubt, spoke to Felix about many of the things written in that epistle. In Romans Paul used the word "faith" 40 times and "believe" 17 times. In one place he wrote: "For in the gospel a righteousness from God is revealed, a righteousness that is by faith from first to last, just as it is written: 'The righteous will live by faith'" (Rom. 1:17).

Life Application
We should never forget that Jesus is the only way to God, both for us and for the ones to whom we minister. It is only thorough faith in Him that anyone can be saved. Christ should, therefore, be at the center of our lives, and He should be the main subject of our preaching and teaching. We must never forget that our primary task is to bring others to faith in Him.

PAUL'S TRIAL BEFORE FESTUS

Reading Assignment: Acts 25:1-12

The Story
Festus Porcius succeeded Felix as governor of Judea. Three days after arriving in Caesarea, he proceeded to Jerusalem. There he met with the chief priests and Jewish leaders, who immediately told him of their charges against Paul and pleaded with him to have Paul transferred to Jerusalem. They were planning to ambush and kill Paul on his way there. Festus, however, denied their request, saying that they could come to Caesarea, where he would listen to their charges against Paul.

The next day, after arriving back in Caesarea, Festus convened the court and summonsed Paul. The Jews who had come with Festus accused Paul of many serious crimes. They were, however, unable to prove any of them.

In his defense Paul denied that he had done anything against the Jewish law, the temple, or Caesar. Festus wanted to do the Jews a favor, so he asked Paul if he was willing to go to Jerusalem to stand trial there. Paul answered, "I have not done anything wrong to the Jews, as you yourself know very well." He then pressed his case: "If, however, I am guilty of doing anything deserving death, I do not refuse to die. But if the charges brought against me by these Jews are not true, no one has the right to hand me over to them. I appeal to Caesar!" After conferring with his council, Festus replied to Paul, "You have appealed to Caesar. To Caesar you will go!"

Commentary

25:11 I appeal to Caesar! Paul's appeal to Caesar was more than a desperate attempt to beat the charges against him. It was a calculated—and possibly Spirit-led—move to ensure that he traveled to Rome. Paul had been compelled by the Spirit to go to Jerusalem (20:22). Although Luke does not say, it is quite possible that he was now compelled by the Spirit to appeal to Caesar. The context seems to indicate that this is the case.

Life Application

As Christ's witnesses we may at times have charges leveled against us. We must live such lives, however, to ensure that these charges are always false. Jesus said, "Blessed are you when they revile and persecute you, and say all kinds of evil against you falsely for My sake" (Matt. 5:11, NKJV). Note that we are blessed only when men speak evil against us *falsely.* The Jews leveled charges against Paul, but they could not prove any of them. Paul wrote that ministers of the gospel "must be blameless" (Tit 1:6).

PAUL'S TRIAL BEFORE AGRIPPA

Reading Assignment: Acts 25:13–26:32

The Story

A few days after Paul had appealed to Caesar, King Agrippa and his wife Bernice arrived in Caesarea. Festus discussed Paul's case with the king, telling him of the recent events. He told Agrippa that the Jews took issue with Paul concerning "a dead man named Jesus who Paul claimed was alive." He further told the king how Paul had appealed to Caesar. Hearing this, Agrippa wanted to speak with Paul himself. A hearing was scheduled for the next day.

The following day Paul was brought before King Agrippa. Festus told the king how the Jews had filed charges against Paul, calling for his death. He, however, had concluded that Paul had done nothing deserving of death or imprisonment. Nevertheless, because Paul had appealed to the emperor, Festus had decided to send him to Rome. The governor, however, faced a dilemma: he had no crime with which to charge Paul. He, therefore, needed the king's help to know what to write to Caesar.

When Agrippa finally gave Paul permission to speak, the apostle began his defense. He explained to the king that his "crime" was nothing more than believing what God had promised to the fathers—that there would be a resurrection of the dead. He told of how he had once persecuted the church in Jerusalem, and how one day, while on his way to Damascus, he had encountered the risen Lord. It was then that Jesus told him that he was to go to the Gentiles.

Paul explained to the king how he was not disobedient to the heavenly vision, and how he immediately began to preach the gospel in Damascus, and later in Jerusalem and Judea, and to the Gentiles in many lands. He preached that they should repent of their sins, turn to God, and live holy lives. And now, Paul continued, "I stand here and testify to small and great alike. I am saying nothing beyond what the prophets and Moses said would happen—that the Christ would suffer and, as the first to rise from the dead, would proclaim light to his own people and to the Gentiles."

At this point Festus became so agitated that he shouted at Paul, "You are out of your mind, Paul! Your great learning is driving you insane." This Paul denied. Then, turning to the king, he said, "King Agrippa, do you believe the prophets? I know you do." Agrippa responded, "Do you think that in such a short time you can persuade me to be a Christian?" Paul replied, "Short time or long—I pray God that not only you but all who are listening to me today may become what I am, except for these chains."

Having heard this, the king and his entourage left the room. After conferring with the others, Agrippa concluded, "This man is not doing anything that deserves death or imprisonment." He then said to Festus, "This man could have been set free if he had not appealed to Caesar."

COMMENTARY

King Agrippa, also known as Herod Agrippa II, was the son of Herod Agrippa I—the one who killed James and imprisoned Peter (Acts 12:1-4)—and was the great grandson of Herod the Great. Agrippa had taken his sister Bernice to be his wife.

Paul's trial before Agrippa is his final trial in Acts. Paul's evangelistic passion is demonstrated in this story as he presses the claims of Christ on Agrippa, Bernice, and Festus.

Festus Consults King Agrippa (25:13-22)

Festus, not knowing how to handle Paul's case, consulted with King Agrippa since the king was better acquainted with Jewish customs (26:3). He was hoping that Agrippa could help him out of his predicament: he was sending Paul to Rome, but he had no crime with which to charge him. When Agrippa heard about Paul's case, he decided to interview the apostle himself the next day.

Paul Before Agrippa (25:23–26:32)
Paul's meeting with Agrippa was a fulfillment of the words of Christ to Ananias that Paul would carry Christ's name "before the Gentiles and their kings and before the people of Israel" (Acts 9:15).

26:16 to appoint you as a servant and as a witness. Jesus appointed Paul as a servant and as a witness of what he had seen and heard. Two primary activities of missionaries are to be servants of God and the people to whom God has sent them, and to be witnesses to Christ and His finished work on the cross. Verses 17-18 recount Jesus' commission to Paul to preach the gospel to the Gentiles. His commission was fivefold:

1. to "open their eyes"
2. to "turn them from darkness to light"
3. to turn them "from the power of Satan to God"
4. to see that "they may receive forgiveness of sins,"
5. to see that they may receive "a place among those who are sanctified by faith" in Christ.

As Christ's ambassadors, we have been given that same responsibility today (cf. 2 Cor. 5:18-20).

26:19 I was not disobedient to the vision from heaven. More than 20 years after first receiving his commission from Christ, Paul testified that he had remained faithful to his original vision. He had traveled thousands of miles, often on foot. He had lived in constant danger. He had been beaten, stoned, and harassed by both Jews and Gentiles. He had, at times, gone without shelter, food, water, and sleep, laboring tirelessly for the cause of Christ (cf. 2 Cor. 11:23-28). In all of this he had endured and had not lost his vision. Neither had he wavered from his original commitment.

26:20 I preached that they should repent and turn to God. Not only did Paul remain true to Christ and His mission, he also remained true to Christ's message, that is, the message of the gospel. He faithfully preached about Christ's death and resurrection and how, through faith in Him and repentance toward God, people could turn to God and find life everlasting (cf. 20:21).

Life Application
Above all else, Christ demands faithfulness of His servants. No matter what the circumstances or the cost, we must remain faithful to Christ and His calling on our lives. Paul wrote concerning himself

and his own ministry, "So then, men ought to regard us as servants of Christ and as those entrusted with the secret things of God. Now it is required that those who have been given a trust must prove faithful" (1 Cor. 4:1-2). We are stewards of the "mysteries of God," that is, the gospel, and we must faithfully preach that message, no matter what the cost.

CONCLUSION

Paul had finished his trials in Jerusalem and Caesarea. He would soon be on his way to Rome, but not as he had previously expected. When he was departing from Ephesus during his Third Missionary Journey, Paul had stated, "I must visit Rome also" (Acts 19:21). A few weeks later, when from Corinth he wrote to the Roman Christians, he told them, "I pray that now at last by God's will the way may be opened for me to come to you" (Rom. 1:10). Now, Paul was indeed on his way to Rome; however, he was going, not as a freeman, but as a prisoner.

QUESTIONS FOR REFLECTION AND REVIEW

1. What did Paul discover when he arrived in Caesarea?
2. Why do you think Luke mentions Philip's four daughters who prophesied?
3. What warning did Paul receive from Agabus and others while in Caesarea? How did Paul respond?
4. How did the elders in Jerusalem receive Paul's report concerning his missionary ministry among the Gentiles?
5. Why was Paul arrested in Jerusalem?
6. List Paul's five trials in Acts 22-26. What was the result of each trial?
7. List and describe three ways that Holy Spirit enables the church to fulfill its mission to preach the gospel to all nations.
8. Paul spoke to Felix about "faith in Christ Jesus." Explain the importance of this message.
9. What prompted Paul to appeal to Caesar?
10. According to Paul's testimony before King Agrippa, what fivefold commission had Christ given him?

QUESTIONS FOR CLASSROOM DISCUSSION

1. In Caesarea Philip had four unmarried daughters who prophesied (21:9). In 2:17-18 Peter quoted the prophet Joel, saying, "Your sons and daughters will prophesy . . . Even on my servants, both men and women, I will pour out my Spirit in those days, and they will prophesy." What are the implications of these verses concerning

women in ministry today?
2. After rereading Acts 11:28-30, 13:1-3, and 21:10-14, discuss the value of prophetic ministry in the missionary advance of the church? What are its blessings? What are its limits? How can it best be utilized?
3. Reflect on the entire book of Acts. In what ways did the Holy Spirit enable the mission of the church throughout the book? How will he enable us today?
4. Before Felix, Paul "spoke about faith the Christ Jesus." Why should faith in Jesus remain the church's central message, whether it is engaged in evangelistic or discipleship ministry?
5. Paul told King Agrippa that he preached that people "should repent and turn to God." How important is the message of repentance in our preaching of the gospel? (cf. 20:21).

– Chapter 14 –

To Rome

PRE-LESSON READING ASSIGNMENT

Acts 27:1–28:30

INTRODUCTION

Because Paul had appealed to Caesar, his path was set. In this chapter we will look at his perilous journey to Rome. In it we will see God at work through His Spirit and His providence. He will direct Paul both by the Holy Spirit and by His controlling hand over nature.

THE JOURNEY TO ROME

Reading Assignment: Acts 27:1–44

The Story

At Caesarea, Paul, under the guard of a Roman centurion, boarded a ship for Rome. With him were Luke and Aristarchus, a Christian brother from Thessalonica. Setting sail, the ship traveled northward then westward until it arrived at Myra, a coastal city of Lycia. There the party changed ships and set off again. After many days of slow and difficult sailing, they finally arrived at Fair Havens on the southern tip of the island of Crete. By this time winter had arrived, an extremely dangerous time for marine travel.

Chapter 14: To Rome

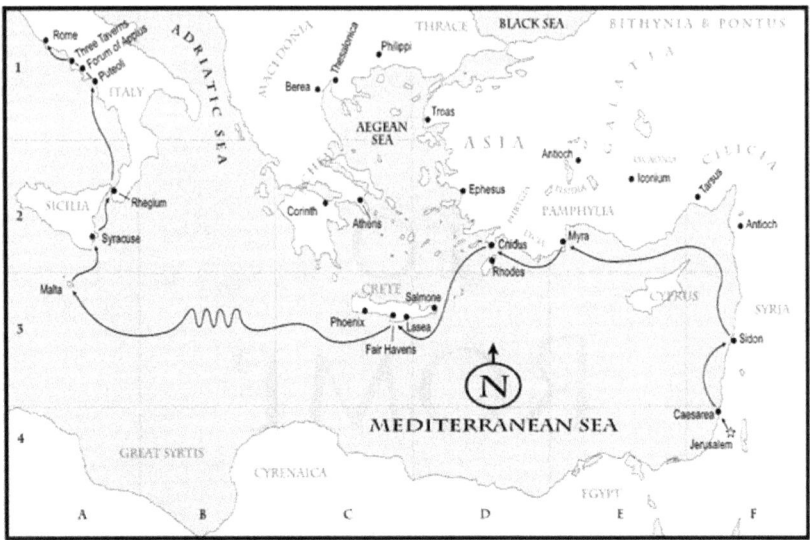

Figure 14.1 Paul's Journey to Rome ©2005 Biblical Studies Press

At Fair Havens Paul warned his fellow travelers, "Men, I perceive that our voyage is going to be disastrous, resulting in great loss to the ship, its cargo, and even to our own lives." Nevertheless, those in authority ignored Paul's warning and decided to cast off for a nearby port in Phoenix, where there was a more suitable harbor to winter in. When a soft southerly wind began to blow, the crew thought that they had attained their purpose. They, therefore, weighed anchor and sailed off to the west, staying close into the Cretan shoreline. Without warning a great storm arose, and a powerful hurricane-force wind blew in from the northeast. It drove the ship out from land into the roiling sea. Day after day the crew and passengers struggled desperately to keep the battered ship afloat. Finally, after many harrowing days, they gave up all hope of being saved.

Paul then encouraged the famished crew to eat. He reminded them that, if they had heeded his advice, this tragedy would not have happened. He urged them to take heart and put their faith in God, for an angel of God had visited him in the night and had told him not to be afraid of dying, because he must stand before Caesar. The angel also told him that God had given him everyone who was with him on the ship. The ship, nevertheless, would be wrecked on some island.

On the fourteenth night the ship did, indeed, come upon an island, and was about to run aground. Some tried to escape in the lifeboat, but Paul warned them, saying, "Unless these men stay with the ship, you cannot be saved." Then, just before dawn, Paul urged everyone to eat so they would have the strength for the ordeal ahead. He encouraged them, saying, "Not one of you will lose a single hair from his head." Then, after he had given thanks to God, they ate together. Altogether there were 276 people on board.

At daylight they spied a sandy beech and decided to let the ship run aground there. So, hoisting the foresail to the wind, they made for the beach. When the ship struck a sandbar, the bow stuck fast, and the waves began pounding against the stern, breaking it into pieces. The centurion ordered everyone to abandon the ship and head for land. In this way everyone was saved.

COMMENTARY

A Warning from the Spirit (27:1-12)

Before the ship departed from Fair Havens, Paul, speaking by the Spirit, gave the sailors a warning: If they tried to move the ship to another harbor, disaster would ensue.

27:10 Men, I can see that our voyage is going to be disastrous. It seems that Paul here is speaking by revelation. Other translations render the phrase "I can see" as "I perceive" (RSV, NKJV, NASB). The phrase likely indicates a manifestation of the gift of the word of knowledge (cf. 1 Cor. 12:8). This same spiritual dynamic may be taking place 8:23, 10:34, 14:9, 17:22, and 28:26.

27:12 the majority decided. God's will is not decided by majority vote but by the word of God and by spiritual discernment.

Hurricane (27:13-26)

27:14 a wind of hurricane force ... swept down. The sea storm was providential, that is, it was by the will of God. It was God's hand directing Paul's pathway to Rome.

27:23 an angel of the God ... stood beside me. The angel ministered to Paul by giving him encouragement and hope. Paul was then able to share that same hope with his fellow shipmates. Angels are "ministering spirits sent to serve those who will inherit salvation" (Heb. 1:14).

27:25 I have faith in God. This confession of Paul's faith sums up the core of his life and ministry. Once he wrote, "I have been crucified with Christ and I no longer live, but Christ lives in me. The life I live in the body, I live by faith in the Son of God, who loved me and gave himself for me" (Gal. 2:20). This should be the confession of every minister of the gospel.

Shipwreck (27:27-44)

After many days at sea, the ship ran aground on a remote island and broke to pieces. As Paul had prophesied, not one life was lost.

27:35 gave thanks to God in front of them all. Paul's giving of thanks in this instance served two purposes: First, it was an expression of genuine gratefulness to God. Next, it served as a witness to those who heard his prayer. Paul's confidence in God in this dire circumstance encouraged the others to trust in God also.

Life Application

How we act—or react—in trying circumstances will influence others. Paul's steadfast confidence in God encouraged others to trust in Him. If we act in confident faith, it will witness to others. They, too, will be encouraged to put their faith in God. However, if we react in fear and unbelief, others will be reluctant to trust in God. We witness to others, not only with our words, but also by the way we conduct our lives, and by the way we respond to life's problems.

MINISTRY IN MALTA

Reading Assignment: Acts 28:1-10

The Story

Once Paul and the others were safely ashore, they discovered that they had landed on the island of Malta. The islanders immediately displayed kindness. They built a fire for the beleaguered survivors to warm themselves. Paul, as was his nature, pitched in and began to help gather firewood. As he put some sticks into the fire, a poisonous snake came out and latched hold of his hand. Seeing the viper hanging from Paul's hand, the islanders exclaimed, "This man must be a murderer. Although he escaped from the sea, Justice has not allowed him to live." However, when Paul shook off the snake into the fire and suffered no ill effects, they changed their minds and said he was a god.

Publius, the chief Roman official of the island, invited Paul and his colleagues to his estate nearby and took care of them for three days. During that time, Paul prayed for Publius' father, who was sick in bed suffering from fever and dysentery. Laying hands on him, Paul healed him. When this miracle was noised abroad, the rest of the sick on the island came, and they too were healed. When Paul and his colleagues were ready to sail, the islanders furnished them with whatever supplies they needed.

COMMENTARY

The battered sea travelers were shipwrecked on the island of Malta. They stayed there for three months. During that time Paul preached the gospel and demonstrated the power of the kingdom to the inhabitants of the island. And, as was his custom, he planted a church on Malta. Thus, a providential event led to the expansion of the kingdom of God on an isolated island in the Mediterranean Sea.

Divine Protection (28:1-6)

On the island of Malta God miraculously delivered Paul from a venomous snake bite.

28:1 we found out that the island was called Malta. Malta is a tiny island in the Mediterranean Sea just south of Sicily and Italy. The guiding hand of God caused Paul's ship to wreck on a sandy beach of that remote island.

28:4 This man must be a murderer. Seeing the snake attach itself to Paul's hand, the Maltese interpreted the event according to their own pagan worldview. They assumed that Justice had caught up with Paul. Then, when he shook the snake off and suffered no harm, they changed their minds and thought that he was a god. Missionaries must be aware of, and sensitive to, the worldview of those to whom they minister. They must not, however, compromise the gospel to accommodate a people's worldview. (For another example of people interpreting an event according to their own worldview and Paul's reaction, see 14:8-18.)

28:5 Paul ... suffered no ill effects. This miracle, and the subsequent healing ministry of Paul on Malta, is a fulfillment of Jesus' prophecy in Mark 16:18: "They will pick up snakes with their hands; and when they drink deadly poison, it will not hurt them at all; they will place their hands on sick people, and they will get well."

The Sick are Cured (28:7-10)

The healing of Publius' father opened a door for Paul to minister the gospel to many.

28:8 Paul ... placed his hands on him and healed him. Healing is an integral part of the gospel message and should thus be an integral part of ministry, as Paul's ministry on Malta illustrates. A miracle of healing can open up people's hearts to hear and respond to the gospel (cf. Acts 3:11-16; 4:4; 8:4-8, 14; 9:34-35, 40-42).

Life Application

As we go into the world preaching the gospel, we should expect the Lord to confirm the word by performing miracles (cf. Mark 16:15-20). We are not only to proclaim the truth of the gospel, but also we are to demonstrate its power. We can do this only if we are daily walking in the power and anointing of the Holy Spirit.

OPEN DOORS IN ROME

Reading Assignment: Acts 28:11-30

The Story

After a stay of three months on the island of Malta, Paul and his companions put out to sea and sailed to Sicily and then to the Italian mainland. In the city of Puteoli they found some brothers with whom they stayed for a week. Leaving there, they headed for Rome. The brothers in Rome, hearing that Paul and his companions were coming, sent an advance party to greet them on the way. When they finally arrived in Rome, Paul was allowed to live by himself in his own rented house with only a soldier to guard him.

After three days Paul called a meeting of the Jewish leaders in Rome. When they had assembled, he presented his case to them, saying that he was innocent of all charges that the Jews in Jerusalem had lodged against him. He concluded by saying, "It is because of the hope of Israel that I am bound with this chain." The Jews replied that they had not received any bad reports about him from Jerusalem. Nevertheless, because people everywhere were speaking against the Christian faith, they wanted to hear what Paul had to say. So they arranged a meeting with him on a certain day.

When the day came, an even larger group of Jewish leaders gathered to hear Paul's words. From morning until evening he taught them concerning the kingdom of God. He tried to persuade them about Jesus from the Law and the Prophets. Some were convinced, but others rejected Paul's teaching. Quoting from Isaiah 6:9-10, Paul chided the Jews for their unbelief. "Therefore," he concluded, "I want you to know that God's salvation has been sent to the Gentiles, and they will listen!"

Paul stayed in his own rented house for two whole years and received everyone who came to visit him. So, boldly, and without opposition, he preached the kingdom of God and taught the people about Jesus Christ.

COMMENTARY

Arrival at Rome (28:11-16)

After the long eventful journey from Caesarea, Paul and his fellow missionaries finally arrive in Rome.

28:13-14 Puteoli ... There we found some brothers. Puteoli is a costal town about 80 miles (130 kilometers) south of Rome. The fact that Paul found some brothers there indicates that there was a church in this place. Could this have been a church plant from the church in Rome?

we came to Rome. How Paul must have rejoiced when he finally arrived in Rome. Even though he had come as a prisoner, he knew that he was moving in the will of the Lord.

Preaching the Kingdom in Rome (28:17-31)

When he arrived in Rome, Paul took every opportunity to preach and to teach about Jesus Christ, both to the Jews and the Romans.

28:23 From morning till evening. Paul's extended teaching session shows both his zeal for the gospel and the Jews' interest in what Paul had to say. It reminds us of his ministry in Troas, where he taught all night (Acts 20:7-12).

tried to convince them about Jesus from the Law of Moses and from the Prophets. Just as Jesus, after His resurrection, had taught His disciples about himself from Moses and the Prophets (Luke 24:27), Paul used the Old Testament Scriptures to teach the Jews about Jesus, their Messiah and Savior of the world. Apollos had also used the Old Testament Scriptures to prove that Jesus was the Christ (Acts 18:28). Whether preaching from the Old Testament or the New, our teaching and preaching should center on the person and work of Christ.

28:27 God's salvation has been sent to the Gentiles, and they will listen! This verse is, in some ways, a summary of the book of Acts. The salvation of God is for all peoples, and it must be preached to them in the power of the Holy Spirit (cf. Acts 1:8).

28:31 he preached the kingdom of God and taught about the Lord Jesus Christ. The book of Acts began with teaching about the kingdom of God (1:3); it ends the same way. The kingdom of God is the overarching context of the entire book (cf. 1:6; 8:12; 14:22; 19:8; 20:25; 28:23, 31).

Life Application

When a door to proclaim the gospel is opened to us, we should not hesitate to walk through it. Just as Paul did with the Jewish leaders in Rome, we must "make the most of every opportunity" to preach Christ (cf. Eph. 5:16). We should be prepared to preach the word "in season and out of season" (2 Tim. 4:2).

CONCLUSION

So ends the book of Acts. Paul has safely arrived in Rome. According to Jesus' prophecy in 1:8, the gospel has been preached in the power of the Spirit "in Jerusalem, and in all Judea and Samaria, and to the ends of the earth." Although the part of the prophecy concerning the "ends of the earth" had not been fulfilled completely, its process had begun, and it had been fulfilled symbolically.

In the next chapter we will ask, *What is the message of Acts? What does it teach us concerning our lives and ministries today?* We will also discuss some of the theological and practical issues that arise from the study of the book, such as the Pentecostal doctrines of subsequence and evidential tongues. We will also answer the important question, *How can one be baptized in the Holy Spirit today, just as were those first Christians in the book of Acts?*

QUESTIONS FOR REFLECTION AND REVIEW

1. What warning from the Spirit did Paul receive? Rather than follow the voice of the Spirit, what did the sailors do?
2. What was Paul's confession to the others in the midst of the great storm? (cf. 27:25).
3. What prophecy of Jesus was fulfilled when the poisonous snake failed to harm Paul on the island of Malta?
4. What was the result of Paul's healing ministry there?
5. Even though Paul was a prisoner, what did he do when he first arrived in Rome?
6. What was his central message? (cf. 28:23, 31).

QUESTIONS FOR CLASSROOM DISCUSSION

1. Through the Spirit Paul understood that their sea voyage would experience disaster. Can we expect the Spirit to warn us of coming dangers today? Will He always do this? What should our attitude be toward these things?
2. Paul gave thanks to God, even as their boat was breaking apart. How can our reaction to danger and threats serve as a testimony to those around us?
3. God used Paul to heal many people on the island of Malta. What is the place of divine healing in evangelistic and missionary ministry?

4. While under house arrest in Rome Paul continued to preach and teach about Christ. How can Paul's ministry in Rome serve as an example for Spirit-filled ministers today?

Chapter 14: To Rome

– Part VI –
Application

– Chapter 15 –
Pentecostal Baptism

We have completed our exegetical study of Acts. In this study we have discovered how the early church found its power and its passion for the lost in the Spirit of God. As believers were repeatedly filled with the Holy Spirit, the church became an irresistible force in the earth. It rapidly advanced from Jerusalem, a remote outpost on the eastern edges of the Roman Empire, westward across frontier after frontier until it finally arrived in Rome, the empire's capital city. In this chapter and the next, we will draw some conclusions and discuss some lessons learned from Luke's narrative.

One important lesson concerns Christian experience. In Acts Luke reveals that God's power can be appropriated into the Christian's life through a dynamic, life-changing experience called the baptism in the Holy Spirit. Let's review what the book of Acts teaches about this experience using the hermeneutical principles outlined the first chapter of this book.

SPIRIT BAPTISM DEFINED

Definition

The baptism in the Holy Spirit, according to Lukan teaching, is a universal Christian experience, separate from salvation, whose primary purpose is to empower believers for missional witness (Acts

1:8).[32] Note that there are four theological concepts included in this definition: First, the baptism in the Holy Spirit is *an experience*. Spirit baptism is more than a theological concept; it is a powerful, present-day, life-changing experience with a living God. It's full meaning, therefore, is not to be found in theological reflection, as important as that exercise is. Rather, it's full meaning can only be found in personal experience.

Next, the baptism in the Holy Spirit is a *universal experience*. On the Day of Pentecost "all of them were filled with the Holy Spirit" (Acts 2:4), thus setting the pattern for the entire church age. Explaining the experience of Pentecost, Peter stated, "The promise is for you and your children and for all who are far off—for all whom the Lord our God will call" (2:39).

Further, the baptism in the Holy Spirit is an experience *separate from salvation*. The experience is not identical with the new birth, as some teach. It is rather, as Luke clearly presents throughout Acts, an experience distinct and separate from salvation. (This issue will be discussed in more detail below.)

Finally, the primary purpose of the experience is *to empower believers* for missional witness. Jesus could have not been clearer as to the purpose of the experience when he said, "But you will receive power when the Holy Spirit comes on you; and you will be my witnesses in Jerusalem, and in all Judea and Samaria, and to the ends of the earth" (Acts 1:8). And, as we have demonstrated in this book, Luke sought to emphasize that fact in Acts by showing repeatedly how people's being filled with the Spirit resulted in powerful missional witness.

Designations in Acts

In Acts Luke uses three designations, or names, to describe the experience of Spirit baptism. Each helps us to understand something about the experience. He describes the experience as a gift, a promise, and a baptism. Let's look briefly at each of these three designations:

---

[32] Paul speaks of baptism in relation to the Holy Spirit only one time in 1 Corinthians 12:13 where he says, "For we were all baptized by one Spirit into one body—whether Jews or Greeks, slave or free—and we were all given the one Spirit to drink." In this passage, Paul describes the work of the Holy Spirit in baptizing repentant sinners into the body of Christ. In Acts, Luke uses similar terminology, however, he speaks of a different spiritual experience than Paul. He speaks of an empowering experience, separate from conversion whose purpose is empowerment for witness (Acts 1:8).

A Gift. In Acts the experience of Spirit baptism is called a "gift" four times, as follows:

- 2:38   "the gift of the Holy Spirit"
- 8:20   "the gift of God"
- 10:45   "the gift of the Holy Spirit"
- 11:17   "the same gift"

The designation "gift" helps us to understand the nature of the experience. Since it is a gift, it cannot be earned, either by achieving a certain level of good works or by attaining a certain state of personal holiness. On the contrary, it is given freely by God to all of His children (Luke 11:9-13). The only requirement is sincere asking in faith. Jesus said, "If you then, though you are evil, know how to give good gifts to your children, how much more will your Father in heaven give the Holy Spirit to those who ask him!" (v. 13).

A Promise. On three occasions Luke describes Spirit baptism as a "promise," as follows:

- 1:4   "the gift my Father promised" (literally "the promise of the Father," NKJV, RSV).
- 2:33   "the promised Holy Spirit"
- 2:39   "the promise"

Jesus also used the phrase "promise of the Father" in Luke 24:49. It each of these four instances, the designation "promise" refers to the promise made by God in Joel 2:28-29:

> And afterward, I will pour out my Spirit on all people. Your sons and daughters will prophesy, your old men will dream dreams, your young men will see visions. Even on my servants, both men and women, I will pour out my Spirit in those days.

We know this is so because it is this promise that Peter cited on the Day of Pentecost (Acts 2:17-21). The phrase "promise of the Father" could additionally refer to the promise made by Jesus when He said that the Heavenly Father will give the Holy Spirit to any of His children who will ask Him (Luke 11:13). Joel universalized the promise; Jesus personalized it. Because the experience of Spirit baptism is freely given and expressly promised, we can approach God with confidence, knowing that He will give us what He has promised (Mark 11:24; Heb. 4:16).

A Baptism. Twice in Acts the experience is described as a "baptism," as follows:

- 1:5 "you will be baptized with [or "in"] the Holy Spirit" (cf. Luke 3:16)
- 11:16 "you will be baptized with [or "in"] the Holy Spirit"

The experience is also designated a baptism in each of the four gospels (Matt. 3:11; Mark 1:8; Luke 3:16; John 1:33). Spirit baptism thus speaks of an immersion in the Spirit. When one is baptized in the Spirit, he or she is immersed in, and overwhelmed by, the Spirit of God. Baptism further speaks of initiation. Spirit baptism is an initiation—not into the body of Christ—as Paul describes in 1 Corinthians 12:13 (cf. Rom. 6:3-4; Gal. 3:27), but into the mission of Christ, as Jesus promised in Acts 1:8. Those who have been baptized into Christ, and have thus been born again, can also be baptized in the Holy Spirit, and thus be "clothed with power from on high," resulting in power for witness (Luke 24:48-49; Acts 1:8).

Descriptions in Acts

In Acts, Luke employs various words and phrases to describe the Spirit's coming upon and filling believers. Some of these descriptions point to God's work in giving the Holy Spirit; others point to the believer's response in receiving the Spirit. An investigation of these various descriptions helps us to better understand how, in Luke's understanding, the experience is given and received. They are as follows:

God's work in giving the Holy Spirit. In Acts, Luke describes the work of God in giving the Holy Spirit to believers in two ways: First, He *gives* the Holy Spirit to believers. Second, He *pours out* the Spirit on believers. Luke presents this work of God as follows:

1. God/Christ gives the Holy Spirit to believers:
   - 8:18 "the Spirit was given" (cf. Luke 11:9-13)[33]

2. God/Christ pours out the Spirit on believers:
   - 2:33 "poured out what you now see and hear"
   - 10:45 "the gift of the Holy Spirit had been poured out"

The believer's response to God's giving the Holy Spirit. In Acts Luke describes the response of believers to the Spirit's coming in

---

[33] Note: Appropriate cross references are made to the gospel of Luke.

three ways: (1) the Holy Spirit comes, or falls, upon believers, (2) believers receive the Holy Spirit, including the Spirit's power, and (3) believers are filled with the Holy Spirit. These responses are listed below:

1. The Holy Spirit comes, or falls, on believers:
   - 1:8 "when the Holy Spirit comes on you" (cf. Luke 1:35; 2:25; 3:22; 4:18; 24:48-49)
   - 8:16 "the Holy Spirit had not yet come upon any of them"
   - 11:15 "the Holy Spirit came on them"
   - 19:6 "The Holy Spirit came on them"

2. By faith believers receive the Holy Spirit, including the Spirit's power:
   - 1:8 "you will receive power"
   - 8:15 "that they might receive the Holy Spirit"
   - 8:17 "they received the Holy Spirit"
   - 10:47 "They have received the Holy Spirit just as we have."
   - 19:2 "Did you receive the Holy Spirit when you believed?"

3. Believers are filled with the Spirit:
   - 2:4 "All of them were filled with the Holy Spirit" (cf. Luke 1:15, 41, 67; 4:1 10:21).
   - 4:31 "they were all filled with the Holy Spirit"
   - 9:17 "and be filled with the Holy Spirit"

Note the logical progression concerning receiving the Spirit indicated in the above verses: First, as disciples seek the face of God, He gives the Holy Spirit to—or pours the Holy Spirit upon—them. As a result, the Spirit comes, or falls, upon these same disciples. Further, they are immersed in the Spirit's power and presence. Then, by faith, these disciples receive the Holy Spirit and are thus filled with (and empowered by) the Spirit. According to Luke, then, every believer should earnestly seek God, and joyously anticipate receiving, this blessed and powerful spiritual experience.

PENTECOSTAL DISTINCTIVES

In the book of Acts Pentecostals find the primary basis for two cardinal Pentecostal doctrines sometimes called "Pentecostal distinctives." These are the doctrine of *separability* (sometimes called *subsequence*) and the doctrine of *normative tongues* (sometimes called *evidential tongues*). These two distinctive teachings in some ways define the modern Pentecostal Movement. Let's now take a moment and talk about each.

SEPARABILITY

The doctrine of separability is the teaching that the baptism in the Holy Spirit is an experience separate from and subsequent to (if not always chronologically, at least logically and theologically) the new birth. A primary tenet of the classical Pentecostal view of separability is that the primary purpose of Spirit baptism is empowerment for mission.

The theology undergirding this biblical doctrine is based on an understanding of Luke's intent in writing Acts. He wrote to call the church back to Spirit-empowered missional witness. In Luke's portrayal, the Spirit came on the disciples at Pentecost, not to bring about their new birth, since they were already saved (Luke 11:11-13; John 15:3; 20:22), but to empower them for effective missional witness (Acts 1:8). Because Christ has called every believer to be His witness, He has also commanded every believer to be baptized in the Holy Spirit (Acts 1:4-8).

Historically, Pentecostals have sought to demonstrate the validity of this doctrine through a systematic inquiry into three incidences in Acts where disciples were initially filled with the Spirit. Those three incidences are the Samaritan Outpouring, the Damascene Outpouring, and the Ephesian Outpouring. Let's look briefly at each incident:

The Samaritan Outpouring (8:4-17)

A thoughtful reading of the story of the revival that came to Samaria under the ministry of Philip reveals that the Samaritan converts were first saved, then later received the Holy Spirit. Their conversion is indicated by three facts:

1. The Samaritans heeded the message of Christ. Luke says that the Samaritans "paid close attention" ("gave heed," KJV, RSV) to Philip's preaching of the gospel (v. 6).

2. They experienced the joy of salvation. As a result of their receiving the message of the gospel, "there was great joy in that city" (v. 8; cf. Ps. 51:12; Isa. 12:3).

3. They believed and were baptized in water: "But when they believed Philip as he preached the good news of the kingdom of God and the name of Jesus Christ, they were baptized, both men and women" (v. 12). Philip, a man full of the Holy Spirit and wisdom (6:3-5), would never have allowed these people to be baptized in water had they not been truly born again.

And yet, "the Holy Spirit had not yet come upon any of them; they had simply been baptized into the name of the Lord Jesus" (v. 16). Later, when the apostles, Peter and John, prayed for them, "they received the Holy Spirit" (v. 17). There is, thus, a clear time lapse between the Samaritans' receiving Christ and their receiving the Holy Spirit. We conclude that the two are separate and distinct experiences.

The Damascene Outpouring (9:1-9)

Saul of Tarsus (Paul) was converted on the Damascus Road. Three days later he was filled with the Spirit when Ananias prayed for him. We know that he was truly converted when he encountered Jesus on the Damascus Road for several reasons:

1. Saul called Jesus "Lord" (v. 5). Paul himself later wrote, "No one can say, 'Jesus is Lord,' except by the Holy Spirit" (1 Cor. 12:3). As Saul of Tarsus lay on the ground before the resurrected Christ, he submitted himself completely to His lordship. (See comments on 9:5)

2. He obeyed Jesus and submitted to His will (vv. 6-9). One clear proof of a person's being truly born again is submission to the will of Christ (John 14:15). Jesus commanded Saul to go into the city of Damascus to receive further instructions. Though he was blind, Saul submitted himself totally to the will of his newly-found Savior and followed His instructions explicitly.

3. Ananias called him "Brother Saul" (vv. 17; Acts 22:13). Ananias knew who Saul was and that he had come to Damascus to persecute the believers there. Ananias would have never called Saul, "Brother," unless he believed that he was indeed a brother in Christ.

It was, thus, three days after Saul became a Christian that Ananias placed his hands on him and he received the Holy Spirit (vv. 17-18). Again, as with the Samaritan believers, Saul's experience of being filled with the Spirit was distinct from and subsequent to his new birth.

The Ephesian Outpouring (19:1-7)

The twelve Ephesian disciples were saved, baptized in water, and then later filled with the Spirit when Paul laid his hands on them. The fact that they were truly converted is demonstrated by the following three facts:

1. Paul called them "disciples" (v. 1). In Luke's writings, when he uses the word disciple without a qualifying adjective (such as "John's disciples" or "disciples of the Pharisees," Luke 5:33) he always refers to the disciples of Jesus. These men were clearly Christian disciples and were likely members of the emerging church in Ephesus (see comments on 18:27 and 19:1).

2. They had been instructed to believe in Christ (v. 4). John taught his disciples "to believe in the one coming after him, that is, in Jesus."

3. Paul had them baptized in water (v. 5). If these disciples were not truly converted when Paul found them, as some claim, certainly they must have been converted before they were baptized in water.

It was after all of this that Paul laid hands on them, and "the Holy Spirit came on them, and they spoke in tongues and prophesied" (v. 6). Their Spirit baptism, as with the Samaritans and Saul, was thus distinct from and subsequent to their new birth.

Having examined these three cases, we can logically conclude that the baptism in the Holy Spirit is an experience following, and in addition to, the new birth. In each of the above three cases, the believers' baptism in the Holy Spirit resulted in powerful missional witness, as our study of the book of Acts has shown.

NORMATIVE TONGUES

The doctrine of evidential, tongues is the biblical teaching that everyone who is baptized in the Holy Spirit will speak in tongues as the Spirit gives utterance. It is also called the doctrine of normative tongues, meaning that the experience is for all Christians, of all cultures, of all times until Jesus comes again. We will first examine the doctrine from a biblical theological approach and then from the traditional classical Pentecostal approach.

Biblical Theological Approach

From a biblical theological approach the doctrine of evidential tongues finds its basis in the prophetic and charismatic character of Luke's pneumatology. Luke, in both his gospel and Acts, invariably connects the infilling of the Spirit to prophetic utterance and inspiration. The very nature of the Pentecostal gift is thus prophetic and charismatic.[34] Using a biblical theological approach we discover the following truths about speaking in tongues. We will first look at

---

[34] For extended teachings on this subject see Robert P. Menzies, *Empowered for Witness;* Roger Stronstad, *The Charismatic Theology of St. Luke*; and Denzil R. Miller, *Empowered for Global Mission.*

Luke's approach to tongues and then Paul's. Finally, we will draw some logical conclusions concerning evidential tongues.

Luke on tongues. In examining the writings of Luke (Luke-Acts) we discover the following about tongues:

- Tongues are intimately connected with Pentecostal baptism (Acts 2:4; cf. 1:4-5).
- Tongues are equated with prophetic utterance (2:16-17).
- Tongues are a prominent form of inspired speech (2:4; 10:45-46; 19:6).
- Tongues possess unique evidential character (10:45-46). In Acts tongues have "sign value" as follows: At Pentecost tongues were God's original "initial physical evidence" of the Spirit's outpouring. At Caesarea tongues were the decisive sign of God's favor on the Gentiles.
- Tongues are a fulfillment of Old Testament prophecy (2:14-18; cf. Joel 2:28-29).
- Tongues are the sign of the new prophetic community (2:4, 16-21; cf. Joel 2:28-29).
- Tongues are a powerful reminder of the church's missionary task (2:5-11).

Additionally, for Luke tongues were a powerful reminder of two facts: that the church is a Spirit-endowed, prophetic community (compare Num. 11:29; Joel 2:28-29; Acts 2:16-18), and that tongues are connected to the church's missionary task, as is indicated by the fact that the disciples at Pentecost spoke in Gentile languages (2:5-11).

Paul on tongues. In examining the writings of Paul (Romans and 1 Corinthians), we discover the following about tongues:

- Tongues are edifying (1 Cor. 14:4)
- Tongues are desirable (1 Cor. 14:5, 18).
- Tongues are universally available (1 Cor. 14:5, 26).
- Tongues are useful in intercessory prayer (Rom. 8:26).
- Tongues are a fulfillment of Old Testament prophecy (1 Cor. 14:21-22; cf. Isa. 28:11)
- There are tongues of men and of angels (1 Cor. 13:1).
- Tongues are not to be forbidden (1 Cor. 14:39).

Further, from the teachings of Paul we learn that some believers should, in the context of proper decorum, exercise the gift of tongues in tandem with the gift of the interpretation of tongues (1 Cor. 14:20-

33). We further learn that all Spirit-filled believers can and should pray in tongues during their private devotions (1 Cor. 14:4-5, 14-15). Finally, we learn that believers should practice Spirit-inspired intercessory prayer (Rom. 8:26-27). Thus, from the teachings of Paul we conclude two things about tongues: all *can* speak in tongues and all *should* speak in tongues.

Conclusions. In combining the theologies of Luke and Paul concerning speaking in tongues, we can draw the following conclusions concerning normative tongues:

- Tongues serve as the uniquely demonstrable sign of Spirit baptism.
- Every Christian should expect to speak in tongues when he or she is being baptized in the Holy Spirit.[35]

Classical Pentecostal Approach

Such an understanding of the biblical theology of tongues helps strengthen the classical Pentecostal approach to evidential tongues. This approach is based on five incidences in Acts of people being initially baptized in the Holy Spirit. In three incidences speaking in tongues is explicitly stated as occurring. (In one of these instances tongues is specifically assigned evidential value, 10:46.) In two more incidences speaking in tongues is strongly implied.

Tongues Explicitly Stated. There are three incidences in Acts where tongues are explicitly stated as occurring as a result of people's being filled with the Holy Spirit. Those three incidences are the Day of Pentecost (2:1-4), the Caesarean Outpouring (10:44-46), and the Ephesian Outpouring (19:1-7). When the 120 received the Spirit on the Day of Pentecost, "all of them were filled with the Holy Spirit and began to speak in other tongues as the Spirit enabled them" (2:4). When the Gentiles received the Holy Spirit at Caesarea, "the circumcised believers who had come with Peter were astonished that the gift of the Holy Spirit had been poured out even on the Gentiles. For they heard them speaking in tongues and praising God" (10:45-46). Here Luke assigns clear evidential value to speaking in tongues. It was "because" (Gk: *zar*) the Jewish believers heard the Gentiles speaking in tongues that they knew that they had been baptized in the Holy Spirit. At Ephesus, twenty-five years after the day of Pentecost, "When Paul placed his hands on them, the Holy Spirit came on them, and they spoke in tongues and prophesied"

---

[35] The above discussion was adapted from Robert P. Menzies, *Empowered for Witness: The Spirit in Luke-Acts,* Chapter 13. "Evidential Tongues," 244-254.

(19:6).

Tongues Strongly Implied. In addition to the three incidences in Acts where speaking in tongues is explicitly stated, there are two other incidences where speaking in tongues is strongly implied. These five incidences represent every account in Acts where people are initially filled with the Spirit. The two implicit occurrences are the Samaritan Outpouring and the Damascene Outpouring (i.e., Paul's infilling with the Spirit).

1. The Samaritan Outpouring. When the Spirit is given to the new believers in Samaria, there is no explicit mention of their speaking in tongues. Speaking in tongues, however, is strongly implied because, when Peter and John laid hands on the Samaritans to receive the Spirit, "Simon saw that the Spirit was given at the laying on of the apostles' hands." He was so impressed with what he saw that he offered them money and said, 'Give me also this ability so that everyone on whom I lay my hands may receive the Holy Spirit'" (8:18-19). What Simon saw was likely the Samaritans speaking in tongues, since this is the stated evidence in three other cases in Acts.

2. The Damascene Outpouring. When Paul was filled with the Spirit at Damascus, it is not explicitly stated that he spoke in tongues. (In fact, it does not even state explicitly that he was filled with the Spirit, which is, itself, only inferred.) Although tongues are not mentioned in this account, it is significant that Paul later claimed to be an ardent speaker in tongues (1 Cor. 14:18). When did he begin this practice? Is it not reasonable to assume that he began when he was baptized in the Spirit, as did other believers in Acts? In Acts 19 Paul laid hands on the Ephesian believers when they were filled with the Spirit and spoke in tongues (v. 6). Is it not reasonable to assume that he had received the same experience, with the same evidence, when Ananias laid hands on him?

In all of the accounts in Acts where people were initially filled with the Spirit, speaking in tongues is either explicitly stated or strongly implied. It is, therefore, logical to assume that, when people are baptized in the Holy Spirit today, they will experience the same. We are thus compelled by the testimony of Scripture to teach that speaking in tongues as the Spirit gives utterance is the normative sign for believers being baptized in the Holy Spirit.

IMPORTANCE OF THE DOCTRINES

Pentecostal scholars and historians have suggested that the movement's adherence to the doctrines of subsequence and evidential tongues has been instrumental in its tremendous evangelistic and missionary success.[36] After only one century, the movement, according to some estimates, has grown to more than one-half billion adherents in more than one million churches around the world. Pentecostals are second only to the Roman Catholic church in the number of adherents worldwide. Pentecostal scholars believe that this phenomenal success is due in large part to the spiritual dynamic that the teaching and practice of these two doctrines brings to the church. There are five reasons why the Pentecostal movement must hold fast to these clear teachings of Scripture:

1. Promotes Missional Understanding. The doctrines of separability/subsequence and normative/evidential tongues, properly taught, promote a true missional understanding of the Pentecostal gift. Subsequence reminds believers that they have been called to bear witness unto Christ to the lost, and in order to do this with the greatest effect, they must seek God for His empowering presence in their lives (Acts 1:8). Evidential tongues reminds them of the missional purpose of the Pentecostal experience. As Spirit-filled believers pray in languages they do not understand, they are reminded that they have been empowered by the Spirit to take the gospel to "every tribe and language and people and nation" on earth (Rev. 5:9; cf. Acts 2:5-11; Rev. 7:9).

2. Nurtures Desire. When purposefully taught, the doctrines of subsequence and evidential tongues can help to birth in the hearts of believers a desire to seek God for the gift of the Spirit. If believers are taught to believe that they "got it all" when they were born again, their desire for deeper spiritual experience is dampened. However, when believers are taught that there is available to them such a powerful, life-changing experience, an ardent desire is born in their hearts to seek God. As they observe others being filled with the Spirit, evidenced by speaking in tongues, their desire is intensified. Such has been the testimony of millions of Christians worldwide.

3. Creates Expectancy. When any believer, or group of believers, embrace the New Testament doctrines of subsequence and evidential tongues, it helps to produce in their hearts a strong sense of expectancy. As they pray to receive the Pentecostal gift, the knowledge that this empowering experience is available to all believers beckons them to seek God with great earnestness. The

---

[36] See: Vinson Synan, "The Role of Tongues as Initial Evidence" in *Conference Papers on the Theme 'To the Ends of the Earth' Presented at the Twenty-third Annual Meeting of the Society for Pentecostal Studies* (November 11-13, 1993).

expectation that they will supernaturally speak in tongues when they receive the Spirit heightens that sense of expectancy in their hearts.

4. Confirms Faith. When one is filled with the Spirit and begins to speak in tongues as the Spirit gives utterance, his or her faith is confirmed and strengthened. A wonderful and powerful release takes place in their spirits. They are encouraged to repeatedly ask God for His empowering Spirit. They are further inspired to allow the Spirit to speak through them as they share Christ with others. In addition, they are prepared to believe God for the manifestation of spiritual gifts in their lives and ministries.

5. Kindles Passion. Millions around the world can testify about how an experience subsequent to the new birth and evidenced by speaking in tongues has dramatically changed their lives. It had created in their hearts a passion for God, His mission, and for the lost. Now is not the time for the movement to abandon its commitment to its two Pentecostal distinctives. It is rather a time to hold fast to these important doctrines. The world awaits the gospel. And God waits for the church to move out in kingdom power and preach the gospel to all nations before Christ's soon coming (Acts 1:8; cf. Matt. 24:14).

RECEIVING THE HOLY SPIRIT

Prerequisites to Receiving

Having said all of this, we must not forget that the primary issue at hand is not merely understanding the doctrine of Spirit baptism. The primary issue is receiving the Spirit and leading others into the experience. Jesus has called us to be His witnesses, but He has commanded us to first be empowered by the Spirit. How then is the Holy Spirit received? The Scriptures teach that there are three prerequisites to one's being filled with the Holy Spirit:

1. Salvation. The first prerequisite is salvation. The baptism in the Holy Spirit is an experience reserved for believers. Jesus taught that the experience is for the Father's children, that is, for Christians (Luke 11:13). He further taught that the "world cannot receive" the Holy Spirit "because it neither sees Him nor knows Him" (John 14:17, NKJV, RSV, NASB). Since the purpose of Spirit baptism is to empower believers for missional witness (Acts 1:8), it follows that one must be born again before he or she can receive the experience.

2. Spiritual hunger. A second prerequisite for Spirit baptism is spiritual hunger. Jesus taught that "those who hunger and thirst for righteousness ... will be filled" (Matt. 5:6). One day He cried out, saying, "If anyone is thirsty, let him come to me and drink" (John

7:37). The power of the Spirit is not given to those who are casual or complacent about God and His mission. It is given to those who are passionate about the things of God. Jesus promised, "Ask and it will be given to you; seek and you will find; knock and the door will be opened to you" (Luke 11:9). Are you passionate about Christ and His Great Commission? Then you, my friend, are a candidate for Spirit baptism.

3. Consecration. A final prerequisite to receiving the Spirit is consecration of heart and life. Peter declared that God gives the Holy Spirit "to those who obey him" (Acts 5:32). In context, the obedience to which Peter was referring is obedience in witnessing for Christ in the midst of persecution (vv. 29-31). God is prepared to give His Spirit to those who will obey Him and consecrate themselves to His will and work.

Receiving the Spirit by Faith[37]

As with all of God blessings, the Holy Spirit is received by faith (Gal. 3:14). Jesus said that the Holy Spirit flows through those who believe (John 7:37-38). As you come to Jesus to be filled with the Spirit, believe that He will grant your request. He has promised that He would (Luke 11:13). There are three "faith steps" you can take in receiving the Holy Spirit:

1. Ask in faith. Jesus promised, "Ask and it will be given to you..." (Luke 11:9). Begin your quest by sincerely praying this simple prayer:

> Jesus, You promised. You said that if I would ask, I would be given the Holy Spirit. You said that everyone who asks receives. So, I ask You now, give me the Holy Spirit. Fill me and empower me to be Your witness.

As you pray, believe that God is hearing your prayer, and that, at that very moment, is answering your prayer and filling you with His Spirit. Focus your attention on what God is doing for you and in you. You will begin to sense the Spirit's presence as He comes upon you.

2. Receive by faith. The act of receiving the Spirit is closely akin to asking. Receiving, however, is a definite act of faith. It occurs at a distinct moment in time when the gift of the Holy Spirit is fully accepted and appropriated. It can be compared to Peter's step of faith

---

[37] The following instructions on how to receive Spirit baptism are adapted from the author' book, *From Azusa to Africa to the Nations*, 2005, 47-54.

when he, at the command of Jesus, stepped from the boat and began to walk on water (Matt. 14:29).

Jesus told us to ask for the Holy Spirit (Luke 11:9-13). He also told us how we are to ask: "Therefore I tell you, whatever you ask for in prayer, believe that you have received it, and it will be yours" (Mark 11:24). Do not think of this faith as a passive or future-oriented faith. It is rather an active faith, located in the immediate present. Notice that Jesus did not say, "believe that you *will* receive," He said "believe that you *have* received." The act of receiving the Spirit is a bold present-tense step of faith.

At this point, pray with complete confidence in the promises of Christ. Say and believe, "I truly believe that *I have received* the Holy Spirit!" In response to your act of faith, the Holy Spirit will fill you with His presence and power. If you will remain sensitive to what God is doing, you will, deep within your spirit, sense the Spirit's coming.

3. Speak in faith. All that remains for you to do is to speak out in faith. On the Day of Pentecost, the 120 disciples "were filled with the Holy Spirit *and began to speak* ..." (Acts 2:4). As they spoke, the Spirit flowed into, through, and out of them. As a result, they "began to speak in other tongues as the Spirit enabled them." When you are filled with the Spirit, you too should expect to speak in tongues. Further, you should expect the Spirit to come upon you again and again empowering you to speak for Christ.

SPEAKING IN TONGUES

You should know, however, that, when you speak in tongues, the words you speak will not come from your mind, as in natural speech, but from deep inside, from your spirit. Jesus said, "Whoever believes in me, as the Scripture has said, streams of living water will flow from within him" (John 7:38). Speaking in tongues is not an activity of the human mind but of the human spirit. It is not a mental but a spiritual exercise. It proceeds from one's "innermost being" (NASB), that is, from his spirit. Paul wrote, "For anyone who speaks in a tongue does not speak to men but to God. Indeed, no one understands him; he utters mysteries with his spirit" (1 Cor. 14:2). He further stated, "For if I pray in a tongue, my spirit prays, but my mind is unfruitful" (v. 14).

When you come to God to be filled with the Spirit, you should relax and open your heart fully to Him. Then, in faith ask for the Holy Spirit, fully expecting God to answer your prayer. As you wait on God, sense the presence of the Spirit coming upon you. Then, through a conscious act of faith, believe that you have received. You will sense the Spirit's powerful presence deep within, filling and empowering you. By this you will know that God is indeed filling you with the Holy Spirit! You should, at this point, begin to *speak from the Presence,* that is, from where you sense God's presence deep within. It will not be a forced effort, but a natural flow of supernatural words. You should simply allow it to happen, and cooperate fully with the Spirit by boldly speaking out in faith. You will begin to speak words you do not understand, words that are coming from the Spirit of God.

Although no two people's Spirit baptisms are exactly the same, everyone can expect certain things to happen. First, as mentioned above, you will speak in tongues as the Spirit enables (Acts 2:4; 10:44-46; 19:6). Second, you will receive zeal and boldness to share Christ with others (Acts 2:14, 4:31). In addition, you can expect a greater awareness of the Spirit's presence in your life. There will be a greater liberty in worship and prayer (2 Cor. 3:17; Eph. 5:18-20) and an increased flow of the Spirit, resulting in more effective ministry (John 7:37-38).

CONCLUSION

We have no valid scriptural warrant, as some have taught, to believe that the power appropriated by the early church is no longer available to Christians today. We today can receive the same power as did those first disciples on the Day of Pentecost. That power comes as we open our lives fully to the work of the Holy Spirit. Jesus promised His disciples, "Ask and it will be given to you ... for everyone who asks receives" (11:9-10). That promise still applies today. We too can be "clothed with power from on high" (Luke 24:49). Simply ask, believe, and receive!

QUESTIONS FOR REFLECTION AND REVIEW

1. Discuss the four theological concepts found in a proper definition of Spirit baptism.
2. Cite four references in Acts where Spirit baptism is defined as a gift.
3. Cite three references in Acts where Spirit baptism is defined as a promise.
4. Cite two references in Acts where Spirit baptism is defined as a baptism.
5. Based on your study of the references cited in Question 2 above, describe how God works in giving the Holy Spirit to believers.
6. Based on your study of the references cited in Question 3 above, describe how a believer responds to God in receiving Spirit baptism.

7. Define and demonstrate the Pentecostal doctrinal distinctive of separability/subsequence.
8. Define and demonstrate the Pentecostal doctrinal distinctive of normative/evidential tongues.
9. Demonstrate the validity of the doctrine of normative/evidential tongues by using both a biblical and a systematic theological approach.
10. List and discuss three truths that demonstrate the importance of the Pentecostal doctrines of separability and evidential tongues.
11. List and discuss three prerequisites for receiving Spirit baptism.
12. List and discuss three "faith steps" one can take to receive Spirit baptism.
13. Discuss this statement: "Speaking in tongues is not an activity of the human mind but of the human spirit."

QUESTIONS FOR CLASSROOM DISCUSSION

1. Why is it important that we as ministers and missionaries understand Luke's unique emphasis on Spirit baptism as an experience for all believers, subsequent to salvation, whose purpose is empowerment for witness? How does this understanding affect the way we do missions?
2. What are some implications of Spirit baptism being a "gift" from God?
3. How can a proper understanding of God's work in giving the Holy Spirit and the believer's response in receiving the Spirit aid someone in being filled with the Holy Spirit?
4. What would be the effect on the missionary advance of the church if Pentecostals abandoned or modified their doctrinal stance on subsequence and evidential tongues?
5. Have you been baptized in the Holy Spirit according to Acts 1:8 and 2:4? Are you, as a minister of the gospel, faithfully preaching and teaching on the subject and leading people into Spirit baptism? Why or why not?

CHAPTER 16

THE MESSAGE OF ACTS

We near the end of our study. From the book of Acts we have learned many things. Most importantly, we have learned about God's mission and how the first-century church went about fulfilling that mission. Hopefully, we have applied what we have learned to our own lives and ministries. And hopefully, we have personally experienced the same power of God in our own lives as did the apostles and early disciples. As we end our study, we ask a final question: What is the message of Acts for the church today?

THE MESSAGE OF ACTS

The messages of Acts can be said to be as numerous as its readers, for, like any part of God's word, the Holy Spirit can take and apply the individual passages and incidences of the book to the specific situations of the reader. If, however, we are to take Acts seriously, we must find its message in the book's literary and historical context. Before we can really know what Acts has to say to us today, we must first determine what it had to say to its first-century readers.

In this study we have discovered that Luke wrote with clear purpose. That purpose was then, and remains today, the primary message of Acts. Luke's primary purpose in writing Acts is found in 1:8, the hermeneutical key to the book: "But you will receive power when the Holy Spirit comes on you; and you will be my witnesses in Jerusalem, and in all Judea and Samaria, and to the ends of the earth." Luke thus wrote to call the church back to its Pentecostal and missionary roots.

Remember, Luke wrote to a second generation of Christians who lived remotely from Jerusalem. These believers, because of the persecution they were enduring, had lost their spiritual fervor and missionary zeal. In Luke's mind, they desperately needed to hear (or to hear again) the story of the church's powerful beginning and irresistible missionary advance. Luke thus wrote to demonstrate to his original readers the absolute necessity of the church, including every member, being empowered by the Holy Spirit.

He further wrote to demonstrate that such an empowering comes as a result of a powerful spiritual experience called the baptism in the Holy Spirit. If Luke's readers would be thus empowered, and remain resolutely focused on, and radically committed to, Christ's mission, they too could become a powerful missionary force, fully equipped to proclaim the gospel at home and abroad, just like the first church. What's more, this could happen even in the midst of severe persecution.

This, then, is the message of Acts. It is the same for us today as it was for those first-century believers: If we are to powerfully participate in Christ's mission to take the gospel to all nations before His soon return, we, too, must be empowered by the Holy Spirit. We as church leaders, missionaries, and pastors must work tirelessly to ensure that in our churches every member has been clothed with power from on high. And we must further work to ensure that our congregations clearly understand the church's—and thus their—mission in the world. If we will do these things, we will have gone a long way to making the church the effective force in the earth Christ intended for it to be.

A MISSIONS STRATEGY FOR THE TWENTY-FIRST CENTURY

Acts can also serve as a manual for missions strategy for today's church. In it we find the "strategy of the Spirit" employed by the early missionaries—especially Paul. It was a strategy that transformed a small group of beleaguered disciples into an unstoppable global missions force in just a few years time.[38]

We have learned that any missionary strategy aimed at effectively penetrating an unreached area with the gospel must contain certain essential elements, including the empowering presence of the Holy Spirit and a clear and convincing declaration of the gospel with signs following. An effective strategy must also include the intentional planting of Spirit-empowered missional churches. In these churches new disciples will be empowered by the Spirit, equipped to reach the lost and plant other Spirit-empowered missional churches, and then, mobilized and sent near and far to proclaim Christ to those who have not yet heard the good news.

TODAY'S CHALLENGE

The church faces a great challenge. More than two thousand years ago Jesus commissioned His church to take the gospel to every nation and people on earth (Matt. 28:18-20; cf. 24:14). Today, as never before, that goal is within reach. Missiologists today talk of *closure,* or completing Christ's commission.

According to the Joshua Project, there remain 6,871 people groups who have yet to be adequately reached with the gospel.[39] The Joshua Project defines an unreached people group as "a people group among which there is no indigenous community of believing Christians with adequate numbers and resources to evangelize this people group." Who will reach these yet-to-be-reached peoples with the gospel of Christ? As did the prophet of old, we must answer, "Here am I. Send me!" (Isa. 6:8).

Today Christian missions is in transition. Once, missions flowed almost entirely "from the West to the rest," that is, from America and western Europe to the rest of the world. But today this is no longer the case. Now, with Christian churches worldwide mobilizing for missions, the face of missions is quickly changing. Missions can now be best described as "from all nations to all nations." With ever more churches rising up and boldly proclaiming, "Missions—we can do it, too!" closure is more doable than ever.

New technological tools and techniques are enhancing the church's ability to spread the good news. The church now utilizes computers, the Internet, and the mass media to reach the lost and

---

[38] Paul's missionary "Strategy of the Spirit" was discussed in chapter 12, "Paul's Third Missionary Journey."

[39] Joshua Project Website: http://www.joshuaproject.net/ accessed February 3, 2011.

penetrate unreached areas with the gospel. Leadership studies abound, teaching the latest leadership and managerial techniques to missionaries and pastors.

We must not neglect any of these means that can enhance our effectiveness in reaching the nations. However, in the midst of these methodological advances, the church faces a great challenge. In acquiring all of the latest technology and leadership methods, we can be tempted to abandon our divine resource—the power of the Holy Spirit. The book of Acts speaks forcefully to this issue.

While not neglecting any means at our disposal, we must again ask the question, "How can we recapture the same power and zeal of those first-century Christians?" Even though they were poor, isolated, and possessed none of the modern technological aids we have today (even the printing press would not be invented for fourteen hundred years!), in a short time, they subdued the Roman Empire and changed the course of history.

How did they do it? The book of Acts answers our question: *They were filled with the Holy Spirit!* The secret of the New Testament church's success was that it was empowered by the Spirit of God and radically committed to the mission of God. Those first disciples were convinced that the power of God came as a result of a powerful life-changing experience—the baptism in the Holy Spirit. Just as Jesus had demanded that His disciples be filled with the Holy Spirit before they began their ministries, the apostles demanded that their disciples be filled with the Spirit before they began their ministries. In that way, the work would continue to progress and move forward unabated.

The book of Acts teaches us that the hope of bringing closure to the Great Commission does not lie in any humanly-devised means. It lies, rather, in our commitment to remain committed on the mandate of Christ, and our insistence that every believer be empowered by the Holy Spirit. We must herald the message of Jesus far and wide: "You will receive power when the Holy Spirit comes on you; and you will be my witnesses in Jerusalem, and in all Judea and Samaria, and to the ends of the earth" (Acts 1:8).

QUESTIONS FOR REFLECTION AND REVIEW

1. Why did Luke write Acts?
2. What is the message of the book of Acts for the church today?
3. How important is the baptism in the Holy Spirit in fulfilling the mission of God?

Chapter 16: The Message of Acts

QUESTIONS FOR CLASSROOM DISCUSSION

1. In your own words, summarize the message of the book of Acts for the church today.
2. How can Acts serve as a book of strategy for the twenty-first century church?
3. What doctrines and practices taught in the book of Acts are being neglected by the church today? What steps should be taken to remedy this situation?
4. In light of what you have learned from this study, what is the greatest challenge for the Pentecostal church today?

Chapter 16: The Message of Acts

– Appendix 1 –

Episodes in Acts[40]

Definitions:

- *Episode:* A story which is complete in itself but is itself part of a larger story.
- *Episodic Series:* A series of episode which form a complete story in themselves but are part of a yet larger story.

Episode	Text/Date

Episodic Series 1: Beginnings in Jerusalem
Introductory words (Summary Statement 1) (1:1-4)

1.	Final instructions	1:5-8
2.	The ascension of Christ	1:8-11
3.	In the upper room	1:12-26
4.	Pentecost: **The First Jerusalem Outpouring**	2:1-42
		A.D. 28

Summary Statement 1 (2:43-47)

5.	Healing at the Beautiful Gate	3:1–4:3

Summary Statement 2 (4:4)

6.	The trial and release of Peter and John	4:5-22
7.	**The Second Jerusalem Outpouring**	4:23-31

Summary Statement 3 (4:32-35)

8.	Barnabas/Ananias and Sapphira	4:36-5:10

Summary Statement 4 (5:11-16)

9.	The apostles are imprisoned, threatened, and released	5:17-41

Summary Statement 5 (5:42)

10.	The seven are chosen	6:1-6

Summary Statement 6 (6:7)

11.	Stephen's capture, sermon, and martyrdom	6:8-7:60a
12.	Saul is introduced	7:60b-8:3

Summary Statement 7: (8:4)

Episodic Series 2: Outreach in Samaria

13.	Philip's revival in Samaria and	8:4-24
	The Samaritan Outpouring	8:14-17

---

[40] Appendix 1 is taken from the author's book, *Empowered for Global Mission: A Missionary Look at the Book of Acts,* pp 339-343.

Appendix 1: Episodes in Acts

	A.D. 31
14. Philip and the Ethiopian	8:25-39
15. Philip preaches from Azotus to Caesarea	8:40

Episodic Series 3: Saul's Conversion and Early Ministry
16. The conversion of Saul	9:1-9
17. The commissioning and empowering of Saul, including	
The Damascene Outpouring	9:10-19
	A.D. 32
18. Saul in Damascus	9:20-25
19. Saul in Jerusalem	9:26-30
Summary Statement 8 (9:31)	

Episodic Series 5: Peter's Ministry in Greater Judea
20 Peter's ministry in Judea	9:32-43
21 **The Caesarean Outpouring**	10:1-48
	A.D. 34
22 Peter reports to Jerusalem	11:1-18

Episodic Series 6: Intervening Events
23 The church at Antioch	11:19-26
24 A great famine	11:27-30
25 Peter arrested and delivered	12:1-19
26 Herod judged by God	12:20-23
Summary Statement 9 (12:24)	

Episodic Series 7: Paul's First Missionary Tour
27 Paul and Barnabas sent out and	
The Antiochian Outpouring	13:1-4a
	A.D. 45
28 Ministry in Cyprus	13:4b-12
29 Ministry in Pisidian Antioch	13:13-43
30 Driven out of Antioch	13:44-51
Summary Statement 10 (13:52)	
31 Ministry in Iconium	14:1-5
Summary Statement 11 (14:6-7)	
32 Ministry in Lystra and Derbe	14:8-20
33 Strengthening the churches	14:21-26
34 "Missions convention" in Antioch	14:27
Summary Statement 12 (14:28)	

Episodic Series 8: The Jerusalem Council
35 The council at Jerusalem	15:1-29
36 Report and ministry in Antioch	15:30-34
Summary Statement 13 (15:35)	

Episodic Series 9: Paul's Second Missionary Tour
37 Dispute over John Mark	15:35-41

Appendix 1: Episodes in Acts

38	Timothy is chosen and circumcised	16:1-3
	Summary Statement 14 (16:4-5)	
39	The Holy Spirit directs the missionaries	16:4-12
40	Ministry in Philippi	16:13-40
41	Conversion of Lydia	—:13-15
42	Demonized girl delivered	—:16-18
43	Paul and Silas delivered from prison	—:19-40
44	Ministry in Thessalonica	17:1-9
45	Ministry in Berea	17:10-15
46	Ministry in Athens	17:16-34
47	Ministry in Corinth	18:1-17
48	Journey back to Antioch	18:18-23

Episodic Series 10: Paul's Third Missionary Tour (Ephesus)

49	The story of Apollos	18:24-28
		A.D. 53
50	Ministry in Ephesus	19:1-20:1
	The Ephesian Outpouring	—:1-7
51	Missionary outreach to Asia	—:8-10
52	Challenging sorcery	—:11-19
	Summary Statement 15 (19:20)	
53	Disturbance in Ephesus	19:20-20:1

Episodic Series 11: Journey to Jerusalem

54	Travels through Macedonia, Greece, Troas	20:1-6
55	Ministry in Troas (Eutychus healed)	20:7-12
56	Journey to Miletus	20:13-16
57	Farewell to Ephesian elders	20:17-38
58	Journey to Jerusalem	21:1-13
59	Prophecy of Agabus	21:10-14

Episodic Series 12: Trials

60	Paul at Jerusalem	21:15-23:10
	—Report to James and the Elders	—:17-26
	—Paul seized in the temple	—:27-36
	—Paul's defense in the temple	21:37-22:30
	—Paul before the Jewish Council	23:1-10
61	Vision of the Lord in the night	23:11
62	Plot to kill Paul, transfer to Caesarea	23:12-35
63	Paul before Felix	24:1-27
64	Paul before Festus	25:1-22
65	Paul before Agrippa	25:23-26:32

Episodic Series 13: Journey to Rome

66	Journey to Rome	27:1-8
67	Shipwreck	27:9-44

68	Ministry at Malta	28:1-10
	—Snakebite	—:1-6
	—Healing of Publius and others	—:7-10
69	Journey through Italy to Rome	28:11-15

Episodic Series 14: Ministry in Rome

70	Ministry in Rome	28:16-31
	—To the Jewish leaders	—:16-29
	—Two full years of unhindered preaching	—:30-31

– APPENDIX 2 –
SPIRITUAL GIFTS IN ACTS

Revelation Gifts in Acts		
Category	**Event**	**Reference**
Readiness to receive healing revealed	• Revelation at the Beautiful Gate. • The Spirit reveals the lame man's faith to Paul.	Acts 3:4 Acts 14:8-11
Motive of a person's heart revealed	• Ananias and Sapphira's deception Revealed. • The intention of Simon's heart is revealed to Peter.	Acts 5:3-6, 7-11 Acts 8:18-23
Seeing into the spiritual realm	• Stephen sees into heaven.	Acts 7:55-56
Divine guidance received	• Philip receives guidance. • The vision of Ananias. • Peter testifies in Jerusalem concerning the Spirit's guidance. • Paul is directed by the Spirit to Macedonia. • The Spirit directs Paul to go to Jerusalem.	Acts 8:26-30 Acts 9:10-17 Acts 11:12 Acts 16:6-10 Acts 19:21
The presence of visitors revealed	• The presence of Visitors is revealed to Peter.	Acts 10:19
God's will revealed	• God's will for the Gentiles is revealed to Peter. • Peter testifies concerning His revelation. • The Lord tells Paul that he will go to the Gentiles. • It is revealed to Paul that he must go to Rome.	Acts 10:9-17 Acts 10:27-29 Acts 22:21 Acts 23:11

Revelation Gifts in Acts (Continued)		
Category	**Event**	**Reference**
Future events revealed	• The Holy Spirit reveals to Paul what awaits him in Jerusalem.	Acts 20:22-23
	• The Spirit reveals to Paul that the voyage will be with great loss.	Acts 27:9-10
	• God reveals the fate of the ship to Paul	Acts 27:21-26
	• The believers warn Paul "through the Spirit"	Acts 21:4
Warning of danger given	• The Spirit warns Paul to leave Jerusalem.	Acts 22:17-18

Appendix 2: Spiritual Gifts in Acts

Prophetic Gifts in Acts		
Category	**Event**	**Reference**
Speaking in tongues	• Tongues at Pentecost. • Tongues and prophetic speech at Caesarea. • Tongues and prophetic speech at Ephesus	Acts 2:4 Acts 10:46 Acts 19:6
Prophetic proclamation	• Peter's *pneuma* discourse • Peter's second *pneuma* discourse. • Bold proclamation following the Second Jerusalem Outpouring. • Powerful proclamation in Jerusalem. • Stephen's *pneuma* discourse • The persuasive preaching of Saul (Paul). • Paul and Barnabas' bold proclamation in Iconium. • Paul's bold proclamation in Ephesus.	Acts 2:14 Acts 4:8 Acts 4:31 Acts 4:33 Acts 6:10; 7:1-53 Acts 9:22 Acts 14:3 Acts 19:8
Predicting the future	• Prophecy of Agabus. • Prophets warn Paul in Tyre. • Agabus prophesies in Caesarea.	Acts 11:28 Acts 21:4 Acts 21:10
Launching a missionary journey	• The Holy Spirit speaks through prophets in Antioch.	Acts 13:1-4
Women prophets	• Philips four daughters.	Acts 21:9

Appendix 2: Spiritual Gifts in Acts

Power Gifts in Acts		
Category	**Event**	**Reference**
Signs and wonders	• Wonders and signs through the apostles. • Signs and wonders. • Stephen performs great wonders and signs. • Philip Performs signs, casts out demons, and heals the sick. • God grants Paul and Barnabas signs and wonders. • Paul and Barnabas testify concerning signs and wonders.	Acts 2:43 Acts 5:12-13 Acts 6:8 Acts 8:6-8 Acts 14:3 Acts 15:12
Healing	• A Cripple is healed. • Many healed and delivered. • Philip performs signs, casts out demons and heals the sick. • Simon observes signs and miracles. • Ananias heals Saul. • Peter heals Aeneas. • Lame man is Lystra is healed. • Paul is healed in Iconium. • Paul testifies about his healing by Ananias. • Paul heals the father of Publius and many others.	Acts 3:6-7 Acts 5:13-16 Acts 8:6-8 Acts 8:13 Acts 9:17-18 Acts 9:34-35 Acts 14:8-10 Acts 14:19-20 Acts 22:13 Acts 28:8-9
Demonic deliverance	• Many are healed and delivered. • Philip performs signs, casts out demons, and heals the sick. • Paul casts a demon out of a slave girl.	Acts 5:13-16 Acts 8:6-8 Acts 16:16-18

Power Gifts in Acts (Continued)		
Category	Event	Reference
Raising the dead	• Peter raises Dorcas from the Dead. • Eutychus is raised by Paul.	Acts 9:40-42 Acts 20:9-10
Extraordinary miracles	• Peter's shadow heals the sick. • Extraordinary miracles of healing and exorcism are done by Paul. • Paul is delivered from a snake bite.	Acts 5:15 Acts 19:11-12 Acts 28:3-5

– RECOMMENDED READING –

Arrington, French, L. *The Acts of the Apostles: An Introduction and Commentary.* Peabody, MA: Hendrickson Publishers, Inc., 1988.

_____. "Acts of the Apostles." In *The Full Life Bible Commentary to the New Testament.* Edited by French L. Arrington and Roger Stronstad. Grand Rapids, MI: Zondervan Publishing House, 1999.

_____. "Luke." In *The Full Life Bible Commentary to the New Testament.* Edited by French L. Arrington and Roger Stronstad. Grand Rapids, MI: Zondervan Publishing House, 1999.

Assemblies of God, "The Initial Physical Evidence of the Baptism in the Holy Spirit." In *Where We Stand: The Official Position Papers of the Assemblies of God.* Springfield, MO: Gospel Publishing House, 1997.

Bennett, Dennis and Rita Bennett. *The Holy Spirit and You: A Study Guide to the Spirit-Filled Life.* Plainfield, NJ: Logos International, 1971.

Bruce, F. F. *The Book of the Acts,* rev. ed. Grand Rapids, MI: William B. Eerdmans Publishing Co., 1988.

Ervin, Howard M. *Spirit Baptism: A Biblical Investigation.* Peabody, MA: Hendrickson Publishers, Inc., 1987.

Gee, Donald. "Spiritual Gifts in World Evangelization." In *Azusa Street and Beyond: Pentecostal Missions and Church Growth in the Twentieth Century.* Edited by L. Grant McClung, Jr. South Plainfield, NJ: Bridge Publishing, 1986.

Horton, Stanley M. *What the Bible Says about the Holy Spirit.* Springfield, MO: Gospel Publishing House, 1989.

_____. *The Book of Acts: The Wind of the Spirit.* Springfield, MO: Gospel Publishing House, 1996.

Jepson, J. W. *What You Should Know About the Holy Spirit.* Springfield, MO: Gospel Publishing House, 1986.

Johns, Donald A. "Some New Directions in Hermeneutics of Classical Pentecostalism's Doctrine of Initial Evidence." In *Initial Evidence: Historical and Biblical Perspectives on the Pentecostal Doctrine of Spirit Baptism.* Edited by Gary B. McGee. Peabody, MA: Hendrickson Publishers, Inc., 1991.

Appendix 2: Spiritual Gifts in Acts

Klaus, Byron D. "The Mission of the Church." In *Systematic Theology,* rev. ed. Stanley M. Horton, ed. Springfield, MO: Logion Press, 1995.

Menzies, William W. and Robert P. Menzies, *Spirit and Power: Foundations of Pentecostal Experience.* Grand Rapids, MI: Zondervan Publishing House, 2000.

Michaels, J. Ramsey. "Luke-Acts." In *Dictionary of Pentecostal and Charismatic Movements.* Grand Rapids, MI: Regency Reference Library, Zondervan Publishing House, 1988.

Miller, Denzil R. *Power Ministry: A Handbook for Pentecostal Preachers.* Springfield, MO: Africa's Hope, 1998.

_____. *Empowered for Global Mission: A Missionary Look at the Book of Acts.* Springfield, MO: Life Publishers, 2005.

_____. *Acts: The Spirit of God in Mission.* Springfield, MO: Africa's Hope, 2007.

_____. *In Step with the Spirit: Studies in the Spirit-filled Walk.* Springfield, MO: AIA Publications, 2008.

_____. *The Kingdom and the Power: The Kingdom of God: A Pentecostal Interpretation.* Springfield, MO: AIA Publications, 2009.

_____. *Experiencing the Spirit: A Study of the Work of the Holy Spirit in the Believer.* Springfield, MO: AIA Publications, 2009.

_____. *Power Encounter: Ministering in the Power and Anointing of the Holy Spirit: Revised.* Springfield, MO: AIA Publications, 2009.

_____. *You Can Minister in the Spirit's Power: A Guide for Spirit-filled Disciples.* Springfield, MO: AIA Publications, 2009.

_____. *The 1:8 Promise of Jesus: The Key to World Harvest.* Springfield, MO. PneumaLife Publications, 2012.

Palma, Anthony D. *Baptism in the Holy Spirit.* Springfield, MO: Gospel Publishing House, 1999.

_____. *The Holy Spirit: A Pentecostal Perspective.* Springfield, MO: Logion Press, 2001.

Riggs, Ralph M. *The Spirit Himself.* Springfield, MO: Gospel Publishing House, 1977.

Stott, John R. W. *The Message of Acts: The Spirit, the Church and the World.* Leichester, ENG: Inter-Varsity Press, 1990.

Stamps, Donald. Study notes and articles for "Acts." In *The Full Life Study Bible.* Springfield, MO: Life Publishers International, 1990.

Stronstad, Roger. *The Charismatic Theology of St. Luke.* Peabody, MA: Hendrickson Publishers, Inc., 1984.

_____. *Spirit, Scripture, and Theology: A Pentecostal Perspective.* Baguio City, Philippines: Asia Pacific Theological Seminary Press, 1995.

_____. *The Prophethood of All Believers: A Study in Luke's Charismatic Theology.* Irving, TX: ICI University Press, 1997.

Synan, Vinson. "The Role of Tongues as Initial Evidence." In *Conference Papers on the Theme 'To the Ends of the Earth' Presented at the Twenty-third Annual Meeting of the Society for Pentecostal Studies,* November 11-13, 1993.

Williams, J. Rodman. "Baptism in the Holy Spirit." In *Dictionary of Pentecostal and Charismatic Movements.* Grand Rapids, MI: Regency Reference Library, Zondervan Publishing House, 1988.

Wagner, C. Peter. *The Acts of the Holy Spirit: A Modern Commentary on the Book of Acts.* Ventura, CA: Regal Books, 2000.

York, John V. *Missions in the Age of the Spirit.* Springfield, MO: Logion Press, 2000.

– Other Books by the Author –

Power Ministry: How to Minister in the Spirit's Power (2004)
(also available in French, Portuguese, Malagasy, Kirnirwanda, and Chichewa.)

Empowered for Global Mission: A Missionary Look at the Book of Acts (2005)

From Azusa to Africa to the Nations (2005)
(also available in French, Spanish, and Portuguese)

Acts: The Spirit of God in Mission (2007)

In Step with the Spirit: Studies in the Spirit-filled Walk (2008)

The Kingdom and the Power: The Kingdom of God: A Pentecostal Interpretation (2009)

Experiencing the Spirit: A Study of the Work of the Spirit in the Life of the Believer (2009)

Teaching in the Spirit (2009)

Power Encounter: Ministering in the Power and Anointing of the Holy Spirit: Revised (2009)
(Available in Kiswahili. Soon to be available in Urdu and Mandarin Chinese)

You Can Minister in God's Power: A Guide for Spirit-filled Disciples (2009)

Proclaiming Pentecost: 100 Sermon Outlines on the Power of the Holy Spirit
(Associate editor—2011)

The 1:8 Promise of Jesus: The Key to World Harvest (2012)

The above and other books are available from
PneumaLife Publications,
3766 N. Delaware Ave.
Springfield, Missouri, USA 65803

A current price list may be obtained by contacting
the above addresses or by visiting
www.PneumaLifePublications.org

© 2013 Denzil R. Miller